# Building
# Design
# Strategy

# Building Design Strategy

## Using Design to Achieve Key Business Objectives

Edited by
Thomas Lockwood
and
Thomas Walton

**ALLWORTH PRESS**
NEW YORK

DESIGN MANAGEMENT INSTITUTE

12   11   10   09   08      5   4   3   2   1

Published by Allworth Press
An imprint of Allworth Communications, Inc.
10 East 23rd Street, New York, NY 10010

Cover design by Continuum
Interior design by The Roberts Group
Page composition/typography by SR Desktop Services

ISBN-13: 978-1-58115-653-9
ISBN-10: 1-58115-653-7


Library of Congress Cataloging-in-Publication Data
    Building design strategy : using design to achieve key business objectives / edited by Thomas Lockwood.
        p.    cm.
    ISBN-13: 978-1-58115-653-9
    ISBN-10: 1-58115-653-7
    1. Design, Industrial.    2. Industrial design coordination.
    I. Lockwood, Thomas.
    TS171.4.B85    2008
    658.4'03—dc22

                                                        2008034920


Printed in the United States of America

# DEDICATION

*This book is dedicated to all of the DMI members and stakeholders around the world that have supported the Institute since its founding in 1975.*

# Contents

# Acknowledgments

I am grateful to all of the authors whose work is included in this book. In addition, I would like to acknowledge and thank all of the other authors who have contributed articles to DMI's *Design Management Journal* and *Design Management Review* publications over the years: They have made this body of knowledge the most extensive resource on design management in the world. I must especially credit the outstanding work of the former president of DMI, Mr. Earl Powell, PhD (hon), who not only founded these publications and served as their publisher but was also responsible for their content since the beginning in 1985. His efforts have increased our understanding and advanced the role of design in business immensely. And finally we must thank Dr. Thomas Walton, PhD, for his outstanding work as the editor of the *Design Management Journal* and *Design Management Review*, also since their inception. Dr. Walton has reviewed every article published and has opened every issue with his well-known and informative "Editor's Notes." Without their hard work, commitment, and significant contributions over the years, this anthology would simply not be possible.

# Introduction

"The problem with communication is the illusion it has occurred."
—GEORGE BERNARD SHAW

ONE OF THE most interesting things about this book is its title—the reason being, there are about as many different opinions of the definition of "design" as there are for "strategy." Nonetheless, we know that design strategy is important, and that if you want to bring true value to a corporation, design strategy is one of the best possible ways to do so. Let's take a look at what this involves by looking into those definitions.

## DESIGN AS A PROCESS

According to Webster's, one of the broad definitions of design is along the lines of "a plan to make something." This is actually quite informative when you really think about it, because the key words are *plan*, *make*, and *something*. Today there is much discussion in the design community and in the business and design press regarding the idea of "design thinking." This, too, is hard to define, but a general idea would involve a deep understanding that would help identify challenges and frame opportunities (in other words, *plan*) in order to create (*make*) new solutions (*something*). Generally this entails observational or ethnographic research, visualization of ideas, and rapid iteration of prototypes—all techniques very common to the design practitioner but relatively new to the business manager or executive. I once heard Steve Jobs referenced at Pixar Animation Studios as saying that the goal is to fail as quickly as possible, so that a better solution can be rapidly explored. This is an example of using design and design thinking as a business process, and it is an integral part of Pixar's strategy. Our argument is that design strategy is not only a relevant business process but in fact can also be a key advantage for businesses.

## DESIGN AS AN ARTIFACT AND SERVICE

Equally important, design represents an outcome, as an artifact or service. This also is very broad. Charles Eames was once asked, "What are the boundaries of design?" and his answer was "What are the boundaries of problems?" In effect, design's range and ability to solve problems is immense. Consider that everything ever made by human beings required design. To simplify this into categories, many would agree that there are traditionally four main types of "design as an outcome": product, communication, interface/information, and environment.

▲ **Product design.** Products are generally the most visible aspect of a company. They are often how we know the company, and they drive our attitudes toward it as well.

▲ **Communication design.** Equally important, communication design affects all touch-points that rely on visual communications—from symbols and corporate identity to packaging, advertising, instructions, and directions. Consider the impact of election ballots, for example: The importance of communication design cannot be underestimated.

▲ **Information design.** We have all come to rely on the importance and functionality of information design, from Web interfaces to product interfaces, from signage to wayfinding, from information architecture to managing our bank accounts. Without information design, our society could not function.

▲ **Environment design.** Affecting everything from branded retail environments to showrooms, from exhibitions to our workspaces, from business architecture to that of our homes, the design of our environments can be extremely influential in our professional as well as our personal lives.

I would like to add a fifth category to these four: service design.

▲ **Service design.** This is emerging as a discipline unto itself. Consider that all services, from bank-teller processes to restaurants, from hospitals to governments, from hotels to travel carriers, are designed. The question is whether they are well designed or simply a reflection of the status quo.

## STRATEGY AS A WAY TO ACCOMPLISH OBJECTIVES

Here, too, we find a rather broad interpretation of strategy. Webster's would define the word as "a careful plan or method" or as "the art of devising or employing plans." It's not too difficult to see the similarities between design and strategy; however, in today's typical large corporation, the strategy department and the design department are most likely worlds apart. As Hartmut Esslinger, the founder of renowned Frog Design, recently noted, "Businesspeople are from Mars, and designers are from Venus." While this may be not too far from the truth, our challenge in building design strategy is to bring these two disparate worlds into alignment. They share a common ground in the desire to accomplish business objectives. So the strategist and the designer, each with a clear understanding of business goals and objectives, can be a powerful force by working together. No one really expects the strategist to become a designer, but it's not so unlikely that the designer will start strategizing. This is precisely one of the roles of design management: to bring design and design thinking into organizations, in support of the development of corporate strategy.

## DESIGN STRATEGY FOR THE TRIPLE BOTTOM LINE

Probably the broadest overlap in strategy and design comes when a business is evaluated in light of the "triple bottom line": from an economic, social, and environmental viewpoint. I would argue that no other business discipline or function has greater potential to affect that triple bottom line than does design. And obtaining that result is the true value of design strategy. As stated above, when one considers the values of design as a process, and also as an artifact or service, its benefits are virtually unlimited. That's why design strategy is so important.

## A WEALTH OF OPINION

Twenty-three authors contributed to *Building Design Strategy*. Each article was originally published by the Design Management Institute in the *Design Management Journal* or the *Design Management Review*, and we chose them for their excellence and their relevance to the goal of building a design strategy. The great thing about this approach is that we can present a range of ideas from across industries and disciplines. Not only are the results diverse, opinioned, reflective, and thought-leading, but they also represent some of today's leading firms, from Procter & Gamble to Caterpillar, Target, and Microsoft, and such well-known design thought leaders as IDEO, Ziba, PARK, Jump, Teague, IIT, and, of course, DMI.

We hope this book will be the first in a series of DMI anthologies. Over the years, the Institute has published more than eight hundred articles covering many aspects of design management as well as design strategy, design leadership, and design as related to brand-building and innovation. There is a wealth of knowledge here to be shared. This first book is our pilot, and we hope the market responds positively. If you have ideas about content you would like to see us publish, or feedback on this project, please let me know. I trust you will find the insights in this book beneficial to you, and I thank you for your interest in DMI.

THOMAS LOCKWOOD, PHD
PRESIDENT
*WWW.DMI.ORG*
LOCKWOOD@DMI.ORG

# CREATING CORPORATE STRATEGY
# AND CREATING DESIGN STRATEGY

The first section of our first DMI anthology looks into the subject of design strategy. Here we explore the organizational need to have a shared strategic vision—a vision it can achieve with the help of a design strategy. We all know that there is often a gap between strategy and execution, and our point of view is that design can fill this gap, and indeed it is absolutely crucial to that end.

Early thought leaders like Wally Olins and Robert Blaich have long promoted identity design as a means to make corporate strategy visible and demonstrated how product design supports corporate strategy. Let's go a step further: *All* design can and should support corporate strategy. In fact, design has grown beyond merely supporting corporate strategy to become a means of informing and even guiding its development.

I have the honor of opening this discussion with the first article in this section, which discusses how to value design. My argument is that design benefits the "triple bottom line" of economic, social, and environmental value and thus has potentially more influence on a corporation than any other business discipline. And because one can't see the value in design strategy without first understanding the complexity and values of design. Next, Ravi Chhatpar challenges traditional strategy development processes with a look at design's contributions. Frans Joziasse helps us clarify how integrating design management functions into business strategy help guide design as corporate strategy. Robyn Waters explains how the work at Target taps into the emotional qualities of design as it supports key business initiatives, with a reminder of how design adds to the head, handbag, and heart. Jacoby and Rodriguez look into design thinking and design process as a way of structuring innovation in support of organizational strategy.

This chapter presents several key insights that should guide your point of view about design strategy:

**Design can help create corporate strategy.** According to Gary Hamel, some 90 percent of strategy fails due to poor execution. As a process and a tool, design can greatly improve those odds. In fact, design methods and techniques such as observational and ethnographic research, visualization of ideas, challenging the status quo, and rapid prototype iteration can make design strategy and corporate strategy symbiotic. There is so much more to corporate strategy, and to design strategy, than meets the eye—literally.

**Design strategy is as much about process as it is about artifacts.** The word "design," of course, has many meanings. According to Webster's, at its most basic, design can be defined as simply "a plan." But all too often design is merely associated with a stylish product, a new fashion, or a company logo, when it involves so much more. We urge you to consider design with a capital "D," because it is actually a way of thinking and a process, as well as a product, service, or communication. All kinds of issues and entities—from business processes to collaborative work teams—can benefit from design.

**Innovation is dependent upon design.** In fact, one could argue that innovation is simply invention plus design. Consider, for example, the Industrial Revolution. It was truly a marriage of invention and design—a powerful combination. But business generally did not recognize the role of design at that time, even though today we can see very clearly that invention is not of much value without design, which makes it tangible and usable. If a company wants to improve its innovation competencies, it should begin by improving its design competencies.

**Strategic design requires management.** All design output, whether it centers on products, communications, interactions, identity, or environment, has to be managed. Strategic design rarely just happens; it develops from specific methods and purposes. There was a time, not too long ago, when some companies depended on a few "star designers" to make an impact. But we now realize that using design to develop sustainable advantages requires much more, and design management is the gateway to integrate design at the corporate, business unit, and operational levels. There is an art and a science to design management that supports integrated work teams and building design strategy.

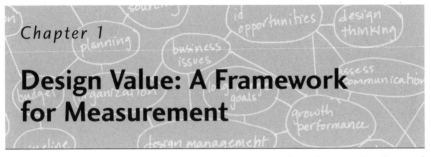

# Chapter 1

# Design Value: A Framework for Measurement

*Design may enhance performance, but unless there are metrics to gauge that benefit, the difference it makes depends on conjecture and faith. Confronting this perennial challenge, Thomas Lockwood enumerates ten categories in which design value and performance can be evaluated. They vary from time-to-market and cost savings to customer satisfaction and the ability to influence preferences, but all of them should serve as useful ammunition for the designer, design manager, and business executive.*

AS BUSINESSES INCREASINGLY recognize the power of design to provide significant benefits, business executives increasingly are asking for metrics to evaluate the performance of design. What is needed, and presented here, is a framework for measurement, a specific set of criteria and methods to be used as a structure to define and measure the values of design.

As design has caught the attention of the business world, so too we must strive to better understand and consider design on business terms. But there is a traditional mindset gap between business people and designers. As Darrel Rhea, CEO of Cheskin, notes, "The central challenge of the design profession is to make ourselves relevant to business leaders." There is a chasm between design and business, particularly when it comes to measuring design.

To analyze design, we must find a balance between creative intuition and research sensibilities. Jerome Kathman, CEO of LPK, the largest independent design firm in the

3

world, recently noted that often designers state that qualitative research is for "us," and quantitative research is for "them"—and that designers tend to underline their importance with anecdotes and quotes ("good design is good business" comes to mind) rather than with numbers, because "creativity resists quantification." The design and creative communities at large are traditionally known to resist quantification. Gus Desbarats of Alloy Ltd. in London agrees, stating that "Designers are not numbers people." Even so, he calls for what he describes as a results-oriented creative culture, noting, "It's not necessarily about numbers, but it is about being rational about emotion."

To an extent, being rational about emotion is something designers already do. The problem comes when they try to convey those thoughts to company management; that requires either design-aware executives or a leap of faith. Unfortunately, not many companies are led by design-aware executives, making design a rather mysterious ingredient for many business managers. But if the design industry is to capitalize on its new popularity in business, it needs to do so in ways that business executives understand— that is, with measurements.

## A FRAMEWORK FOR VALUE

The following identifies ten categories of design measurement, all of which are relevant to business criteria and are presented here as a framework for measuring the value of design. These measurements represent areas in which design contributes; and when design can be isolated, the contribution areas can be measured. This framework stems from research and from various inputs, including thoughts emerging from two recent DMI conferences, one held in the United States and one in Denmark.[1] We have conducted this research and assimilated this point of view because businesses need to capture real value from their investments in design, and design managers and leaders are increasingly asked to provide evidence of success. The most difficult part is isolating the role of design and design management, a task this framework can help to accomplish.

The ten categories of this framework to measure design are

1. Purchase influence/emotion
2. Enable strategy/enter new markets
3. Build brand image and corporate reputation
4. Improve time to market and development processes
5. Design return on investment (ROI)/cost savings
6. Enable product and service innovation
7. Increase customer satisfaction/develop communities of customers
8. Design patents and trademarks/create intellectual property
9. Improve usability
10. Improve sustainability

This framework is not meant to suggest that each category is required for each design project, but rather to suggest that any project will find one or more categories relevant to setting measurement criteria. Let's look more closely into these categories in terms of measuring the values of design.

## PURCHASE INFLUENCE/EMOTION

Design has the ability to influence purchase preferences, to support premium pricing, and to improve product sell-through. And it can have a positive effect on the customer's emotional relationship with a brand. According to Esslinger, "Money buys, but emotion sells." Consider the Mini Cooper automobile, an emotional attraction indeed; its parts cost about the same as those of other vehicles of similar size and quality, yet it maintains a premium price based on the emotional connection people have with their Minis—from ordering to ownership. Design is, of course, an imperative in the shift from selling products to selling experiences. And experiences can be measured, as well as designed; simply remove the intended design elements, then ask your customers about their experience.

Target, for example, looks to set an emotional connection and measure the impact of product design on customer experience—and on sales. Robyn Waters, president of RW Trend and former vice president of trend, design, and product development at Target, notes that the business world is beginning to lose its "analysis paralysis"—the belief that "if it can't be counted, it doesn't count." At Target, it became clear that shopping can be an emotional experience ("It's about the treasure hunt," says Waters, "not the saved nickel"), so Waters began to evolve a philosophy she refers to as "trend from the inside out." Target's new mission was to be "trend right, guest-focused, and design-driven." Trends were not sufficient by themselves to create product success; they had to be interpreted and translated into something that made sense in customers' lives. Design, in this context, needed to be the tool that could translate a trend into something fun and meaningful that would inspire desire, as well as fulfill a need. There have been many successful new products that use design as a key selling point at Target, and these have been isolated and tested on the retail shelf.

In a related model, the role of design in purchase influence is particularly measurable in packaging design. Rob Wallace, managing partner of Wallace Church, in New York, has isolated the role of design in packaging numerous times and has demonstrated incredible return on investment for design activities. One client achieved a sales increase of 30 percent and more than $300 million in incremental sales gains based solely on a new suite of packaging. Same product, new packaging. Wallace argues that design can be quantified, and that design generates the highest ROI of the marketing mix. The measurement is not too difficult: Design new packaging, put it on the shelf side-by-side with the old, and see what sells. Then deduct the cost of design from the new sales . . . and voila: ROI design based on actual numbers. Eventually, says Gus Desbarats, you will arrive at this equation: Design's value equals attributes affecting sales (trial or repeat) minus the extra cost due to design's input.

## ENABLE STRATEGY/ENTER NEW MARKETS

A second way to measure the value of design is through its ability to enable corporate strategy or to enter new markets. One only has to mention iPod, Dyson, OXO Good Grips, or Amazon to get the idea here. And the design of these products, communications, interfaces, and experiences can be isolated. Here's a simple example: British Airways had built a business strategy around increasing its long-haul international flights. So the company looked to see how the interior design of its planes could be improved to offer more comfort to customers. BA's designers flew all over the world, for days on end—as passengers. What resulted was the first seat in the industry that could lie completely flat, allowing customers to sleep prone rather than simply slouch as in conventional airline seats. The result was a significant increase in sales and profitability for long-haul international flights. Design alone made the difference, because everything else remained the same. Granted, in some product situations the difference between design and engineering is vague, but at minimum the two should be symbiotic, and design must always involve multidisciplinary work teams engaging in design thinking processes.

Many firms, of course, use design competencies to help visualize business strategy. At the Danish National Railway (DSB), according to design director Pia Bech Mathiesen, design is used to create strategic maps for departments, and this helps to visualize DSB strategy goals. And at Philips Electronics, says design director Clive Roux, "design direction-setting" takes place across Philips product lines. Going even further, Harry Rich of the British Design Council claims that sustained design strategy allows companies to take leadership positions in their sectors. He compares the electronics firms Sony and Panasonic, noting that Sony prefers to innovate and be known as a design-driven company, and Panasonic, which prefers to follow trends, is more of a design follower. Both have sales of about $62 billion; yet Rich notes that Sony has a brand value of $12 billion and a brand rank of #26—three times that of Panasonic's brand value and rank. He attributes this difference to the value of design strategy and to making design part of the corporate strategy.

## SHAPING BRAND IMAGE AND CORPORATE REPUTATION

Here's another comparison: Apple achieves about half the amount of profit as Dell, but it does so with only about a third of the revenue and is thus much more profitable. Esslinger believes this demonstrates that it pays to invest in design and in your suppliers. In fact, Apple reported 34 percent revenue growth of an astounding 33 percent gross margin for Q3 2007. Target has clearly established a brand image and set itself apart in the discount category by being about design (and value). In the United Kingdom, interestingly, brand value is quantified on the balance sheet, noted as goodwill.

Design that receives design awards also contributes to corporate reputation and brand image. By providing an independent and expert critique of design, awards can provide valuable feedback, help build company pride, and confer prestige upon the business—prestige that is valued by the consumer, as well. I've toured many design studios and corporate design centers all over the world that proudly display their collections of design awards.

According to Cathy Huang, president of China Bridge International, there are four types of design award providers: professional award organizations (such as IF, Red Dot, and Good Design); governments and institutions (such as country design councils and design schools); companies (such as Braun and Sony); and the media (such as BusinessWeek/IDEA, HOW, and Communication Arts). Design award competitions generally seek to identify excellence in design aesthetics and design innovation. Unfortunately, today most award competitions, notably those administered by the media, government/institutions, and companies, take the easy (and efficient) way out by having judges simply review online pictures or PDFs of design entries, which can of course be misleading.

Generally, the professional award organizations provide the most thoughtful design award processes. Germany's Red Dot, for example, insists that the judges evaluate all submissions in person and abide by strict criteria. However, physically collecting all the award entries and physically assembling an expert panel of judges for days of thorough inspection and evaluation is costly and difficult. Yet this process and attention to quality has elevated the Red Dot Award, which has become the seal of design quality throughout Europe and Asia.

Denmark's Index Award looks at the environmental benefits of design. Britain's Design Effectiveness Awards are judged purely on commercial results, based on written documentation. More akin to an analysis of the success of a new-product launch, these entries must prove their merit by demonstrating improved bottom-line performance. To do so, they must be able to isolate the contributions of design.

## IMPROVING TIME TO MARKET AND DEVELOPMENT PROCESSES

It is also possible to measure design based on process and time to market. Here, the design manager is always looking for the best combination of process efficiency and design success. One common way to do that is by establishing design standards or at least design guidelines. Today it is becoming more common to have guidelines. The thinking is that this improves design flexibility because it allows the brand to demonstrate innovation while giving designers parameters to work within so that they don't have to reinvent the wheel with every new project. When I was responsible for design at StorageTek/Sun Microsystems, we established simple guidelines and a design platform approach. Graphic guidelines included typography, color, photography style, diagram style, and iconography. Product guidelines included a common platform for computer hardware and a standardized chassis and interface, as well as other shared components. In this way, our engineers didn't have to design components, only functions; development time was greatly reduced. The cost and time savings based on platform design, guidelines, or even standards can be easily evaluated; just watch your project costs rise without them.

Han Hendriks, a vice president at Johnson Controls, notes a methodology for measuring design performance internally and with customers in the car industry. The company's design-quality metrics look at craftsmanship, perceived quality, design-to-cost ratio, and ROI for design processes. The main metric for ROI is based on asking internal customers how the design solutions compare to those of external design firms; in this way, process efficiency also involves a comparison of internal design service performance to that of other providers.

## DESIGN ROI/COST SAVINGS

Julie Hertenstein and Marjorie Platt, from Northeastern University's School of Business, have conducted research in conjunction with DMI on the financial performance of design since the mid-1990s. In their first study, they identified a set of fifty-one firms in four industries that positioned design as a key strategic advantage. They chose a panel of design management experts from DMI to rank the design effectiveness of the sample firms. They then evaluated the financial performance by using traditional financial ratios, such as return on assets and net cash flows to sales, for the sample period. They found that firms rated as having good design were stronger on virtually all financial measures, from a practical and managerial perspective as well as from a statistical perspective. By looking at the study sample as companies, not products, this research also suggests that "good design" is a characteristic of a company and indicates many financial successes in a variety of industries.

Similarly, for more than a decade, the British Design Council has been tracking the performance of the stocks of design-aware companies on London's FTSE 100 and FTSE All-Share indices. The original Design Index, which ran from 1993 to 2003, followed sixty-three companies recognized as effective users of design (they were grouped together as a result of their consistently winning design awards). Those companies outperformed the rest of the FTSE by 200 percent in that decade. The Design Council has continued to follow the Design Index, as well as a broader Emerging Index of companies identified as emerging users of design, and has found that the performance of both groups has continued to outpace their peers. Since March 2003, the Design Index has risen by another 43 percent and the Emerging Index has gone up by 74.3 percent, while the FTSE 100 and All-Share indices have grown by 26.2 and 32.1 percent, respectively. (Note that this is a long-term study and has covered both bull and bear markets.) Companies whose success could be seen as merely the result of transient consumer or business trends are not likely to have lasted this long.

Further Design Council research, in an independently run study, is based on 1,500 British businesses across all sizes and sectors. Titled "Design in Britain, 2003–2004," the study indicates that the U.K.'s most successful businesses rate design as the second most important factor for success (only marketing is judged more important). However, U.K. companies as a whole rate financial management as the number-one factor, with design running in seventh place.

These are some telling numbers. They go a long way toward demonstrating the financial value of design in business.

## ENABLE PRODUCT AND SERVICE INNOVATION

Design is also a critical component for product and service innovation and can be measured as such. What if a car dealer used design to create the perfect customer experience and increased sales by more than 25 percent? Open Road Toyota, working with Karo Design in Canada, did just that. They redesigned all their touch-points for a specific customer experience, and in 2006 they became the number-one Toyota dealer in Canada. The cars did not change, but the design of everything else did, and sales skyrocketed. We see similar results from Portland-based Umpqua Bank's work with Ziba Design. Both of these successes stemmed from a deep understanding of customers, which was used to design the desired customer experience, and then to design every touch-point so that it would support that experience. These projects can isolate design on a before-and-after basis with any number of customer satisfaction methods.

Sophie Bartlett of consulting firm Kaiser Associates notes that companies often measure what can be counted, not what counts. Many firms simply don't have an appropriate measurement protocol—they use too many metrics, or they fail to standardize and align their metrics, or they don't have clear processes for measurement. Kaiser's metrics measure output rather than input, studying parameters such as revenue, organic growth, and something Kaiser calls "IGPM"—innovation for growth performance measure. Bartlett points out that companies are always looking for new ways to create value or to reinvent value. It is easy to develop one successful idea, but finding a model for innovation is difficult. Companies need to integrate and orchestrate innovation across the whole company. This is an area in which design can help by integrating multifunctional input and bringing in design thinking techniques.

IDEO's Diego Rodriguez is a believer in metrics for innovation—with reservations. As he likes to say, "Measure less; understand more." Rodriguez recently identified two kinds of metrics: generative (designed to get you somewhere) and general (to be used as a tool for design teams, managers, and stakeholders). Either kind should be fodder for an ongoing conversation. Moreover, because every company is unique to itself, there is no one silver bullet metric. However, good metrics do exhibit some shared characteristics. They are simple, but not simplistic; they are "sticky"; and they are actionable. Rodriguez asks, "What's the point of measuring things if you're not going to do anything with the results you get?" Innovation is important because it leads to improvements in a company's bottom line, promotes organic revenue growth, and (one hopes) creates a better quality of life. All these factors are part of creating value. And measurement is important when guiding innovation; it can improve efficiency, boost effectiveness, and make the whole process less of an art and more of a science.

Design is often considered an intangible, notes Pamela Cohen of Communications Consulting Worldwide (CCW). Coauthor of *Invisible Advantage: How Intangibles Are*

*Driving Business Performance*, Cohen insists that such intangibles as communications and design are actually measurable, and that the data needed to evaluate them often already exist. Factors that contribute to communications, for example, include relations with analysts, customers, employees, shareholders, and suppliers, as well as capital structure and brand. This framework does so for design.

## INCREASE CUSTOMER SATISFACTION/DEVELOP COMMUNITIES OF CUSTOMERS

Many new companies have been tremendously successful in developing new communities of customers. Consider Facebook and Google among these companies; design not only plays a role but is partially carried out by customers. This is engaging, sticky, and extremely effective. At times, the professional designers need to allow the customers to play a part. Hard to measure? Not really, since it's based on individuals. Effective? Yes indeed; consider the usage and rapid growth of online communities of customers.

Some more traditional companies, such as Procter & Gamble, take a keen interest in the measurement of intangibles in customer satisfaction. P&G has always measured the "first moment of truth" (purchase decision) and the "second moment of truth" (repeat purchase), but it now includes the role of design as an influence. Today, more and more designers and design managers are gaining important insights from qualitative types of research—ethnography, focus groups, directional learning. And that research is based on what best solves customer needs. As a measurement, Kathman notes that "consumer-preferred design outperforms management-preferred design." Designers might argue that metrics can lead to formulaic decisions and that the rush to numbers can limit interest in improving on concepts. However, synthesis of the quantitative and the qualitative is needed, and designers should be conversant in all areas of generally accepted research methods. Above all, Kathman notes, designers should always engage the reasonability test—examining the metrics they use to ensure their relevance and efficacy.

## DESIGN PATENTS AND TRADEMARKS/CREATING INTELLECTUAL PROPERTY

Another way to measure design's contribution is to consider how much you've lost if it's stolen. In today's economy, a company's IP assets are often more valuable than its physical assets. Consider Coca-Cola's signature bottle, or Nike's swoosh. Joshua Cohen, of intellectual property firm RatnerPrestia PC, notes that IP laws do not give us the right to do things in the marketplace; however, they do give us the right to exclude others from using our designs. That's what patents—either for design or for utility—do, along with copyrights and trademark and trade-dress protection.

Because any product can, and often does, include features that provide brand identity or aesthetics along with features relating to performance and manufacturing advantages, comprehensive IP protection often calls for separate protections covering various aspects of the same product. A product or a package can benefit from utility patent or trade secret protection for its functional features, while the aesthetic elements of that same product or package can enjoy protection through design patents, copyright, and trademark and trade-dress protections. Strategies aimed to maximize the ROI of design efforts by securing comprehensive IP protection, avoiding the IP rights of others, and integrating IP-building efforts into design processes can be isolated and are of significant value. The concept of design ownership is central. Nearly every day, brand acquisitions take place in which the purchase price greatly exceeds the value of the plant and equipment assets.

## IMPROVE USABILITY

There are many ways to isolate, measure, and improve design based on usability. Very often, the usability of an interface design is measured by analyzing the efficiency of user navigation through observation, click-through, or interviews. Web sites are constantly monitored for user performance, and most Web marketers watch our behaviors very closely and make design adjustments to improve performance. All manner of design-based usability issues can be isolated and evaluated.

Lavrans Lovlie, of the U.K.'s Live/Work, has developed a usability index to help companies better understand how their businesses are experienced by their customers. The index starts with broad questions and then goes deeper to assess how the customer's experience ranks at each touch-point. Experience can be evaluated at call centers, online, through marketing materials and retail environments, and the design of that experience can be changed to reflect customer feedback.

Measuring design by usability also includes areas such as signage, wayfinding, and employee experience, which can also be measured. At StorageTek, we introduced an interior design program that affected about five thousand employees and garnered astonishing returns in employee satisfaction. First, we benchmarked via an employee survey and interviews; then we implemented a fairly modest interior design renovation that involved artwork, paint, carpet, and lighting in common areas, corridors, and cafeterias, as well as about seventy-five conference rooms. A second employee survey carried out after the renovation found these results:

- ▲ 72 percent of our employees said the new design reduced their stress
- ▲ 84 percent said it improved their mood or attitude
- ▲ 69 percent said it improved their morale
- ▲ 60 percent said it improved wayfinding
- ▲ 91 percent felt it demonstrated company efforts to improve the work environment

Perhaps the most influential direct impact of design for usability was the 2000 U.S. presidential election that pitted George W. Bush against Al Gore. Famously, the ballots used in the state of Florida featured a very poor graphic design that made it difficult for some voters to know exactly which hole to punch for the candidate of their choice. The consequences were far-reaching and permanent.

## IMPROVING SUSTAINABILITY

It's a fact: Good design is good for all. We must all look to measure design in terms of its ability to improve the world and improve people's lives. We all have an obligation to practice responsible design, inclusive design, and design that has minimal impact on the environment.

Hartmut Esslinger has called on designers to help move our world forward toward sustainability and toward creating a more adequate and balanced model. The creative economy is a greener economy, and we all need to help; designers and design managers have considerable influence in this area. Valerie Casey, a creative director at Frog Design, argues that green design is a business issue and a moral issue, and designers and design managers who have the freedom to adopt some design criteria and on this basis make what, in their view, are better choices. In effect, given that ethics is defined as dealing with good and bad, right and wrong, designers have to make ethical choices. Casey suggests a Kyoto Treaty for Design featuring collective and individual criteria— the goal being to advance our intellectual understanding of environmental issues from a design perspective. Undoubtedly, design has considerable impact on our environment, and that impact is easily measurable.

## CONCLUSION

Indeed, there are many ways to measure the value of design; one can even divide them into ten categories, as this research suggests. We have to consider design as integral to the triple bottom line—which consists of economic benefits, social benefits, and environmental benefits. What's more, managing design is a science, as well as an art, and requires the integration of the two; in effect it is the convergence of business, strategy, and customer experience.

Brigitte Borja de Mozota has been researching design performance for many years, much of them as a life fellow at DMI. She argues that there are four powers of design: as differentiator, as integrator, as transformer, and simply as good business. One model she has adopted and modified to reflect design value is the Balanced Scorecard, which should be eminently familiar to any business manager.

As this framework demonstrates, measuring the value and performance of design does not need to be complex or foreboding. There is a case for intuition, a case for qualitative research, a case for quantitative research, and a case for synthesis. And there is even room for imponderables, because some things are simply beyond definition or measurement. Indeed, we must continue to appreciate that at the heart of creativity and design is not just design skill but also intuition. I hope this framework will empower that intuition and creativity and yet help all concerned find a more definitive way to value design solutions. And I hope this framework for design value is embraced by design owners, practitioners, and educators everywhere, so that we don't fall prey to the wiles of the bean counters.

## *Endnote*

1. All the quotes in this article are derived from DMI conference proceedings in Vermont and Copenhagen.

## Chapter 2

# Analytic Enhancements to Strategic Decision-Making: From the Designer's Toolbox

by Ravi Chhatpar

*In today's fast-paced consumer market, strategic decision-making has changed in fundamental ways. Ravi Chhatpar argues that the iterative, user-centric methodologies of design can supplement the rigor of traditional analytical approaches to allow for more accurate and flexible evaluation of strategic options.*

THE ROLE OF the designer has traditionally been viewed as distinct from the corporate strategy process. The designer's methods, largely qualitative approaches that seek to generate the market and user insights that spark creativity in execution, have long been considered incongruent with the highly analytical and quantitative approaches required in strategic planning.

The view of conventional strategists essentially boils down to this: first, make the key business decisions; then, codify them into business strategy; finally, bring in designers (among other parties) to make that strategy a reality. There has been some change in this perception recently. The high-profile success of well-designed products and the emergence of design as a serious competitive differentiator have made executives look at designers in a new light. As a result, design has expanded beyond its product-level execution category. The growing and currently trendy field of innovation strategy, which seeks to systematize creative thinking in a corporate environment using methods that draw from the design world, is just one example of this expanded role.

But strategic planning is still viewed as the turf of corporate strategy groups and management consultants. Opportunity portfolios, business cases, and road maps are core elements of business strategy, and all are most successful when supported by deep, analytical methodologies, which are not yet characteristic of the designer's toolbox.

I maintain, however, that a change is occurring in today's market that calls for a fundamentally different approach. The goal of this chapter is to demonstrate that success today requires a new view of strategic decision-making, particularly (but not exclusively) in fast-moving, consumer technology industries. This new view suggests an evolved role for the designer, a role in which design methods are melded into traditional strategy methods to ensure that strategy translates into market success. To illustrate this point, I will discuss two methodologies in detail.

## A MESSY SITUATION

Over the past few years, it's been startling to observe leading brands, both established and new, make serious missteps in their product decisions.

The consumer technology space offers numerous examples. Consider the emergence of mobile virtual network operators (MVNOs) in the mobile phone industry. Every quarter, we see new strategies—sports phones (Mobile ESPN), social networking phones (Helio), and teen-targeted phones (Amp'd Mobile and Boost). ESPN, an established brand with a strong track record across a broad range of ventures, folded its MVNO after investing more than $100 million. In hindsight, it seems obvious that consumers would be unwilling to pay more than $400 for a premium-priced phone with sports content. Handsets with better design (such as the Motorola RAZR) and heavy price competition among carriers on basic features (plans and minutes) made it clear that ESPN's original assumptions about its value proposition to consumers were flawed.

Similarly, the music industry failed to respond effectively to consumer interest in music downloading and allowed the newcomer, Apple, to enter and control the space. Moreover, Sony let that same newcomer take the lead in the portable music device segment, losing its decade of Walkman dominance.

Other industries have comparable stories of strategic errors based on misunderstood consumer behavior. The airline industry failed to respond effectively to consumer desire for simplification and allowed newcomer JetBlue to become the most favored airline brand today. Most car manufacturers missed the hybrid boat and let Toyota's Prius make strong gains in the sector. And Friendster lost its first-mover advantage in the social networking arena due to poor feature planning and scaling.

## WHAT'S GOING ON HERE?

In the consumer technology space, it's convenient to place blame for these missteps in the standard places. The competitive pressure is higher than ever before, as low barriers to entry have resulted in a field crowded with new innovations, technologies, and approaches to marketing and distribution. Consumer needs are harder to anticipate, as consumers have become more technology savvy, more connected in complex technology and social ecosystems, more fickle, and less brand loyal. Internal organizations are often siloed, with disparate business groups structured for success in the "old world" tossing around ideas for new directions and tactics, as management struggles to organize them.

But if this were truly the case, then we're essentially describing classic strategy problems that should be resolvable using classic strategy approaches. They just happen to be contextualized in an environment that is faster-moving and more dynamic. Are we simply asking companies to make better strategic decisions—on what their vision is, on what products to release and when, on what features these products should have, on what to do next?

Let's explore this line of reasoning. Corporate strategy groups, consultants, and academics have invested much effort over the years into developing methodologies and tools to support strategic decision-making in every imaginable context.

The business case is the core tool used to quantify the impact of a strategic decision. The business case rigorously considers benefits and costs involved around a given decision point, whether it's investing in a new venture, expanding into new product lines, or adding a new feature. Any uncertainty around the decision can be managed through a variety of other formal approaches, including game theory, decision trees, opportunity portfolios, real options, scenarios, simulations, and numerous variations.

A host of approaches also exist when less rigor is required, such as when filtering options to the most attractive ones, which will then be evaluated with a business case. These approaches include rapid analysis frameworks (such as SWOT), scorecards and weighting systems, and evaluation processes (such as Stage-Gate).

All these approaches are supported by a large body of both rigorous mathematical theory and less rigorous, but equally vigorous, discussions of topics such as decision styles, roles, and emotions.

These fast-moving consumer companies, being leaders (or former leaders) in their fields, clearly have employed many of these approaches over their years of corporate existence, making good and bad decisions along the way. They have access to the same body of decision-making intellectual capital that any company has. They take strategic decision-making very seriously, as any major company does.

So why does it seem as if so many poor decisions are being made in today's market— poor decisions that lead to failure?

One obvious answer is that poor decisions are being made now for the same reason poor decisions have always been made: incorrect assumptions of risk and uncertainty. Business case inputs may be wrong due to improper forecasting. Decision tree probabilities may be off due to misconceptions of what choices are available. Scorecard options may be ranked incorrectly because intangibles such as strategic fit and degree of asset leverage are too subjective.

While this may often be true, we believe in many cases there is a deeper issue at play. The answer to our previous question—"Are we simply asking companies to make the right strategic decisions?"—is yes, we are, but to do so requires a different approach because the nature of decision-making has fundamentally changed.

## THE REAL ISSUE

There is a common thread running through the prior examples of strategic missteps. In each example, businesses were unable to respond with agility to change in the market. Based on Frog Design's extensive work with companies in the consumer technology space, we see two primary reasons why companies experience this inertia:

1. The traditional approach to decision-making, from strategy formulation through product development, is too rigid in its requirements for buy-in.

2. The traditional approach to decision-making does not position companies for successful execution, because it fixes execution plans based on old assumptions.

The first of these reasons is rooted in historical product development processes. Product development is often a lock-step process, building alignment through consensus around key decision points, such as the set of initial strategic options, the business plan, product design attributes, and development constraints, among others. In effect, product development becomes a narrowing of options to a final solution, which is then driven into production. The Stage-Gate process for product innovation is one example of such a process used by many businesses.

The first issue with this process is that the product development timeframe becomes extended, as time required for acquiring buy-in must be built into the development plan. Furthermore, each decision is based on the decisions made previously, meaning the product is often representative of assumptions made several months (if not more) before. In the rapidly changing consumer technology market, in several months much can change.

It's useful to assess the second of these reasons from a platform strategy lens. A platform has always been considered the Holy Grail of product strategy. A platform allows businesses to lock consumers into their product offerings for extended durations. For classic platform strategy case examples such as Intel, this duration can be several years, due primarily to proprietary technology.

Nowadays, however, the elements that constitute a platform have changed. Proprietary technology may be part of it, but less-proprietary technology and services also constitute platforms. For example, Amazon's one-click ordering, co-branded login system (such as that used by Amazon and Target), recommendation engines, and user experience based on stores (the tabs in their navigation) all are elements of the Amazon platform. And many of these platform elements (patent issues aside) can be easily replicated by competitors.

What this means is that anyone can have a platform strategy. In the rapidly changing consumer technology market, competing at a platform level means competing with products, services, experiences, and technologies in an agile way that is responsive to new market developments. An execution plan locked in and based on old assumptions becomes ineffective in this context.

To succeed in today's market, businesses must instead adopt a new view of decision-making. It is not consensus and buy-in around fixed decision points rooted in old assumptions. It is a coordination of roles across an organization to support broad, less-bounded strategic approaches that permit action in a more responsive way.

## A NEW APPROACH

To support this new view of strategic decision-making, we have developed a set of approaches, some formal and some less so, to enable organizations to make more successful decisions. The common theme in these approaches is the juxtaposition of design methodologies, which tend to be qualitative methods that uncover market and user insights, with traditional decision-making approaches (or adaptations thereof), which tend to be more rigorous and analytical.

In this chapter, I focus on two approaches we believe are particularly effective in helping organizations make successful decisions.

1. The first enhances the business case. In this approach, a business case is developed iteratively, incorporating data from prototypes and associated design research methods, to improve underlying assumptions around user adoption and behavior.

2. The second focuses on evaluation of multiple strategic options in the context of a platform. The core of this approach is a formal analytical framework that evaluates experience with the same rigor as business impact and feasibility. This framework in turn directly enables the traditional strategic planning and roadmapping process to be more responsive to new market developments.

## AN ENHANCED BUSINESS CASE

Ask any consultant and you'll hear the same line: "Business case development is part science, part art." Business case templates exist for virtually every type of business problem conceivable and are easily adaptable to any unforeseen problem. The key challenge is always in the assumptions—the variables that drive the business case output. The way to ensure a business case is accurate is to ensure that the assumptions are accurate. To do this, you research, model, forecast, and test. If certain assumptions can't be determined, you break them down into their component parts, you restructure parts of the business case into a new logical model, or you guess. Then you run sensitivity analyses to make sure you've put enough effort into ensuring that the most important assumptions are accurate. Repeat until satisfied. Then make your decision and plan around the output.

The conventional approach says that at this point, you plan for execution. Designers come in to design products (physical products, applications, Web sites, services, environments, and so forth), which are then passed into development. In parallel, branding, marketing, and distribution strategies are refined.

Most designers prototype as an interim step. Prototyping, at low or high degrees of fidelity, has numerous benefits—key being that it may serve as a tool for user validation, which in turn often helps achieve buy-in within an organization and among other stake-holders. Findings from the prototyping process also help refine the design, ensuring that the product is the best it can be when it moves into development.

When the business then fails, it's hard to place blame. The business case convinced the financial decision-makers. The prototypes were validated by users and convinced everyone else. Clearly one or both were off target, but everyone bought in.

Let's start at the source and consider the business case in more detail. Many a sensitivity analysis reveals that the key assumptions in any business case are related to user adoption—take rates, purchasing patterns, behavior over time. Not surprisingly then, there is a wide body of theory that seeks to describe user adoption in a more refined way. Bass diffusion and other diffusion of innovation models, technology adoption curves, variations on standard statistical distributions, and many others are all theoretical approaches that seek to quantify user adoption so that the key business case assumptions are more accurate.

The unfortunate truth of these approaches, however, is that they are indeed theoretical, designed to describe macro trends and behaviors. A real-world understanding of user adoption and behaviors could greatly improve the accuracy of a theoretical model. We have found that the prototype, in conjunction with a range of other methods from the designer's toolbox, can provide this real-world understanding.

A first set of insights comes from the prototype itself. Product prototypes can be used in usability studies and conjoint analyses to evaluate feature usage and comparative preference. Web site and application prototypes can be used in similar fashion to evaluate user paths, behaviors, drop-off points, and conversions.

A second set of insights comes from contextualization of the prototype. Many design research techniques seek to understand a user's behavior in context. Participatory design brings users into the design process and examines usage in the context of the user's product ecosystem. This allows a Web site prototype, for example, to be understood in the context of the user's broader online experience with competitive and unrelated sites. Similarly, it would allow product prototypes to be seen in the context of the usage of other devices throughout a daily routine.

The results from these efforts help to refine the prototype for successive, more detailed evaluation and to directly feed the business case assumptions of user adoption and behaviors. Indeed, this approach can be used at an earlier stage to inform the ingredients of an opportunity portfolio—test multiple prototypes to determine the most compelling concepts. In turn, the refined business case improves definition of constraints as the product moves into development.

In the end, this interdisciplinary approach results in a more accurate business case and a more validated product, allowing for a better strategic decision to be made. The combination of approaches is synergistic. The best way is not to hand off from business case to design, but instead to conduct both efforts in a parallel and interweaving way. The diagram opposite (Figure 1) illustrates this process.

**Traditional approach:** Independent, sequential business validation track leading to a business case, and user validation track leading to prototypes.

**New approach:** Parallel business and user validation tracks in which design research activities bridge the tracks and improve the output of both (first two cycles depicted).

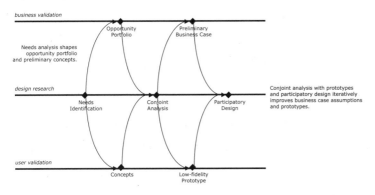

**New approach:** Parallel business and user validation tracks in which design research activities bridge the tracks and improve the output of both, directly feeding strategic planning and pilot activities.

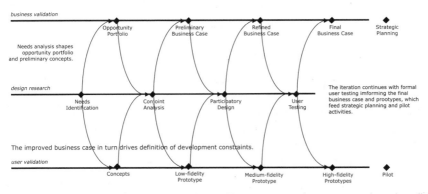

Figure 1. Comparison of independent, sequential business case and prototype tracks and parallel tracks joined by design research methods.

## EVALUATING THE PLATFORM EXPERIENCE

While the business case is the core decision-making tool for evaluation of a single strategic option, a related need is evaluation of multiple strategic options. This step often occurs in a blue-sky situation, when many options are under consideration or when market or competitive activity has changed the business climate in a significant enough way that multiple counter-options to a previously selected path need to be evaluated.

The ideal solution would be to create a business case for every option. But few businesses have the time and money to take this approach. Fortunately, many options can be eliminated from consideration on the basis of other criteria: Is there a strategic fit? Is the option consistent with the brand? Is it organizationally feasible? Is it bold enough?

The tools used to make these types of decisions fit under the category of evaluation frameworks, many of which look like scorecards with weighted criteria. These frameworks often include in a less rigorous way standard business case elements, such as financial impact and cost. They also tend to include other elements important to the business, such as fit, feasibility, and degree of asset leverage. In addition, they may have elements unique to the specific decision at hand, such as opportunity for brand extension or degree of Wow factor. Many of these frameworks have also been codified into processes, such as the Stage-Gate process for product innovation, which uses a series of evaluation scorecards that become increasingly rigorous as products pass through stages and gates of evaluation.

We have found that for businesses to make successful decisions in today's environment, the classic dimensions on which these frameworks are based are often insufficient. Understanding such attributes as strategic fit, business impact, ROI, cost, and feasibility are not enough.

A few real-world examples highlight a key issue with these frameworks. Consider product feature decisions. Most well-thought-out features rate highly on all scorecard dimensions, resulting in feature overload. We've seen examples everywhere—mobile phones with high-resolution cameras, Bluetooth add-ins, MP3 players, and more that still offer only a low-quality speaker and microphone for completing its core function. As another example, consider the many portals and e-commerce sites exhibiting a lack of focus in their vision, crowded with content, user networking features, promotions, video, and multiple navigation schemes.

These examples support the point that competing in today's environment requires competing at the platform strategy level, meaning competing not only with products but also with services, experiences, and technologies in an agile way.

What does this mean for decision-making? The gut answer is that there's some filter related to simplicity, usability, and a clean, well-thought-out experience that dictates which options are right. But how do these general tenets translate into specific decisions around strategic options? What is needed is a method to understand these tenets in a formal way, one that allows for evaluation of the platform experience alongside traditional evaluation framework attributes, such as business impact, feasibility, and cost.

To that end, we use what we call the "experience architecture," a set of criteria related to experience that can be scored and evaluated in terms of clearly defined interrelationships.

Let's break this concept down. The first component is that there are criteria that can be scored. These criteria are derived in the same way in which other scorecard criteria are derived—from key business drivers. Just like the financial driver of "be profitable" translates into "ROI impact" as a scorecard criterion, the experience driver of "clean experience" may translate to "low number of clicks" for a Web site, or the driver of "engaged experience" may translate to "extent of cross-product interaction" for a mobile phone.

The second component is the architecture. The use of this term is deliberate and gets at the crux of how an evaluation framework based on the experience architecture operates. Most attributes in a traditional evaluation framework are independent and can be scored as such—strategic fit can be high, net benefit can be medium, and feasibility can be low. There does not have to be a correlation between cost, benefit, and feasibility. Weightings are used to determine the relative importance of one attribute versus another.

But experience is not a standalone construct. Products compete for mindshare and use with other products in the user's ecosystem. Product features compete with others on the same product. This competition varies by situation, timeframe, and context. The term "architecture" gets at the fact that there is a relationship among criteria—scoring higher on one criterion may have an impact on another, depending on the situation, timeframe, or context. In short, the attributes are no longer independent. Attributes that score high may cause other attributes to score lower.

How do we define this architecture? We use a number of design research tools. Experience models describe a user experience in the context of a user's product ecosystem. User archetypes and customer journey maps describe a customer's experience over time or through stages of engagement. Each of these tools helps describe the components of the platform experience.

From these descriptions of experience we then derive the evaluation framework. The framework often resembles some of the more sophisticated evaluation systems, such as hierarchical systems in which criteria are organized so that changes to one criterion affect others at the same hierarchical level, nodal systems in which changes to one criterion affect others in proximity (which can be defined in various ways), or process models, in which changes to criteria affect successive criteria in a defined process. Often the framework is a hybrid of these, in conjunction with a simple, weighted scorecard.

Frog Design's work with ETS (Educational Testing Service) provides a relevant case study. ETS, the company behind the SAT, TOEFL, and other standardized tests, recognized that today's learning environment is changing in fundamental ways. Education is extending beyond institutional boundaries and competing for share of mind and usage across rapidly evolving technologies. The key insight in our work with ETS was the recognition that educational products are used in the context of a school year, with summer and semester breaks and passage to the next grade as core aspects of the educational experience. We created a time-based experience architecture that structured key aspects of the product experience—such as parental involvement, community engagement, and relationship with nonacademic activities—in the context of the school year and semester milestones. New product ideas were evaluated against this architecture and an adapted Stage-Gate process that measured benefit, cost, and feasibility.

A key benefit of this approach is that it provides a framework to make ongoing decisions about the platform experience. As a result, changes in the market, development efforts, or consumer behavior can be understood in a holistic way, enabling execution planning to be more fluid. For ETS, we used this approach to understand how some parts of the product experience, such as parental involvement, could be achieved quickly, while others, such as learner engagement in a community, would require many steps, given the inherent challenges in growing communities. Figure 2 illustrates this relationship between the experience architecture and the strategic planning process.

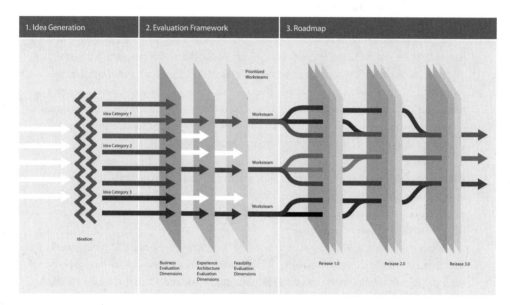

Figure 2. An evaluation process consisting of an experience architecture in conjunction with business impact and feasibility impact dimensions and its relationship to the strategic planning process. The evaluation step is depicted once here, but may be iterated with higher degrees of rigor if a larger screen is required.

## IN CLOSING

The examples of the enhanced business case and the experience architecture represent two approaches we have found to be successful in helping clients make the right strategic decisions in today's frenetic business climate.

But we believe these are symptoms of a broader trend. As the focus of decision-making has fundamentally changed from fixed consensus-building to coordination of roles, there is a significant opportunity for designers to hybridize their more flexible, organic methods with conventional methods that focus on solving point problems. It is this combination of traditional rigor with fluid, dynamic application that is needed to achieve business results in today's market.

# Chapter 3
# Corporate Strategy: Bringing Design Management into the Fold

by Frans Joziasse

*There is clear evidence that firms consider design as one of the issues in developing strategy. Frans Joziasse documents the level of corporate strategy and its implementation and proposes a framework for integrating design within the strategic management process. He examines many points of views, supports conclusions with a wealth of examples and references, and suggests several roles the corporate design manager can take on to influence corporate strategy.*

THE 1990S HAVE seen the design profession come into its maturity. Design managers suggest that design's responsibility goes beyond merely "creating beautiful things"—that it is a source for gaining competitive advantage. The logical outcome of this is that designers will face new responsibilities and challenges, which are exemplified by four major trends in the marketplace.

## 1. DESIGN AS A CORE COMPETENCE

Much more interest is being shown in design as a core competence. Authors such as Rosabeth Moss Kanter, Gary Hamel and C.K. Prahalad, and Gerry Johnson and Kevan Scholes suggest that defining core competencies and organizing to support and augment them ensures continuing success under changing conditions. How is design perceived under these circumstances?

A core competence must make a disproportionate contribution to customer-perceived value, and indeed design has played a prominent and obvious role in the "lifestyle" offerings from companies like Swatch, Nike, and Oakley.

A core competence must be worthy of investments of time and money. For example, in the 1990s, the German auto industry's investments in innovative designs were second only to production outlays in their attempt to gain back market share. Products such as the new VW Beetle, the Mercedes A-Class, and the Audi TT were very public examples of innovative design. Core competencies are now seen to be the gateways to tomorrow's markets. A good example is Dyson Appliances Ltd., the British vacuum cleaner manufacturer. Dyson has clearly shown how design can deliver uniqueness and functionality, helping the company to outsell makers of more conventional products.

## 2. INTEGRATION OF DESIGN INTO THE BUSINESS WORLD

The late 1980s and early 1990s saw such designers as Philippe Starck and Etore Sottsass featured as public figures and artistic heroes. That focus has now widened to include an understanding of designers as influential figures responsible for failure, as well as success. Johann Tomforde, director for product development and design for the Smart, DaimlerChrysler's small-car brand, was forced to resign after it became clear that the company would need to postpone for six months the market introduction for the product. Advertisements in business magazines communicate that successful companies invest heavily in design and that their design directors contribute to the company's success. BusinessWeek, Capital, and *Manager Magazine* pay tribute every year to companies that use design as a source of competitive advantage.

## 3. DESIGN MANAGEMENT AND PLANNING AS A FOCUS FOR CONSULTANCIES

More and more consultancies now offer design management and design planning services. This trend has four origins:

▲ Traditional industrial design agencies, such as IDEO and Ziba, which have extended their services toward integrating design into all business processes.

▲ Traditional management consultancies, such as the Arthur D. Little Group and Andersen Consultants, now offer design services to support the implementation of the corporate strategies they have developed for their clients.

▲ Independent design strategy or innovation consultancies, such as Doblin Group and PARK the design strategists.

▲ Design departments of multinationals, such as Siemens Messe & Design and Philips Design Center, have gone independent and now advocate design management and design planning as a means of positioning themselves in the company and the design industry.

## 4. THE MERGING OF BUSINESS AND DESIGN EDUCATION

Business education all over the world surfs on the waves of design.[1] Three different "merging areas" are in evidence:

- ▲ Traditional executive MBA programs are linking their program with design courses. A good example is the Kenan-Flagler Business School at the University of North Carolina.

- ▲ Years ago, special MBAs and MAs in design management were practicall non-existent. Nowadays, designers with professional experience can take advantage of graduate programs at UK- and Boston-based Westminster University, the Advanced Institute of Science & Technology, in Korea, and others.

- ▲ Several companies—for instance, Korea's Samsung Corp.—now offer their own courses in design management.

### DESIGN AND CORPORATE STRATEGY

> "The effectiveness of design depends on the recognition and place-
> ment of strategic design management as a driver for the organiza-
> tion's leadership. And the conference is dedicated to fostering a
> design-based leadership to shape the 21st century."
> —THE DESIGN MANAGEMENT INSTITUTE, IN ANNOUNCING THE 25TH
> INTERNATIONAL DESIGN MANAGEMENT CONFERENCE

A frequently heard and cited comment from design managers that underlines the demonstrated evolution of design is that designers are currently moving from operational to strategic involvement within corporations. Let's check the reality of this statement. In

The Audi "TT" coupe—an example of the German automotive industry's investment in innovative design (source: *ID Magazine*, Volume 46, Number 5, New York).

1997, two Dutch market researchers[2] asked six hundred business managers of Dutch companies in different industries how they experience the importance of design. The researchers concluded that design is getting more attention within companies and that it is becoming more strategic; however, they were less than clear, at least for readers, in their definition of the word "strategic." A second study, commissioned by the European Community,[3] showed that business managers do believe that design adds value for their companies; at the same time, it was clear that companies still tended to consider design largely as it related to the form and usability of the product.

Consequently, we must ask:

▲ Do business managers truly consider design as a contributor to organizational strategy?

▲ Are there any real differences between design and strategic design? Or does strategic only mean important, as Les Wynn[4] has suggested?

▲ Do design managers know what strategy is? Or have they only adopted it as a useful buzzword?

Dyson "DCO1." Dyson's vacuum cleaner without a vacuum bag (source: *Identity Matters,* 09/00, Art View, the Netherlands).

Many researchers[5] have explored the position of design in the strategy context and have come to the conclusion that the two are indeed linked. They have found, for instance, that

▲ Design is not an isolated process within the business process.

▲ Design and strategy are most strongly linked at the very end of the business process.

▲ The link is one-way, not cyclical or iterative (that is, strategy is fairly inflexible; it does not change as the result of discoveries made in the design process).

▲ Most models show the activity of design as taking place after the business strategy is developed. Only companies with a "design leadership ideology"[6] take design into account when planning the business strategy.

My own research, carried out as part of a dissertation toward an MBA in design management at London's Westminster University, tends to disagree with these observations.

## HOW DO YOU DEFINE STRATEGY? RESEARCH INTERVIEWS

Following the secondary research summarized above, I set about interviewing design managers from six multinational corporations and four design (planning) agencies based in the United States and Europe. Their industries ranged from domestic appliances, footwear, and power tools to computing, telecommunications, industrial machin-

Smart "City-Coupe," DaimlerChrysler's small-car brand
(source: Smart's European advertisement campaign, 1999).

ery, and medical equipment). The multinationals could be identified as having a corporate strategy that supports design. I followed the interviews with a questionnaire.

In the context of the research, interviewees referred to design as *(strategic) design planning, strategic design, visionary design,* and *advanced design.* Most of the design managers I interviewed defined strategy as:

▲ A plan; a direction or course of action

▲ A position; namely, the determination of particular products in particular markets

▲ A perspective; namely, the organization's concept of its business

Many of the interviewees linked these definitions with the words end user, which indicated that they tended to see their strategic role as advocates of consumers' future needs. Moreover, most interviewees seemed to consider the development of their corporate strategy (or that of their clients) to be a process that was at once emergent and deliberate.

## STRATEGIC DESIGN MANAGEMENT

Many strategy theorists[7] agree that there are three levels of strategy within corporations: corporate strategy, business strategy, and operational strategy. For design management to be more fundamentally linked with overall corporate strategy, it is necessary to have an effect on all three levels, as below:

▲ Strategic design management. Design can operate at the corporate strategy level if focus can be placed on its use as a source of competitive advantage and a catalyst for change to the overall scope and direction of the organization. Truly strategic design projects influence a company's direction in terms of structure, finance, and human resources. In this way, a strategic design manager is involved fully in the corporate strategy process.

▲ Business or tactical design management. At this level, design can be managed as a proficiency to generate unique product concepts, as well as search for new market opportunities. Tactical design is executed at the level of single business units within an organization, but it also has interrelationships with design management as it is practiced at the level of corporate strategy. The tactical design manager must always be focused on the extent to which new product concepts meet future customer needs as dictated by the objectives of the business unit.

▲ Operational design management. At the project level, design must concentrate on the efficiency and effectiveness of the design process, the design team, and individual design projects. The operational design manager focuses on how design contributes to the business and corporate level of design management. A successful business strategy depends to a large extent on decisions that are made and activities that occur at the operational level.

Most of my respondents believed that design did indeed contribute on all three levels in their companies. However, although the preoccupation of design could be identified on all three strategic levels, the corporate strategy level clearly underperforms the business and operational strategy levels. How can this situation be improved for design management? First, it's important to consider how corporate strategy tends to be managed.

## THE MANAGEMENT OF CORPORATE STRATEGY

Strategic management on the corporate level is concerned with decision-making about major issues facing the organization, as well as ensuring that the ensuing strategy is put into effect. It can be thought as having three main elements:[8]

▲ Strategic analysis, in which the company seeks to understand the current strategic position of the organization

▲ Strategic choice, which formulates possible courses of action, evaluates them, and chooses one or more of them

▲ Strategic implementation, in which the chosen strategy is planned and the required changes in the organization is managed

My interviewees didn't demonstrate a clear organizational connection between the management of design and the management of corporate strategy, but it was possible to identify four main characteristics of their involvement:

▲ It is driven by the corporate vision and mission

▲ It fundamentally affects the business

▲ It has a long-term impact on the company's competitive position and profitability

▲ It is based on end-user needs

One aspect of my research that was very encouraging was that most respondents believed, and apparently experienced through their projects, that design does create and generate corporate strategy. This could mean that design has a strong involvement in the step between strategic analysis and strategic choice. I believe design is especially well suited to help with this step, because it is able to look beyond the immediate strategic position of an organization and take a wider view.

## THE PERCEPTIVE APPROACH

Second, I suggest design managers develop a new approach toward the management of corporate strategy that goes beyond the standard conceptions.[9] I call this the "perceptive approach." Perceptive in this context means observant and alert but also intuitive, understanding, and sensitive. It is an approach that offers an enlarged perspective on strategy—an approach that perfectly fits the skills of design managers:[10]

Ford "021 C," as a key function to change Ford's DNA, part of Nasser's new corporate strategy (source: *Harvard Business Review*, March–April 1999).

If managers have to "see the big picture" and create strategic "vision"—clearly more than just metaphors—then their perceptions require the soft, speculative information they favor, which is better suited to synthesis than analysis.[11]

Phoenix and npk industrial design, "Objects for children," can be considered as a vision on future needs, integrating new technologies (source: npk-now, issue 4, 1998, Leiden).

Philips Corporate Design, "Updated version of the traditional medicine cabinet," one of many projects in Marzano's "High Design" company-wide design consciousness program (source: *From vision to reality*, Philips, Eindhoven, 1996).

Whirlpool, "Macrowave," of one of the designs out of a project to show design's corporate contribution toward creating strategic innovations (source: *Macrowaves, new frontiers for the modern microwave*, Whirlpool Europe srl, 2000).

My research has convinced me that design management is already beginning to take this role. (See examples at left.) Designers are teaching management about design, thus developing a "design mind" within the company and paving the way for design as a new core competence. They are helping to visualize strategy so that it can be clarified and gain consensus throughout the company. As well, companies are finding that designers are well placed to manage and support brand image, create brand loyalty, develop new product opportunities, and support strategic innovation.

## WHAT FUTURE ROLES SHOULD STRATEGIC DESIGN MANAGEMENT CONSIDER?

Based on my research and professional experience, I assume that the move to design maturity will intensify over the next few years. The signs are everywhere, from business literature to company perceptions; there is an attitude of acceptance rather than avoidance of the challenges of an uncertain and very dynamic future along with a smaller,

| | Strategic Analysis |
|---|---|
| Catalyst | Design management should encourage management to think and plan for the future. |
| Analyst | Design management should challenge management's mental models and mindsets by enabling them to be more explicit in their key assumptions about the future. Through a perceptive and continuous way of analyzing the organization and its environment, design management should set the criteria for new concepts of corporate strategy. |
| | **Strategic Choice** |
| "Synthesyst" | Design management should transform the company's perceptions of its future into designs that harmonize with corporate strategy. Design management should be able to visualize the outcomes of creative transition: This is design's unique core competence. |
| Evaluator | Design management should be an advocate of new designs. It should use its abilities to build connections with users who can critically evaluate these designs. |
| | **Strategy Implementation** |
| Implementor | At the end of a project, design management should be able to transform tested prototypes into a final design that harmonizes with corporate strategy. Design management should use its natural talent and experience to work with and manage multidisciplinary teams for a successful implementation. |

The roles of strategic design management in the management of corporate strategy.

"virtual" world. It is an attitude that accepts the importance of creating fundamentally new products and businesses and that conceives strategy as stretch. Much like good design, a perceptive approach toward corporate strategy is creative and visionary, rational as well as intuitive—and a critical element in the survival of an organization. Design, as well as strategy, is concerned with creating values and making them visible, not to mention profitable. Indeed, design management has developed innovative and imaginative strategic tools—"vision documents" and "strategic concepts"—as well as complete philosophies, such as Philips' High Design. As Alison Rieple[12] has suggested, the building of corporate powerhouses depends very much on a professional group's ability to visualize its core competencies.

Design is truly moving into a more pivotal role within the corporate world, and design managers should rejoice at the prospect of developing design into a continuous element of corporate strategy. Strategic design management should emphasize design as a source of sustainable competitive advantage and as an element that can change the direction of the organization.

## A NOTE ON THE RESEARCH

There may be an unconscious irony about a study that seeks information relating design to corporate strategy by interviewing only design managers. I admit that this may result in a biased view.

My research has focused only on the management of industrial design. I assume that the effect of strategic design management is more powerful when all design disciplines work closely together.

### Suggested Reading

Cooper, Rachel, and Press, Mike. *The Design Agenda: A Guide to Successful Design Management* (Chichester, U.K.: John Wiley & Sons, 1995).

Courtney, Hugh, Kirkland, Jane, and Viguerie, Patrick. "Strategy Under Uncertainty." *Harvard Business Review*, November–December, 1997.

Hamel, Gary, and Prahalad, C.K. *Competing for the Future* (Boston: Harvard Business School Press, 1994).

Hendriks, Hans. "The Strategic Role of Design in Network Organizations." (MBA Design Management dissertation, Westminster University, London, 1999).

Joziasse, Frans. "What Specific Roles Should Industrial Design Consider to Make a Significant Contribution to the Management of Corporate Strategy?" (MBA Design Management dissertation, Westminster University, London, 1999).

Kanter, Rosabeth Moss. *Frontiers of Management* (Boston: Harvard Business School Press, 1997).

Mintzberg, Henry, Ahlstrand, Bruce, and Lampel, Joseph. *Strategy Safari* (New York: The Free Press, 1998).

Peters, Tom. *The Circle of Innovation* (London: Hodder & Stoughton, 1997).

Tushman, L. Michael, and O'Reilly, Charles A. *Winning Through Innovation: A Practical Guide to Leading Organizational Change and Renewal* (Boston: Harvard Business School Press, 1997).

## Endnotes

1. See, for example, the *Design Management Journal*'s Summer 1998 issue.

2. Dirk van Ginkel, in "Design onmiskenbaar in de lift," from *Design in Business*, May 1997.

3. Noted by John Tackara in *Winners* (Amsterdam: BIS, 1997).

4. Les Wynn, "Industrial Design: Crossing the Client/Consultant Divide," *Design Management Journal*, Spring 2000, p. 28.

5. See, for instance British Standard 7000, Part 2 (London: *British Standard*, 1997), Kurzmarski, in Project Management Module 2 for the MBA in Design Management (London: Westminster University, 1998), and Gillian and Bill Hollins in the Corporate Strategy and Design Module for the MBA in Design Management (London: Westminster University, 1997).

6. Wynn, op. cit.

7. Gerry Johnson and Kevan Scholes, *Exploring Corporate Strategy* (New York: Prentice Hall, 1993).

8. Johnson and Scholes, op. cit.

9. See, for example, David Whittington, *What Is Strategy and Does It Matter?* (London: Routledge, 1995).

10. This has also been suggested by Victor Seidel in "Moving from Design to Strategy: The Four Roles of Design-led Strategy Consulting," *Design Management Journal*, Spring 2000, p. 35.

11. Henry Mintzberg, *The Rise and Fall of Strategic Planning* (London: Prentice Hall, 1994), p. 319.

12. Alison Rieple, in the Corporate Strategy and Design module for the MBA in Design Management (London: Westminster University, 1997), Unit 3.

**by Robyn Waters**

*As good design enhances life, it merges with desire and touches the soul, according to Robyn Waters. In the "claustrophobia of abundance," businesses should consider this connection essential to sales and growth. To facilitate such links, Waters highlights a design process and designers who synthesize a focus on the head (need), the handbag (value and price), and the heart (desire).*

**"The heart has its reasons of which reason knows nothing."**
**—BLAISE PASCAL**

WHAT INSPIRES DESIGN? A need for profits? A quest for fame, notoriety, or market leadership? A desire to beautify?

Where does good design come from?

Consider for a moment the obscure cocoa bean. Would you believe the cocoa bean inspired one of our society's most timeless and recognized designs? In designing the iconic Coca-Cola bottle, Swedish immigrant Alexander Samuelsen—an engineer employed by the Root Glass Company in Terre Haute, Indiana—found his inspiration from an illustration of a cocoa bean in the *Encyclopedia Britannica*.

Frank Gehry's Guggenheim Museum in Bilbao is intended to resemble a ship. Its brilliantly reflective titanium panels call to mind fish scales, echoing the other organic and fish-like forms that commonly occur in Gehry's designs.

Did a bug inspire Ferdinand Porsche when he designed the first low, light, aerodynamic, and economical VW Beetle?

The first Vespa was produced in 1946 and became an instant success. When Enrico Piaggio first saw the scooter his designers had developed, he remarked "Sempra una Vespa!" thus instantly naming the design. Vespa is Italian for wasp. Did an insect inspire the design of that first Piaggio scooter?

For Arne Jacobsen, there isn't any question which came first, the chicken or the egg. Jacobsen's Egg Chair was inspired by the elegance and beauty of a hen's egg. The chair is an example of the movement in design that adapts organic forms in such a way as to bring comfort into our living spaces.

## MOTHER NATURE VERSUS HUMAN NATURE

I suppose one could say that nature inspired these designs. Perhaps that's true. But I think it was more than just Mother Nature at work.

I think human nature played a big part in the ultimate success of each of these examples. In fact, I think human nature triumphed. With all of these products, it's the heart that ultimately helped them to become icons in our lives. Think about it.

Coca-Cola once professed that it wanted to "teach the world to sing, in perfect harmony."

The Guggenheim Bilbao is more than a well-designed venue to house modern art. The museum virtually resurrected a dying city in the rust belt of Spain and brought it to world prominence.

The original purpose of the Volkswagen Beetle was to be a car ordinary folks could afford to buy and drive.

The Vespa was designed to help Italians get around a war-torn, war-ravaged country. In post-WWII Italy, the roads were blown up and gasoline was in short supply. Believe it or not, the inexpensive Vespa could accommodate a family of four and get them where they needed to go, in great style.

The Egg Chair was designed to welcome travelers to the lobby of the Royal Hotel in Copenhagen and to help them feel at home, even if they were half a world away from their homes.

I think good design ultimately delivers more than function or beauty. It even does more than bring beauty to the bottom line. Good design makes you feel good . . . it makes your life better. Good design touches your heart. And when it touches your heart, design and desire become one.

## NEED VERSUS DESIRE

Never before in human history have consumers faced so many products . . . or so many choices. Global prosperity is fueling economic growth and mammoth consumption.

Vespa

Coca-Cola

VW Beetle

Egg Chair

Guggenheim Museum

The Internet has spawned a global marketplace. Increasingly sophisticated consumers now have the ability to seek out and purchase whatever they need. There are almost no limits to what any of us can locate and purchase.

Some pundits say that we are living with a claustrophobia of abundance—meaning we have too much stuff, stuff that doesn't always mean a whole lot. Who really needs another pair of jeans? A TV with a bigger screen? Another cup of expensive coffee?

To add to the complexity, we've reached a point where manufacturing and distribution methods are mostly perfected. That means function and value have become minimal expectations for every product we consider.

Professor Robert Hayes of the Harvard School of Business said a few years back, "Fifteen years ago, companies competed on price. Today it's quality. Tomorrow it's design." Well, tomorrow is here. Design has become a powerful advantage in the business arsenal.

But, if our needs have been met and the quality improved to where everything is good and the price is such that most can afford the good stuff, isn't it time to ask ourselves this basic question: What is it that we want, not just need? What will keep us shopping, buying, and coming back for more? What will keep the retail world ka-chinging?

The answers to these questions aren't always found in the marketplace. Numbers won't show you the way, either. Statistics and analysis can't really point us in the direction of what's next. A number or statistic is a measurement telling us what's already happened.

To answer the question: What is it that customers want next? I believe you have to first determine what's important. You have to go inside, into the hearts and minds of consumers, to understand what they value . . . what's important to them. That's the basis of my trend from the inside out philosophy.

My trend philosophy was developed as a result of more than thirty years in the retail trend and product development world. The first half of my career was spent in the department store world, cultivating high fashion and trying to convince fashionistas everywhere that in order to be truly cool they needed to be on trend and if they wanted to remain hip, they had to constantly be on the lookout for the next big thing.

I began to revise my philosophy when I went to work for Target. When I joined the company, there were five people in the trend department and the company had $3 billion in sales. Three years later, I was named trend director, the company had achieved $10 billion in sales, and my department consisted of eight people, including our first designer.

A few years later, I was named vice president of trend, design, and product development. We were growing fast, and over the years I hired many more designers, including graphic designers, CAD designers, industrial designers, technical designers, and clothing and fashion designers. By the time Target reached $48 billion in sales, there were more than 100 designers and trend managers working in design and product development, and Target had become a nationally recognized brand that customers loved.

## THE 3H DESIGN THEORY

My 3H design theory is a basic part of my trend from the inside out philosophy. I developed it as a way of explaining to young designers the three main reasons why a customer would come in to Target to buy something that they were designing.

The head is about need: I'm out of toothpaste, time to buy. The handbag is about value and price: It's on sale, so I'd better stock up. The heart is about desire: I love that and I have to have it.

When it was still a small, regional discounter, Target realized that in order to differentiate itself from the competition it would need to embrace a strategy other than lowest price. It knew the economies of scale realized by the sheer size of WalMart wouldn't be an attainable goal. Design became the ultimate differentiator, the secret sauce in a simple formula that reframed the discount retail landscape and turned Target into the upscale discounter.

The formula is simple—I view it as a three-legged stool. Target's mission is to be trend-right, guest-focused, and design-driven. (Note: Target calls its customers guests, in the Disney tradition.) Trend-right comes out of Target's department store heritage. Notice I didn't say trend-forward. The trend has to be interpreted and translated into something that makes sense for guests' lives.

Guest-focused means that everything Target does should focus on seeing things from the guest's perspective. Target never tries to preach to its customers; instead it seeks to surprise and delight them. The company did that by learning more about its guests than just their ZIP codes, ages, and income levels. A concerted effort was made to really know and understand the lives of customers: what was important, what really mattered, and which issues were challenging them on a day-to-day basis.

At Target, design became a driving factor in the owned-brand product development process. It was about much more than form or function or cutting out costs. Design was the tool used to help translate a trend into something fun and meaningful that would inspire desire, not just fulfill a need.

Target was also ahead of trend in understanding and embracing the idea that a logo could become a lovemark. The idea that you could love a brand wasn't new; what was new was the idea of embracing that concept as a design strategy. The Sign of the Times campaign ultimately put Target on the national map by showcasing its commitment to great design and stamping the brand indelibly as a lovemark in the hearts and minds of its guests. Target continues that tradition today with its Design for All campaign. By leveraging great design with a lot of heart, Target became known affectionately as Tarzhay.

## THE STARCK REALITY SIPPY CUP

One of the strategies Target used to showcase its commitment to great design was to develop unique partnerships with well-known designers and showcase their exclusive products in the stores. Michael Graves was a landmark first, and many others have followed.

When Target embarked on the Starck Reality Design Project with world-famous designer Philippe Starck, none of us really knew what to expect. As the head of the design department, I knew we'd learn a lot about the technical world of design. But I had no idea we'd learn so much about the heart.

One of the first products Starck proposed was a sippy cup, one of those sturdy, unspillable cups with a lid that kids can drink from without messing up the kitchen table or spilling milk onto the new sofa. Most parents consider sippy cups a standard piece of child-rearing equipment . . . a need.

The design that Starck presented was unique, to say the least. It resembled a clear, cut-crystal, double-handled loving cup on a pedestal. Initially the buyers were hesitant to even consider the design. It looked so impractical sitting on the pedestal, as though it were more likely to spill, not less.

To convince buyers to go forward with the counterintuitive design, Starck first demonstrated that if the vessel did tip or was knocked over, the liquid wouldn't spill. Therefore the head was satisfied; the product was useful and it worked. Because we were Target, the design, although chic, could still be made inexpensively and retail for $3.49—still a value for the handbag test.

It was Starck's passionate belief that every little girl should feel like a princess when she drank from the sippy cup, just as Mommy does when she sips champagne from finely cut crystal. Ultimately, he convinced the merchants to think with their hearts about this merchandising decision, and the design moved forward into production.

The sippy cup was displayed on the aisle endcaps and featured in fashion editorials; it ultimately became an icon for the entire Starck Reality Design Project. By leveraging great design that connected with the hearts of Target shoppers, a great product was delivered with a lot of buzz and a big Wow factor.

Target isn't the only company to leverage the idea of design with heart to deliver profits and delight customers. Apple is another great company that has consistently delivered on this equation.

There are many Apple/Steve Jobs stories. My favorite is Jobs talking about the Mac OS X. When he was asked what distinguished the OS X operations system from other operating systems on the market, he reportedly didn't utter a single word about megahertz or gigabytes, but instead replied: "We made the buttons on the screen look so good you'll want to lick them."

Hmmmm . . . Need or desire? Isn't it interesting that the literal translation of the French term for window shopping, *leche-vitrines*, is window-licking? Window shopping is about dreams and desire. And that's what design with heart is about too.

## HEART AND SOUL

A chair must be relaxing. A telephone must be comfortable. A toy must be playful. No doubt it takes design expertise to accomplish these things. But to design a product with heart, you need a designer with soul.

My first book, *The Trendmaster's Guide*, is a simple guide that shows how anyone can become a trendmaster. It's an alphabetical tour of my personal trend philosophy. The letter *s* is for soul.

What is soul? How do you put it into a product? Unfortunately, there is no formula for soul. Products with soul can be big or small, useful or frivolous, cheap or expensive, simple or fancy, elegant or exotic. You can't measure, flowchart, dictate, or expedite soul (much to the chagrin of Six Sigma black belts). Soul is one of the main ingredients that put the heart we all love into our products.

Charles Handy, the preeminent British management guru, said, "Soul is one of those concepts that, like beauty, evaporates when you try to define it, but like beauty it is instantly recognizable when you meet it." Products designed with soul are easy to fall in love with and much sought after in a marketplace awash with mediocrity.

Hiring designers with soul should be a top priority for any company looking to raise the love quotient of their product. Finding them may be challenging. My advice is to look for designers with passion—those who see a world of possibilities as opposed to those who believe there's only one right way to design something.

How to spot a designer with soul? They tend to have voracious appetites for knowledge and a relentless curiosity. They aren't afraid to walk in other worlds, and they aren't afraid to show their enthusiasm and their emotions either.

## MARKETING TO THE HEART

Once you've unleashed the power of design with heart into your product development process, it's important to make sure your customers find out about what you've accomplished. In order to do that, you don't necessarily have to take out a full-page ad in the *New York Times* or unleash a flurry of press releases to the media. Word of mouth will spread infectiously as a result of the genuine enthusiasm generated about your product. But as a marketer, how do you talk to your customer in a heartfelt way and share what you've accomplished?

I believe you need to reframe how you think and talk about your product. Instead of listing features and benefits or plastering a giant price point in the headline, think about how you can reach your customers' hearts with your message.

Pampers was first to market with a practical and affordable disposable diaper. It wasn't necessarily glamorous, but it was well designed, functional, and worth the price. The marketing message was simple: Pampers makes moms happy.

When Kimberly Clark launched Huggies, Pampers had a 75 percent market share. KC added a lot of features and benefits to set the product apart from the competition. Huggies offered a better fit as a result of design improvements such as elastic leg holes and Velcro closures and greater function as a result of better absorbency. Although the product improvements were significant, KC knew that the competition would eventually catch up and even out the playing field.

The smartest thing KC did when it created its marketing message was to reframe Pampers' original value equation to take the heart into consideration. Yes, Pampers made mothers happy, but Huggies made babies happy. Just imagine how that made mom feel! Even the name Huggies implies something soft, loving, and wonderful for babies.

The stakes were effectively raised from a consideration of the next design innovation or technological improvement that would make mom's life easier to what was really important to mom—her baby! Huggies came from behind and ultimately surpassed Pampers as the leading disposable diaper on the market.

Another example of reframing your message to market to the heart is the story I once heard about the London Underground. For years, ridership on the Tube, and on the suburban commuter rail system, had been declining, even while London's streets became more and more crowded, parking spaces became harder to find, and pollution levels skyrocketed.

Transportation authorities knew they had to redesign their product to entice riders back to mass transportation. They set to work, cleaning up the graffiti, installing Wi-Fi in the cars, offering designer coffee in the newly remodeled café dining cars of the commuter trains, and improving overall efficiency and reliability.

They announced these design improvements with a big media campaign that trumpeted: We get you to work faster! The results? Nothing dramatic happened. Ridership levels remained virtually flat, despite the improvements.

After doing a little research and talking to their desired customers, the authorities developed a different approach to their marketing message. They now trumpeted: We get you home faster. Ridership went up dramatically.

Why? It was the same cars on the same tracks going the same direction, back and forth, all day, every day. The new message was a success because it got to the heart of the matter and focused on what was really important to the customers. What really mattered to them was getting home faster, to their families and to their lives. Getting to work on time was a given, a need. But getting home faster was a bonus and a desired outcome as far as the heart was concerned.

## SENSE AND SENSIBILITIES

Today, when a business sets out to design something new, it is often designed around a hard goal—taking into account form and function, materials, desired price points, production capabilities, and necessary profit margins. That only makes sense.

But I believe we have to look beyond the statistics and the numbers and appeal to other sensibilities, such as our emotions. I know that's an unpopular statement in today's numbers- and results-driven world. But I believe that things other than numbers can measure results. I like to quote W.C. Fields: "Statistics are like bikinis. What they reveal is important, but what they hide is vital." Those numbers may be hiding what's really important—like the way a product makes you feel.

Design with heart, I believe, goes beyond what is possible given the numbers and surpasses it. Tom Peters says, "Design is the fundamental soul of a manmade creation; it's why we love something!" These days, if you want to thrive, not just survive, in the crowded marketplace, you need to find ways to put heart into your designs and soul back into the dollar sign. That's what design with heart is all about.

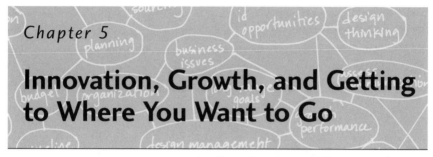

*Chapter 5*

# Innovation, Growth, and Getting to Where You Want to Go

## by Ryan Jacoby and Diego Rodriguez

*Design thinking is a crucial business asset—one that can, indeed, move a company forward and improve the bottom line. To optimize this impact, Ryan Jacoby and Diego Rodriguez advise thoughtfully structuring the innovation process. They stress working on projects that improve people's lives, and they present a "ways to grow" model that helps managers direct and assess innovation efforts.*

"WE NEED TO be more innovative." As a reader of this book, you have probably voiced that sentiment hundreds of times. And no doubt you have heard at least one business leader say, "We want to be our industry's innovation leader," or, "We need a breakthrough innovation." Though lofty and aspirational, these statements belie the complexity and difficulty of innovating in a sustained, effective manner. Indeed, the sheer breadth of the challenge can be paralyzing.

Innovation loves structure. To many new to innovating, this may be surprising. But design thinkers are inspired by constraints,[1] which provide the focus to do generative work in the face of great complexity. At IDEO, we have evolved and refined methods and tools that use design thinking to help our clients structure their innovation efforts. These tools are based not only on lessons learned from the thousands of projects IDEO has done with clients but also on some of the best external thinking in the nascent field of systematic innovation.

We will share with you some of the methods we use at IDEO to uncover "innovation bias," link innovation to growth and outcome goals, match process to desired outcomes, and assess the effectiveness of your efforts. While we recognize that these methods are not the ultimate innovation painkiller, we hope you find them useful in increasing the efficiency and effectiveness of your efforts.

## START BY DETERMINING YOUR INNOVATION BIAS

We like to begin an innovation journey by trying to uncover what we call the innovation bias of the individuals and organizations on our team. We see three types of biases in organizations we work with:

1. Human: "How might we become more relevant to people outside our existing markets?"

2. Technology: "How might we leverage this new technology in the marketplace?"

3. Business: "How might innovation allow us to grab share from our competitors in this growing new market?"

Our experience creating successful innovations at IDEO tells us again and again that the best efforts come from organizations that solve for human desirability, point 1 in the above list, early in the process. You must uncover human needs to design compelling user value propositions. Otherwise, why would anyone want to buy what you sell? Technology and business, points 2 and 3 above, are critical elements of any innovation effort, but we view them as lenses with which to enhance and refine the user value proposition as we proceed with an innovation journey. The trick is to lead with human needs and balance all three perspectives.

The following questions can help assess innovation bias:

▲ Origin and Outlook: Where in an organization—functions, roles, people—do growth projects originate? We have worked for clients in technology-driven organizations in which user-driven insights identified by marketing are less valued. Similarly, we have worked for clients in marketing-led organizations that ignore business model or technology opportunities because of the "risk to the brand." Identifying the dominant point of view helps you to determine whether you are missing opportunities.

▲ Decisions: How are decisions made on innovation projects? Sometimes, promising user value propositions are screened early by powerful veto voices. For example, a manufacturing engineer might say, "It takes $10,000,000 to change our manufacturing lines, I just don't see that being worth it," and effectively kill a human-centric innovation.

▲ Team: Do the people who address human desirability, technical feasibility, and business viability work together on the same team? Or are handoffs required? Often, an innovation team will pass a concept or prototype to a business team to "size the market" or to a delivery team to "figure out how to get this thing made," without a common vision or shared passion for an idea. Recognizing and managing the handoffs is critical.

▲ Iteration: Do you iterate multiple times through human desirability, technical feasibility, and business viability before making decisions to prototype, proceed, or abandon an innovation project? An organization that identifies a seemingly compelling value proposition often takes a concept directly to validation before prototyping or refining the value proposition. Doing so leads to a less balanced perspective and lack of market-based evidence to guide decision-making.

Your answers will indicate whether a different innovation approach—likely a move to a more human-led process—is warranted. Once an organization or a team realizes that innovation effectiveness requires a balance of human, technical, and business factors, it is more likely to consider and frame innovation opportunities in a way that leads to success in the market.

In the early stages of an innovation project, it is the questions you do not ask that bite you later. Better to surface and address your institutional bias early than to ship things that have untested desirability, or to pass on a concept that could have had a real impact in the market.

## GROWTH AND INNOVATION

Once you have assessed your innovation bias, what comes next? First, allow us to ask one of those broad questions we alluded to in the Introduction: Why are you trying to innovate? We hope the answer is "To deliver experiences that make life better for people." Create value and the rewards will follow. However, in a world that focuses more on shareholder value than on the needs of all stakeholders in our society, altruism alone is not sufficient. There must be an economic benefit to justify the expenditure of time, effort, and capital. In the end, the benefit expected from innovating is growth.

Organic growth comes from creating markets that do not yet exist, differentiating within an established

**Ways to Grow**

NEW OFFERINGS

**EXTEND**
- Extending brands
- Share of wallet
- Leveraging users

**CREATE**
- Creating markets
- Disrupting markets

**MANAGE**
- Raising price
- Raising usage
- Winning share

**ADAPT**
- Expanding footprint
- Winning share

EXISTING OFFERINGS

EXISTING USERS                                    NEW USERS

Understand the relationship between your growth intention and the innovation outcome you are seeking. Incremental, evolutionary, and revolutionary outcomes require different approaches and expectations for results.

market, or by jump-starting a declining industry. As a result, it is a natural focus for design thinkers. The results of organic growth may be concentrated on the top line, the bottom line, or both.

But when faced with all these options, where can you start? This is where the next tool, Ways to Grow, can help. It cuts through the fog of innovation by clearly identifying, describing, and prioritizing opportunities for growth in a way that is simple yet actionable.

## Ways to Grow

Before we show you how you can use this tool in practice, let us talk about a few of its important features.

First, the origin of the diagram on the previous page (that is, the lower-left-corner point) is anchored in an organization's existing assets and capabilities. Because each company is different, each company's origin is unique, even within the same industry. For example, we all recognize that Wal-Mart and Target are both discount retailers, but it is easier to imagine Target's brand being able to offer interior decorating services to boomer women than Wal-Mart's brand. What is revolutionary to one company is incremental to another company. It is all relative. Think about your company or your client. Where could it easily go that its competitor could not?

Notice, too, that we have drawn the Ways to Grow diagram using the word "users" instead of "markets." We have found that we reach richer (literally and figuratively) innovation outcomes when we think of markets as the sum of real individuals, rather than as an abstraction of marketing data. It is difficult to design something compelling without picturing a face or feeling empathy for a person's wants, needs, and behaviors.

A wise business thinker once noted that there are no new business ideas under the sun, innovative or not.[2] You have likely encountered similar frameworks in the course of your educations and careers. But though its provenance may be uncertain, the utility of Ways to Grow is undeniable: It brings outcome-centric structure to the innovation process.

## Match Growth Intent to an Innovation Outcome

The first way to use Ways to Grow is to articulate how you intend to grow, then to match that intention to an innovation outcome. This type of brief, yet often skipped, discussion yields shared expectations and helps frame the rest of the innovation journey. To make the discussion of intent more concrete, we will often walk our client through the following set of questions:

## How new is the user?

**Contexts:** Will a user experience the offering in a new context? Is the context new for the offering? On a recent project, an IDEO team found that, due to fundamental differences of culture and infrastructure, the needs of people doing housework in rural Asia were quite different from the needs of people doing housework in rural America.

**Occasions:** Is your offering helping a user at a new time? Food and beverage companies have a deep understanding of occasions. On a recent project, an IDEO team explored the differences between the needs of someone having a glass of wine with dinner versus having a beer after work.

**Jobs:** What is the user trying to accomplish with your offering? Clay Christensen and Michael Raynor nicely describe the concept of jobs-as-outcomes in their book *The Innovator's Solution.* Our colleague Jane Fulton Suri's book, *Thoughtless Acts*, empathetically and elegantly illustrates ways in which people accomplish a variety of desired outcomes, ranging from the seemingly mundane to the deeply meaningful.

**Mindsets:** Are the user's emotions, hopes, and aspirations new to your company or organization? While exploring the future of a popular sport, an IDEO team found that people had three basic mindsets, or approaches, to participating in that sport. These mindsets were not determined by a person's age, physical abilities, or athletic experience.

### How new should you make the offering?

**Value proposition:** Are there new visceral (instinctive feeling), reflective (conveying a sense of identity), and behavioral (functional) benefits and attributes that can be offered to the user?[3] Is it just one new element or a combination of two or even all three? Unfortunately, innovation is often focused on the search for functional benefits, which limits the overall potential for market success. Visceral design (making an offering more beautiful) and reflective design (appealing to a user's desire for meaning and identity) are also valuable ways to create real value.

**Business model:** Are there new demand-side aspects of the business model, such as pricing, frequency of payment, or modes of ownership? When considering your offering, would a person have to shift his personal frame of reference for comparing price or making decisions? A recent success example from the world of financial services is Keep the Change, a service that rounds up purchases made with a Bank of America debit card to the nearest dollar and transfers the difference from individuals' checking accounts into their savings accounts. The convenience and ease helps a member save money over the long run and represents a radically new way to think about saving.

**User (and customer) journey:** Where, when, how, and why might a user experience the offering in the world? Which components of messaging, sample, trial, usage, disposal, reuse, and maintenance are critical in shaping that experience? On a recent project, an IDEO team identified opportunities for wall coverings by understanding the entire social cycle. To do so, they spent time with salespeople, in the store, with installers, and in homes.

**Technology:** In order to deliver on the value proposition, will we—or could we—use technologies that are new to our organization or to the people who will use them? IDEO helped Organ Recovery Systems to design the LifePort Kidney Transporter. The design

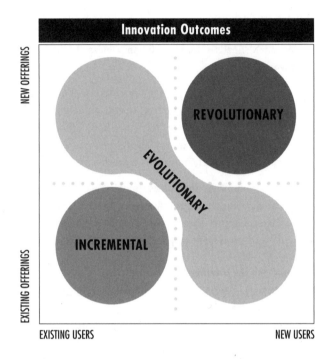

Organic growth can emerge from every quadrant of Ways to Grow. Use
this tool to a) identify the type of growth you intend to create, b) recognize the scope of that challenge and deploy an appropriate innovation
process, and c) assess your portfolio of innovation efforts.

would not have been possible without radical improvements in sensing and micropro-
cessor technologies.

Next, it is important to recognize the outcome associated with your growth intention. Doing so allows you to design the process and assess your efforts with outcomes
in mind. Across IDEO's work, we have seen three basic archetypes of innovation
outcomes:

1.  Incremental innovation: existing users and existing offerings

2.  Evolutionary innovation: existing users and new offerings or new users and
    existing offerings

3.  Revolutionary innovation: new users and new offerings

## MATCH RESOURCES AND PROCESS

Once you have used the Ways to Grow tool to identify your growth and innovation goals,
your innovation team can discuss how to best match resources and processes. To in-

crease the probability of achieving your desired innovation outcome, you need to make choices about the right type of innovation process to use (whose extremes are execution versus exploration), the right type of people to assign to the team, and the right type of outcome measures to measure success. For example, consider the following two recent innovation projects at IDEO.

## INCREMENTAL OUTCOME

At IDEO, we were asked to help reinvigorate and generate growth for a venerable beer brand. First, we facilitated a discussion to identify the client's growth intent. There were differing opinions about whether to pursue new consumers or to develop a more premium offering for existing consumers. As the project continued, our clients felt the brand was ready and able to address existing beer drinkers, given its constraints.

An incremental project requires execution-focused process and people. Our team was staffed with designers who had multiple experiences putting together detailed design documents. On the extended team, we worked with resources skilled at navigating the organizational decision points required to proceed through a more linear process to take an innovation to market, such as a classic stage-gate development flow. Our research was focused on understanding, not exploration. We created prototypes that could be used directly in the existing market validation process, which for this incremental project meant focus groups. When considering our opportunity areas, we were acutely aware of the costs associated with changes to bottling lines and packaging. We understood the incremental consumption and contribution margin required to make these investments worth it in the near term. The company started shipping a new offering in early 2007.

## REVOLUTIONARY OUTCOME

On another recent project, a food manufacturer asked us to imagine the future of cooking and how one of its smaller, but important, brands could play a role in that future as defined by Ways to Grow. Users could be new and so could the offerings. Our client was a person who understood from personal experience what it took to marshal resources and build a new business. He needed help uncovering a revolutionary human-led strategy and making it tangible to inspire his organization.

A revolutionary project requires exploration-focused processes and people. Our research explored food trends both in places in which the brand was entrenched and in contexts and with mindsets outside the field in which the brand currently played. We assessed the capabilities and assets of the company to identify when new manufacturing, supply chain, or distribution models might be needed. Our output was a qualified set of options, as well as an implementation plan detailing how to further experiment to turn those options into real value. Because visceral storytelling is a key way to develop and deliver revolutionary strategies, we visualized new opportunities using three-dimensional prototypes and experiential spaces. That revolutionary vision is still being nurtured through the organization.

These two examples—on opposite corners of Ways to Grow—illustrate the differences in resources and processes required to be successful. Intent was different, process was different, and outcomes were different. Mismatching growth intent and capabilities is the breeding ground of failed innovation efforts. To maximize innovation effectiveness, understand your desired outcome and then match people, capabilities, and processes to the task at hand.[4]

## ASSESS OUTCOMES TO MANAGE INNOVATION AT SCALE

Finally, leaders within an organization can use Ways to Grow to track, understand, and assess an in-progress portfolio of innovation projects.

Each innovation initiative in which you are engaged can be mapped onto this tool simultaneously. The result is a dashboard mapping out your innovation initiatives, which is a useful way to think about your innovation strategy as the sum of many smaller bets. For example, at IDEO we think it is vital to evaluate the different innovation zones on an organization's Ways to Grow tool in terms of the following measures of innovation effectiveness:

▲ Financial: What is the net present value of initiatives? Are you creating or destroying value?

▲ Brand: Are you creating raving fans in the marketplace? Are you building emotional currency? We like to use the Net Promoter[5] score to measure our success with brand factors across initiatives.

▲ Learning: What have you learned? What real options for the future exist?

In our experience, looking at your entire innovation portfolio in this way can be a sobering but illuminating experience. Imagine yourself considering the following questions:

▲ Only half our innovation time and energy is expended outside the incremental zone—do we think that is the right mix, given our growth?

▲ Our ability to build and test prototypes drops precipitously when we undertake revolutionary innovation projects—what can we do about that?

▲ We can't seem to "see" insights generated using ethnographic, rather than quantitative, research methods in order to play in the revolutionary quadrant. How can we see more of our users' lives?

▲ Few of our evolutionary innovation projects are positive from a net present value standpoint—should we put more of an emphasis on profits over growth?

By utilizing Ways to Grow as a true dashboard—updating its content frequently, referencing it regularly—you can make it a generative, strategic engine at the heart of your innovation efforts.

## GET STARTED

Innovation is a fiendishly complex and nuanced subject, and the act of innovating can be simultaneously terrifying and exhilarating. It is difficult to bring something new into the world, and as we noted in our introduction, stasis is often the result. It need not be that way.

We will not pretend to have all the answers, but we do know this: Getting started in the right direction is more than half the battle when it comes to innovating effectively. Ways to Grow can help you to get started. It offers a way of evaluating your organization's opportunities for innovation. It is a simple tool, offering a way to focus conversation and planning to achieve a shared view of desired outcomes and process within the organization. It is useful for understanding your organization's path forward and for targeting the best projects for your particular culture and capabilities. It is a tool that can be used anywhere, anytime to frame next steps. Ultimately, it is a tool for growth.

## *Endnotes*

1. We believe that anyone pursuing innovation, given the right training and mindset, can think of himself as a designer.

2. For a discussion of this topic, see Jeffrey Pfeffer and Robert I. Sutton, *Hard Facts, Dangerous Half-Truths and Total Nonsense: Profiting from Evidence-Based Management* (Boston: Harvard Business School Press, 2006), pp. 42–53.

3. Cf. Donald Norman's *Emotional Design: Why We Love (or Hate) Everyday Things* (New York: Basic Books, 2003).

4. Cf. Steven C. Wheelwright and Kim B. Clark, *Revolutionizing Product Development: Quantum Leaps in Speed, Efficiency, and Quality* (New York: Free Press, 1992)

5. Cf. Fred Reichheld, *The Ultimate Question: Driving Good Profits and True Growth* (Boston: Harvard Business School Press, 2006).

# SECTION 2

# IMPLEMENTING DESIGN STRATEGY

Section I confirms the value of design. More significantly, it makes clear that organizations need a shared strategic vision if design is to be more than a tactical resource managers exploit now and again to address individual challenges. Taking the next step, the chapters in this section probe how this broad vision is implemented.

It's a fascinating collection of insights, amplified with hands-on cases from such companies as Motorola, Microsoft, and KitchenAid. Alonzo Canada, Pete Mortensen, and Dev Patnaik examine how different user groups buy into changes in technology. Kevin McCullagh addresses strategy as a blend of forward-looking thinking and en-route adaptation. Laura Weiss presents a framework that combines expertise in human, technical, and business factors to helps consultants translate innovative ideas into reality. Andy Cargile and Ken Fry tell how their division moved from a commodities-focused business to one based on customer experience. Sohrab Vossoughi probes the relationships among customers, brand, and strategy.

Most valuably, within this diverse collection of perspectives and stories are found several important themes and lessons:

**Understand where you are and where you want to be.** Strategy is not whole cloth. It begins with a candid analysis of where things stand within the organization and where they stand in the marketplace and among stakeholders. This critique can include an assessment of brand, customers, function, and the competitive environment. The counterpoint is a rendering of aspirations across the same criteria. This target can and probably will change, but having that marker on the horizon is critical to successful navigation.

**The strategic journey is one that circles back on itself.** Several of these authors map the milestones along the strategic pathway. That's great, but there are a few points to keep in mind. Implementing a design strategy is really more of a never-ending adventure than a discrete journey. You can't always see exactly where things are headed. Detours and surprises are inevitable, so enjoy and take advantage of discoveries along the way. The process repeats itself, and each new horizon yields a view of the next adventure.

**Success depends on collaboration.** Contributions and insights come from many disciplines, including anthropology, engineering, writing, marketing, cost analysis, production, and, of course, all of the design specialties. Design is a team effort; the quest for innovation and creativity moves from one player to the next and back again. The playing field is shaped by time, resources, imagination, and the competition, and the goal is to keep the ball moving but not kick it out of bounds. Fortunately, there is a breadth of resources to tap for this endeavor, including all manner of consultants and in-house talents ranging from executives to managers to staff.

**Effective strategies merge design and business objectives.** A last message embedded in this section is that design strategy looks in two directions. On the one hand, it must be open to reverie and the exploration of ever-new frontiers. On the other hand, within this creative panorama, decisions must ultimately be down to earth. They might stimulate change in the marketplace, even dramatic change, but they still must be timely and cost-effective. Read on for recommendations on striking this essential but delicate balance.

*Chapter 6*

# Design Strategies for Technology Adoption

## by Alonzo Canada, Pete Mortensen, and Dev Patnaik

*Innovation is one thing; success in the marketplace, quite another. Alonzo Canada, Pete Mortensen, and Dev Patnaik offer a framework in which design becomes the channel for uniting these two realities. Identifying five clusters of users—innovators, early adopters, early majority, late majority, and laggards—and numerous hands-on examples, this trio of authors advocates tailoring designs to the priorities of each group.*

IN 1999, HONDA introduced the Insight (Figure 1), a car promising greater fuel economy than any automobile ever made. Years in the making, the Insight could travel up to seventy miles on a single gallon of gasoline, thanks to a revolutionary gas/electric hybrid engine. Despite the Insight's many innovations, the car was a flop, selling just 13,200 units before Honda pulled the plug in 2006.

The Insight's development team sought to incorporate every possible advance in fuel efficiency into a single car. In the process, they created a vehicle that was far too weird for most mainstream drivers. Honda focused on endorsing the technology as viable, proudly calling the Insight a "real-world product for the global market." But with two seats, an unproven aluminum frame, and a form seemingly borrowed from old Buck Rogers serials, the Insight seemed more like a bleeding-edge prototype than a product that was ready for prime time.

While Honda was working on the Insight, its arch-rival Toyota was developing its own hybrid car, the Prius, capable of forty-seven miles per gallon. Toyota recognized

Figure 1. Though introduced within a year of one another and based on similar hybrid engine tech-nologies, the Honda Insight and Toyota Prius could not have fared more differently in the market. The Insight barely sold 13,000 units and is no longer produced, while the Prius has hit 400,000 cars sold and counting. This is largely because Toyota best understood how to meet the needs of early adopters. Insight photo by Michael Pereckas under Creative Commons Attribution license. Prius photo by Keith and Shane Daly under Creative Commons Attribution Share-alike License.

that the most important problem to solve was not how to maximize fuel efficiency but rather how to develop a car that would maintain the comfort of existing compact sedans but have significantly better fuel economy thanks to advanced engine technology. To highlight its improvements in fuel economy, Toyota kept most things the same when it designed the Prius. The vehicle looked virtually indistinguishable from Toyota's exist-ing Echo model, an economy sedan targeted to younger buyers. Most elements in the initial design spoke to reliability and safety, not advanced technology. By keeping al-most everything else the same, Toyota highlighted the primary benefit of hybrid engine technology—better gas mileage. To help drive that message home, the car manufac-turer built in a computer display dashboard that provided continuous feedback about the car's remarkable efficiency. The Prius was a runaway success and would go on to sell more than 400,000 units in its first seven years in the United States alone.

Toyota and Honda were in competition to define a new technology, and Toyota won. On the face of it, technology played a central role in Toyota's success. Yet other fac-tors were equally important in deciding that contest. One of the means through which

Toyota succeeded was an effective design strategy. Design strategy is an emerging disci-pline created to help firms determine what to make and do, both immediately and over the long term. Design strategy is the interplay between design and business strategy, wherein design methods are used to inform business strategy, and strategic planning provides a context for design. While not always required, design strategy often uses so-cial research methods to help ground the results and mitigate the risk of any course of action. The approach has proved useful for companies in a variety of strategic scenarios. As the Prius case shows, one particularly effective application of design strategy has been in helping to ensure the successful management of new technologies.

Many companies struggle with how to best bring new technologies to market. Like Toyota, some of these firms have developed targeted design strategies to drive the wide-spread adoption of new offerings. By drawing from adoption theory—the study of how new ideas spread to new audiences—these businesses tailor their offerings to meet the different needs people have at various points in a category's lifecycle. Jump Associates has conducted extensive research into design strategies to drive adoption. We've devel-oped six generic strategies that play best at different points in a technology's diffusion, from endorsing a new technology's viability to drastically economizing already success-ful technologies. This chapter will demonstrate how to implement an appropriate de-sign strategy for adoption at a company and also explain the theoretical underpinnings of the practice.

## FROM THE CORNFIELDS TO THE CONCEPT LAB

Technology-driven companies, such as consumer electronics manufacturers, have con-cerned themselves for years with reaching early adopters—a small but influential group of users who are more likely to value new offerings than the rest of the population. Be-cause of the social status of early adopters, other buyers who might not immediately recognize the value of a new product, service, or technology look to these folks to make their purchasing decisions.

As important as early adopters have been to the growth of the consumer electronics industries, adoption theory has relevance for every company. Adoption theory is a well-established body of research that owes its origins to communications theorist Everett Rogers' seminal work *Diffusion of Innovations*—the pre-eminent text on the subject. In that text, Rogers charts the rise and fall of ideas, technologies, products, and nations while teasing out the insights, psychographics, and principles needed to apply adoption theory to new fields. We'll briefly summarize key points from Rogers before explaining the field's implications for design strategy. Ironically, the roots of adoption theory are decidedly nontechnical. The subject was first created in the cornfields of Iowa during the 1940s.

In 1941, two researchers at the Iowa Cooperative Agricultural Extension, Bryce Ryan and Neal C. Gross, began to study the diffusion of hybrid seed corn. Introduced in 1928, it promised boosts in field productivity by as much as 20 percent. Thirteen years after its introduction, the economic benefits were clear. Still, some growers chose not to plant the hybrid product. Ryan and Gross studied the use of this new product to understand how social factors affected economic decision-making. They interviewed 259 farmers to find out when they first began to use hybrid seed corn and to learn why they had made the switch. For some, the change was immediate. In 1928 a small handful of wealthy, educated farmers who lived close to cities adopted the seed corn at once. By 1933, 10 percent of the studied farmers had implemented the new seed. By 1936, just three years later, 40 percent of the farmers had switched over, driven largely by early adopter farmers who shared the benefits of the new product with the wider community. By the time of the study, almost all the farmers in the region were hybrid seed users. In charting how hybrid seed corn gradually infiltrated this farming community, Ryan and Gross observed a pattern for diffusion, which they called the adoption curve (Figure 2).

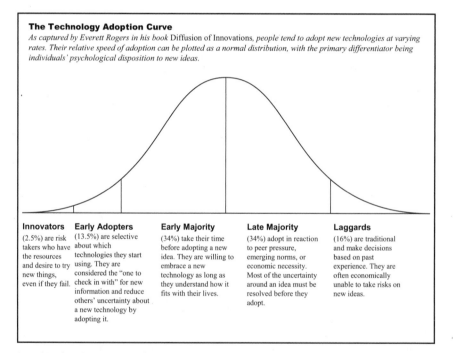

**The Technology Adoption Curve**

*As captured by Everett Rogers in his book* Diffusion of Innovations, *people tend to adopt new technologies at varying rates. Their relative speed of adoption can be plotted as a normal distribution, with the primary differentiator being individuals' psychological disposition to new ideas.*

| **Innovators** | **Early Adopters** | **Early Majority** | **Late Majority** | **Laggards** |
|---|---|---|---|---|
| (2.5%) are risk takers who have the resources and desire to try new things, even if they fail. | (13.5%) are selective about which technologies they start using. They are considered the "one to check in with" for new information and reduce others' uncertainty about a new technology by adopting it. | (34%) take their time before adopting a new idea. They are willing to embrace a new technology as long as they understand how it fits with their lives. | (34%) adopt in reaction to peer pressure, emerging norms, or economic necessity. Most of the uncertainty around an idea must be resolved before they adopt. | (16%) are traditional and make decisions based on past experience. They are often economically unable to take risks on new ideas. |

Figure 2. The adoption curve, first defined by Ryan and Gross in 1941, follows a normal distribution for people and time. All new ideas, products, services, and technologies can be viewed as going through an adoption process.

Over time, the existence of this pattern has been shown across numerous disciplines and industries, always with similar conclusions: The adoption of new ideas follows a standard bell curve, and anyone who engages with a given innovation fits into one of five categories. Each of these groups has unique psychographic characteristics that cause people to be more or less likely to adopt a particular idea at a particular point in time. By understanding the needs of each group on the adoption curve, we can understand how to make an idea more appealing to different types of people.

## INNOVATORS

Innovators, comprising 2.5 percent of the population, are risk-takers who have the resources and desire to try new things. Rogers describes innovators as almost obsessively "venturesome," constantly seeking new ideas, often around the globe. Innovators care less about an idea's success or failure than they do about their need to believe that they are engaging with daring and risky new ideas or technologies. Therefore, while innovators are essential to introducing new ideas, their enthusiasm for both good and bad ideas tends to make their opinions irrelevant to most of the rest of the population.

## EARLY ADOPTERS

Far more important to the spread of ideas are early adopters, comprising 13.5 percent of the population. More than any other group, early adopters differentiate by their propensity to see an unfamiliar solution and map it to their own situation. Because of this ability, they are often considered "the individuals to check with." Early adopters are concerned with maintaining respect in their social circles. They have a need to be perceived as "in the know" and credible and therefore make judicious decisions. Simply by adopting a new technology, early adopters often help to reduce their peers' uncertainty about it. A strong foothold with early adopters is often a good sign that a new idea will ultimately be adopted more widely in a system.

## EARLY MAJORITY

Contrary to the thinking of countless people creating technology-driven products, the vast majority of the population does not value novelty for its own sake. Instead, most of us care more about the benefit we receive from a new idea or technology. We are relatively slow to try new things. The early majority, making up 34 percent of the population, prefer to take their time in adopting new ideas. They adopt new ideas and technologies only if they see tangible benefits that fit into their lives. Members of the early majority often make decisions to try new things by looking to early adopters for guidance.

## LATE MAJORITY

Though members of the early majority won't adopt a new technology until they understand how it fits into their lives, they don't inherently distrust new ideas. By contrast, the late majority, comprising another 34 percent of the population, is openly skeptical of new ideas; the members of this group adopt in reaction to peer pressure, emerging norms, or economic necessity. Because they tend to have limited economic resources, most of the doubt around an idea must be resolved before they will adopt it. Members of the late majority may become motivated to embrace a technology or idea once they think they are the only people they know who haven't already tried it.

## LAGGARDS

The last people to adopt an innovation are laggards, who value tradition. Laggards often make decisions based on past experience. This is in part a social phenomenon, as laggards are often isolated from other social networks. Much as innovators associate with themselves and a few early adopters, laggards generally stick to their own. They are often economically unable to take risks on new ideas, which further prolongs the time they take to adopt something new. Any lingering uncertainty about an idea must be entirely eliminated before laggards will consider it.

## DESIGN STRATEGIES TO DRIVE ADOPTION

New ideas appeal to various groups on the adoption curve at different times for different reasons. Understanding the needs and values of innovators, early adopters, early majority, late majority, and laggards can help determine a set of design strategies that encourage the diffusion of a new product, service, or technology. Thomas Edison was a natural in this area. By examining how he commercialized electric power and the incandescent lightbulb, we can better appreciate how those technologies diffused so rapidly—and why the venture was a long-term success.

## THE EARLY ADOPTION OF ELECTRIC LIGHT

Though popular history points to 1882 as the year the lightbulb was invented, the basic technology had existed for almost a century. Prior to 1882, Edison himself ran the Edison Isolated Electric Company, which provided the homes of wealthy innovators with electricity and light from a proprietary on-site generation system. The reason we actually remember 1882 is because it represents the moment when Edison managed to push the unproven ideas of electric power and light along the adoption curve to the early majority (Figure 3).

Edison's initial electric lights were technologically unimpressive, casting 13 watts of light, imperceptibly brighter than the 12-watt gas lamps he sought to replace. And from a design standpoint, the new electric lamps looked almost exactly like those same gas lamps. Yet it's the very ordinariness of Edison's design that ensured its success. The simple design represented a sublime design strategy, one that reflected a decision to curate the technology and thus meet the needs of early adopters. De-

Figure 3. Thomas Edison designed his first commercial lightbulb, shown above, to recall the form of existing gas lamps. This led the way in which people thought about the technology and put the focus squarely on the observable benefits of electric light.

signing a product that matches the way people already think about a need, and then dramatizing a few key features that distinguish the new from the old, helps get early adopters on board with an idea. Since gas lamps were the dominant solution to the need to light up the inside of a building, Edison designed his electric lights to look and operate almost identically. While the specific solution of a lightbulb powered by a centralized power source was unfamiliar to most people, virtually everyone living in New York in 1882 would have been able to explain the benefits of interior illumination. The technology was new, but the form and function were decades old.

Edison's strategy for rolling out electric light was tailored to fit the way people of the era thought about interior illumination in terms of the design, as well as the function, of his initial lightbulbs. It can also be seen in the opportunity for integration he noticed when determining how to wire homes for electric power. Recognizing that many commercial and residential landowners in New York had invested considerable capital in gas infrastructure to light their buildings, Edison chose to run his first electrical wires through existing gas lines, fitting directly into the system people already understood for the delivery of light. This sped adoption and cut infrastructure costs.

Edison also publicly endorsed the technology's possible benefits through the location of his first customers—financial institutions in lower Manhattan. Seeing the windows of the financial district aglow by night dramatized the technology to the metro population living across the Hudson River in New Jersey. Telling his story on the scale of a city skyline, Edison reached a large audience of early adopters, who then shared the idea with their local communities. By making deliberate design choices, Edison curated his radical innovation by designing it to resemble and function like existing offers, integrated the larger solution by leveraging existing infrastructure associated with the need, and endorsed the use of the technology by demonstrating its use in a visible location that had tremendous influence on the rest of the country.

## SIX STRATEGIES FOR TECHNOLOGY ADOPTION

Like Edison, firms interested in commercializing a new idea can use an appropriate design strategy to promote its adoption. Though Edison provides an excellent case study for how to drive a new idea from early adopters to the early majority, other design strategies can drive further adoption at any phase of a new idea's diffusion (Figure 4). Depending on the situation, a company may choose to:

1. Endorse: Explain the benefits and function of a nascent technology to the world.

2. Curate: Create icons that are selective in their functionality.

3. Integrate: Provide solutions that fit into people's lives.

4. Economize: Drastically cut costs of production on already successful technologies.

5. Play: Find new ways to add value that don't depend on technical differentiation.

6. Refresh: Reinvent existing offerings and renew technical differentiation to reach new markets.

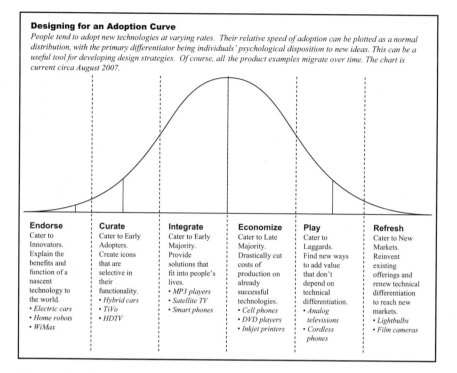

**Designing for an Adoption Curve**

*People tend to adopt new technologies at varying rates. Their relative speed of adoption can be plotted as a normal distribution, with the primary differentiator being individuals' psychological disposition to new ideas. This can be a useful tool for developing design strategies. Of course, all the product examples migrate over time. The chart is current circa August 2007.*

| Endorse | Curate | Integrate | Economize | Play | Refresh |
|---|---|---|---|---|---|
| Cater to Innovators. Explain the benefits and function of a nascent technology to the world. | Cater to Early Adopters. Create icons that are selective in their functionality. | Cater to Early Majority. Provide solutions that fit into people's lives. | Cater to Late Majority. Drastically cut costs of production on already successful technologies. | Cater to Laggards. Find new ways to add value that don't depend on technical differentiation. | Cater to New Markets. Reinvent existing offerings and renew technical differentiation to reach new markets. |
| • *Electric cars* • *Home robots* • *WiMax* | • *Hybrid cars* • *TiVo* • *HDTV* | • *MP3 players* • *Satellite TV* • *Smart phones* | • *Cell phones* • *DVD players* • *Inkjet printers* | • *Analog televisions* • *Cordless phones* | • *Lightbulbs* • *Film cameras* |

Figure 4. By studying the needs of people at different points along the adoption curve, Jump has developed six generic strategies to drive adoption, each of which targets success in a particular stage of diffusion.

## Endorse

When first introducing a new technology to the world, companies often need to appeal to innovators and early adopters. They need to explain the nascent technology's functions and possible benefits to the world, while also proving its viability. At this stage, it's imperative to prove that the new technology is ready for prime time—that it complies with established regulatory standards, for instance. A company might produce an incredible new form of high-speed wireless Internet connectivity, but it will never get beyond the conceptual phase if it has the unfortunate side effect of disabling all cell phones within a five-mile radius. Because a new technology may be spotty in its performance, it's critical to design an offering that leverages its strengths and minimizes any potential glitches. That means constraining not just the feature set but also the settings under which people can experience those features. Designers seeking to endorse a new technology may find it most useful to choose a physical form that doesn't reference any prior art.

Alexander Graham Bell helped fuel the adoption of the telephone by installing the first commercial models at hotels. He did this for both technical and strategic reasons.

From a technical perspective, it's a lot easier to install a hundred phones in one hotel, which all route to a front-desk operator, than to wire a hundred households in a village. Strategically, ensuring that most people's first experience of a phone would occur away from home meant reaching people when they were at their most adventurous. Vacations represent a great new product adoption opportunity because people view travel as a time to experiment. Most importantly from a strategic standpoint, the phones Bell installed at hotels did only one thing—connect a traveler to a front-desk clerk. Bell chose a performance benchmark that would be easy to hit every time—carrying a voice from a hotel room down to a front desk. In a few short decades, the telephone leapt from hotel rooms to most homes in the United States. Having proven that the telephone was ready for the world, Bell could then focus on increasing its capabilities and improving its reliability.

### Curate

As a new offering begins to reach early adopters, companies can further adoption by selectively highlighting aspects of the new technology that demonstrate specific benefits and use. Curating is often achieved through iconic designs that are desirable because they emphasize easily understood and valuable functions. At this stage, clean and simple designs can often help a product to explain itself, and so it's no surprise that so many unfamiliar technologies have leveraged the formal clarity of Bauhaus Modernism and its intellectual successors.

When MP3 players were first introduced in 1997, the market was tiny, and initial designs either compromised storage space for the sake of portability or bulked up on size to allow more storage space. All of them offered a wide range of functionality, but they also required a power user's level of computer expertise. When it was first launched, the iPod was almost simplistic by comparison. The Apple design team ensured that users could convert music from their CD collections into Apple's iTunes software with relative ease. Whenever the iPod was connected, it would automatically load every song in the library. The physical interface was equally simple—an iconic scroll wheel that made navigation through long lists of songs a snap. Yet for all of its benefits, the first iPod was actually a very limited product. It worked only with Macintosh computers. Its hard drive came in only one size. It lacked features such as an FM tuner. Still, the product was iconic. It leveraged a simple geometric form. Rather than release a family of iPods at first, Apple released the one iPod—one model, one color, one size. The company wanted to send a clear message—it had nailed the formula for digital audio players. Designing for early adopters and the mainstream is a lot like being the curator of a museum. You need to select your pieces, have a clear point of view, and guide visitors through the experience.

### Integrate

Unlike early adopters, mainstream users are often unable or unwilling to make the compromises needed to work with a new solution. Companies should therefore look for ways to integrate a technology into people's habits and routines as a product reaches the early majority. Products need to work the way people already work. They need to adapt, connect, or respond to other solutions around them. When appealing to the mainstream, making a product stand out is often less important than "how it will look in the living room." An integrating strategy can help a company take a new technology from novel niche to household name.

In the 1990s, Kodak found new ways to integrate disposable film cameras into the mature photography market. Although Fuji had established itself early on as the market leader, Kodak found a way to take back ground quickly. Rather than enter into a suicidal price war, Kodak realized it could create different kinds of premium disposable cameras by tailoring models to the activities in people's lives. The company developed a model for underwater use at the beach. It sold a wide-angle-lens version at the Grand Canyon. It started to package multiple cameras together for use at weddings. By contextualizing their use, Kodak's designers were able to integrate disposable cameras into the lives of ordinary people, many of whom already owned a traditional camera. Kodak was able to reclaim market leadership and drive the adoption of the technology. Firms sometimes find a single solution insufficient when following an integrating strategy. Often, accessories and ancillary products are needed to respond to a particular application. Flexible platforms may be required to support customization for multiple applications, customer targets, and channels. The ability to integrate a new technology into people's lives often serves the dual purpose of driving sales volumes while keeping margins high.

## Economize

Once an offering achieves widespread adoption, companies can spur further market penetration by appealing to the late majority with cost-cutting and commoditizing strategies. Since the late majority often finds itself trying out a new offering solely out of peer pressure, it may be necessary to create more economical solutions that reduce barriers to adoption. An economize strategy often suits a company in a mature category where the value of a technology is generally accepted.

IKEA has built its global brand on a strategy of designing to economize. The company's furniture is stylish, attractive, and almost inevitably derivative of a classic design. Their Karlstad Swivel chair, for example, looks like a slimmed-down (some would say dumbed-down) version of Arne Jacobsen's Egg Chair. But while Jacobsen's original was designed as an artistic, crafted object and continues to sell for more than $3,000, the Karlstad was designed for manufacturability and retails for less than $500. At $500, there's not much Egg left in the Karlstad. This is what IKEA excels at. Its designers study great, high-end furniture designs, shrewdly identify which features people value most, and then find ways to manufacture and deliver the new version for a fraction of the original's cost. In the case of the Egg and the Karlstad, both chairs have high backs, a swivel base, and a comfortable foam frame. And while the Egg also has an innovative form and a wrap-around seat back, the Karlstad offers nothing else. While one can assume the quality of IKEA's swivel stand may not match Jacobsen's, it's equally likely that the Karlstad feels just as good to sit in. And that's the secret of designing to economize—not cutting corners arbitrarily, but analyzing successful high-end solutions in a market and figuring out which corners could be cut to create a true low-cost alternative.

## Play

To drive adoption of a new technology beyond the mainstream, companies must find ways to appeal to laggards. This involves finding ways to create value that don't depend on technical differentiation. Often, the inherent familiarity of a widely adopted product can give designers an opportunity to do something different. Indeed, many designers thrive on bringing inventive forms to established categories and making the familiar unfamiliar. In recent years, Italian design has made a name for itself through such play strategies.

In the 1970s, the Swiss watch-making industry, world-renowned for its precision and quality, was in crisis. Leveraging low-cost quartz technology, Asian manufacturers had begun to match the Swiss in technical precision for a fraction of the price. Swiss market leader SMH responded by changing the game. The near ubiquity of wristwatches meant that consumers were ready for a little bit of play. The launch of the Swatch brand in 1983 was marked by artsy, cheeky, and irreverent watch designs. Swatch played with watches by positioning them as fashion accessories, not finely tuned timepieces. Over time, Swatch has continued to create new watch styles, soliciting well-known artists like Keith Haring to create whimsical designs that emphasize trend and fashion. An implicit message of the entire product line is that consumers should collect multiple watches to wear on different occasions. The strategy was so successful that SMH went on to rename itself the Swatch Group, and the company is now the world watch leader in both revenue and market share.

## Refresh

Once a technology has reached near-universal adoption, it's incumbent upon existing players and new entrants to reinvent the category. This can mean finding ways to refresh an obsolete technology, often by identifying a novel use for it.

By the early 1990s, digital compact discs effectively replaced vinyl albums as the dominant medium for recorded music. While most people were happy to have pop- and hiss-free CDs, a small but significant audience never stopped using records. Unlike the rest of us, hip-hop and electronic music DJs still use turntables. Since DJs use record players to mix, cut up, and loop existing music tracks into new songs, they have requirements that are very different from those of the mainstream consumers who used to purchase phonographs. Responding to this shift in the market, companies such as Technics have designed turntables to better handle reverse spins, audio fades, and variable speeds. Needles designed for DJs are both more durable and more precise than their mainstream predecessors. These professional models fundamentally work in the same way as every phonograph ever made, but they can handle far greater strain and make it easier for a DJ to be an artist in his own right. By identifying a novel use for an obsolete technology, a handful of companies have enjoyed considerable success catering to a refreshed category.

## THE STRATEGIES IN PRACTICE

Multiple companies in the same market can succeed by leveraging the same technologies at different points in their diffusion. The three top American computer brands, for example, follow drastically different strategies. Apple is the quintessential curate company—for decades, its entire business model has been based on taking nascent technologies and wrapping them in iconic and easy-to-understand packages. Apple tends to do less well, however, when a technology reaches the integration stage, in large part because it involves compromises the company is unwilling to make. HP, by comparison, excels at designing to integrate. The company seeks to create ecosystems of offerings that have greater capabilities than any one component. There are many homes in which families connect their HP cameras to their HP computers that are connected to an HP printer that uses HP ink cartridges to deliver photo-quality prints on HP-branded paper. However, because of a commitment to these larger systems of products, HP's offerings are rarely the cheapest on the market. Dell Computer, on the other hand, has succeeded through economizing. Dell has found ways to drive the cost out of established technologies and replicate the look and feel of competitors. The company's competence in economizing a category has nonetheless failed to help it introduce new ideas or command sustainable price premiums.

Each of these companies plays to its strengths by following a strategy best suited to its abilities—and each has a strategic goal to keep the product categories it operates in stuck at the point on the adoption curve where it succeeds most often. Apple constantly looks for new technologies that it can curate. HP looks for opportunities to integrate disparate solutions into a seamless whole. And Dell looks for new ways to economize already successful technologies. Each has a distinct vision for the technology industry and pursues it accordingly, and each has performed best when focusing on doing things its own way. As long as the bulk of a product category remains in these companies' sweet spots, these players continue to prosper.

## CONCLUSION

Companies continually grapple with how to develop effective design strategies that will minimize the inherent risks involved with launching new products, services, and businesses. Understanding diffusion theory helps to frame the introduction of new offerings as an issue of adoption. This in itself is useful in determining where a new offering might be in its adoption cycle. Applying adoption theory to a firm's design strategy can empower managers to focus design activities on those goals likely to yield the quickest results. Rather than give up introducing new technologies to the market or relying on random luck for success in such endeavors, design managers can craft strategies that play to their strengths, minimize risk, drive adoption, and ultimately fulfill their companies' larger growth objectives.

# Chapter 7

# Strategy for the Real World

## by Kevin McCullagh

*Contending that the contemporary business environment can be tur-
bulent and chaotic, Kevin McCullagh asserts that design strategy is
not about grand conceptual ideas but is instead a pragmatic blend of
thinking ahead and en-route adaptation. Using Motorola's RAZR as a
case study, he explains how strategy is grounded in facts and analysis,
synthesizes disparate thinking, provides a framework for decisions,
and includes an implementation plan.*

"STRATEGY" IS A word managers and consultants use when wishing to sound important and expensive. To a large extent, overuse has emptied it of much of its meaning.
Strategizing also stands for a number of things, some of which smack of ulterior motives,
such as gaining credibility, pleasing investors, and even serving as group therapy for
management.

Yet despite the cynicism surrounding it, strategic thinking in design has never been
in so much demand. This is primarily due to the promotion of design onto the senior
management agenda—witness the Innovation, Creativity and Design Strategy debate
at the Global Economic Forum, in Davos, earlier this year.[1] With this elevation of the
design perspective to board level come greater expectations of design managers. As senior executives learn to deal with soft issues, such as aesthetics and experience, design
managers and consultants are stepping up to deal with the hard stuff—data, rigor, and
the business case.

However, few of those called upon to deliver these strategies have had a classroom education in the subject.[2] They have developed their expertise in the studio through a mix of personal experience, shared war stories with their peer networks, and by reading the odd business strategy article.

The aim here is to capture some of the experiences of those crafting strategies amidst the cut and thrust of business life—both inside and outside corporations.

## STRATEGY AND ITS MISCONCEPTIONS

Since designers love to attach strategic to any big project, it is worth making a few distinctions. Rather than get stuck in turgid definitions of the word, it is probably best to begin with what it does not constitute.

One of the most common delusions is that any project involving future-gazing is by definition strategic. As Clive Grinyer, experience design chief at France Telecom, states, "Design strategy is often confused with future fantasy, which can sometimes be inspirational, but should never be confused with strategy."[3] A distinctive view of the future is central to strategy, but without backup data and a coherent engagement with commercial realities, it remains purely intuitive speculation. While an iconic project, such as Philips' Vision of the Future, was highly inspirational to a generation of young designers, its actual role was one of PR rather than strategy—to project an impression that Philips was a future-focused company.

Rudolf Voigt, design manager for mobile devices at BenQ Corp., points to two other misconceptions: that design strategy is mostly based on consumer trends or visual language and that it can be developed without engagement with the business strategy.

As is true of business strategy, there are many schools of thought on what design strategy constitutes, but most agree that it includes the following.

## BIG-PICTURE PERSPECTIVE

To build a case for a strategy that will be taken seriously outside the design studio, designers must engage with commercial realities and take a board-level perspective. It's vital to demonstrate a firm grasp of what is happening in the worlds of consumers, competitors, and technology if one hopes to articulate possible opportunities for the brand. Personal experience confirms that progressive corporate strategy departments are already reaching out to design strategists with a wide-angle view of consumer, technology, and design developments to help them develop peripheral corporate vision.

Greg Orme, chief executive of the London Business School's Centre for Creative Business, makes this point succinctly: "Design strategy is essentially about envisioning a new future from a 35,000-foot CEO perspective." And Grinyer gives a current example: "The challenge is to demonstrate how design can contribute to corporate strategy. For example, how should the Orange brand articulate itself as it moves toward a four-play offer (TV, broadband, mobile, and landline)? Where should it deliver value?"

## ANALYSIS

For a strategy to be credible to senior management, it must be backed up by analytical rigor, reputable data, and, in case the data are soft or not available—as is often true—explicit assumptions. While this sounds like a snooze to many, it is one of the main reasons why design strategies are not taken seriously within corporations. Effective strategists immerse themselves in the details.

Gary Hamel, the designer's favorite strategy guru, makes it crystal-clear that a business-savvy point of view (POV) must be compelling, coherent, and commercial, but most of all it must be based on unimpeachable data. "A POV can be as bold and far-reaching as your aspirations, but it must have a foundation in fact. Rhetoric isn't enough. You need to wade hip-deep in data to make sure you know what's going on. You have to be ready to back up your bold assertions. And you must clearly separate what can be known from what is unknowable—don't claim to know things you can't."[4]

## SYNTHESIS

At the most abstract level, strategy-making always involves the coupling of rigorous analysis and intuitive synthesis. Creatively fusing disparate data, insights, ideas, and assumptions into a new whole lies at the core of strategic thinking.

Orme underlines this point, noting that "strategy is driven by the synthesis of evidence and expert assumptions," and he goes on to observe that while designers are strong synthesizers, "they tend to lack a big-picture perspective and to be slack about building a base of evidence data."

## FRAMEWORKS

Chris Bangle, design director of BMW, describes one of his key roles as "creating a framework around which senior management can make product development decisions."[5]

Clients tend to call consultants when they have a tough nut to crack, and in my experience the essence of the brief often lies in framing these complex and multidimensional problems. This generally begins with panning out from the issue in hand and defining its boundaries, before zooming back in to break it down into its constituent parts. Then, with the ultimate goal in mind, one can structure these elements into a framework that brings clarity to the front end of a new initiative. To ensure that this provides a robust decision-making infrastructure, internal inconsistencies must be ironed out, terminology defined, and metaphors clarified by testing the framework with key stakeholders.

In sectors as diverse as automotive and fast-moving consumer goods, I have found that the most powerful frameworks help different departments develop a new and shared view of the opportunity space. It must fit with their worldviews and they should be able to position key concepts and data within it.

Richard Eisermann, strategic director for strategic design consultancy Prospect and former design director for Whirlpool in Italy, concurs. "Design strategy is about controlling the amount of subjectivity in the product or service development process. It should provide a decision-making framework and a rationale to stakeholders, including nondesigners. Strategy should not be prescriptive—it cannot be a blueprint for good design."

## IMPLEMENTATION PLANNING

It has been estimated that less than 10 percent of strategies get implemented,[6] and as post-dot-com wisdom has it, "Strategy is easy; implementation is hard." Managers in the real world stress the importance of familiarity with practical implementation issues.

Rudolf Voigt of BenQ comments that designers are being recognized for having a more practical appreciation of a company's intrinsic capabilities, in comparison with their typically more abstract-minded marketing colleagues. "Designers can be more realistic about what can really and credibly be done, because they are more aware of the delivery challenges." Indeed, Ignacio Germade, design director for Motorola Europe, emphasizes that "a key element of a successful strategy is knowing about and thinking through all the steps to get there. It is not just about formulating an implementation plan—it's also familiarity with its different elements."

## THE ROLE OF CONSULTANTS

Few would dispute that strategy formation should be owned, championed, and implemented by internal design managers rather than outsourced to consultants. Most managers also agree that consultants have valuable roles to play. Indeed many of the trailblazers of design planning and strategy, such as Jay Doblin, Larry Keeley, John Rheinfrank, and Patrick Whitney, have operated outside the corporation.

## SKILLS AND PERSPECTIVES

So how are design managers using consultants to help build better strategies? The top-level answer revolves around balancing skill sets and perspectives. Strategic thinking is not a run-of-the-mill activity in most design departments, because most of their work revolves around the tactical implementation of an existing strategy. The skill set managers require in the cut and thrust of the corporate world is distinct, but not mutually exclusive, from that of strategic thinkers. Managers tend to assess their needs and bring in senior talent as required.

Prospect's Eisermann counsels an honest appraisal of internal resources: "No single person possesses all the required skills! Good design managers play to their strengths, acknowledge their weaknesses, and bring in external expertise as required." And France Telecom's Grinyer is also conscious of corporate myopia. "It is imperative to get an outside view and have internal assumptions challenged. Brave design managers consistently look to refresh their knowledge through the involvement of outside consultants with cross-sector experience and strong views of the way the world is changing."

The matrix below summarizes the skill sets and perspectives that tend to be associated with design managers and strategy consultants.

## THE RIGHT RELATIONSHIP

In general, managers strive to achieve a healthy balance between internal and external resources. BenQ's Voigt also stresses the proactive side of the relationship: "Good consultants think like entrepreneurs for their clients—they ask what they should do to keep the company fresh?"

Managers look for strategic inputs at the level of big-picture perspectives, analysis, synthesis, frameworks, and conceptualization; but rarely does it make sense to involve consultants in implementation planning. Grinyer underlines this point. "To have a chance of success, a strategy must be championed by a strong in-house design leader. For a strategy to have real impact, consultants must work with a senior partner and champion to prepare the ground, hone it, own it, sell it, and execute it."

High-profile strategic projects also have a tendency to backfire. A familiar complaint is that consultants dream up pure strategies in glorious isolation on the basis of grand generalizations that ride roughshod over corporate realities and brand values. Grinyer admits to "often being shocked by how little consultants understand about their clients' brands." On the other side of the relationship, Eisermann reflects on "overestimating the appetite for change within the client—the people who clamor most for a strategy are often those least willing or able to implement it."

Probably the most common error on both sides is to underestimate the amount of work needed to prepare the ground and obtain buy-in with all key stakeholders. This work also helps to ensure that the strategy is situated within the needs of the whole company and not just the needs of the direct client contact.

From a consultant's perspective, the most common mistake clients make is to treat strategy passively—as a one-off issue that lands in their lap or even blows up in their face every few years. Strategies should be regularly reviewed, challenged, tested, and adapted to remain alive to change. Smart managers also develop a range of strategic alternatives—or "stratlets"—as a way of testing the primary strategy, as well as having something close to hand in case of a sudden change in the environment.

## ORGANIZATIONAL BARRIERS

The key issue, even contradiction, in strategy is trying to rationally plan in often chaotic and irrational environments—whether in markets, companies, or studios.

Grinyer is worldly enough to accept that "stuff happens"—the world changes, whether it's "a new CEO, a disruptive technology, a bad set of quarterly results, or a new competitor that makes some strategies either redundant or in need of a serious rethink."

Corporate chaos and politics present the biggest and most underestimated barrier to delivery. Companies are far from homogenous units; they comprise disparate departments with conflicting agendas, dysfunctional communications, petty rivalries, and overworked individuals. Getting a new strategy out there and gaining mindshare and traction is a real challenge—not to mention having to compete against or accommodate competing strategies from other departments.

Even when market and corporate conditions are favorable, the design manager can find frustrations closer to home. Designers, especially the most talented, often prove to be the worst barriers to a design strategy when they refuse to work within the constraints of a strategic framework. Germade reflects that recruitment is as much about the culture as raw talent: "You need to get designers to care about the studio's work, not just their own."

## AGILE STRATEGY

Henry Mintzberg, the iconoclast and Woody Allen of business strategy, would recognize the experience of design strategists in the real and often chaotic corporate world. He is dismissive of the traditional MBA school of strategy in which top management makes rational and detached planning decisions that are then implemented by those below. In the real world, strategy emerges through interplay between structured planning and ad hoc responses. Mintzberg speaks of "crafting strategy" according to the needs of the organization and environment. Here, strategy creation and implementation are interdependent. He compares the art of strategy-making to pottery and managers to potters sitting at a wheel molding the clay and letting the shape of the object evolve in their hands.

Design strategists might take comfort in this analogy. While they must be business-savvy analysts and synthesizers, they should also stay alive to their intuition and environment. This is not to justify strategy on the fly or post-justified rationales, but it is to make the case for agile strategy. Maxims for strategy in the real world include the following: get hold of what facts you can; where the data are soft or absent, make your assumptions explicit; build frameworks and hypotheses; and then review, test, learn, and adapt them on a regular basis.

Strategy in the real world involves some thinking ahead and some adaptation en route. Thought needs to dynamically interplay with action, not dictate it from a lofty ivory tower.

|  | Skills | Perspectives |
|---|---|---|
| Design managers | Motivation and mentoring<br>Internal and external communication<br>Culture creation and management<br>Cross-department alliances<br>Budgeting | Corporate culture<br>Political/diplomatic<br>Internal capabilities<br>Brand<br>Sector<br>Target consumers |
| Strategy consultants | Bi-polar—analytical and intuitive<br>Thought leadership<br>Empathy with corporate pressures<br>Ability to produce tangible, engaging,<br>    and stand-alone deliverables | Objective<br>Big picture<br>Cross-sector<br>External possibilities<br>Challenging<br>Consumers in general |

## THE RAZR AS CATALYST FOR MOTOROLA'S STRATEGIC RENEWAL

The success story of Morotola's RAZR cell phone is emblematic of the more active role design departments are playing in the formulation of corporate strategy in progressive companies.

The RAZR has now sold more than 50 million units, nearly as many as Apple has sold iPods—but in less than half the time. Like the iPod, it has also been called a company-changing product. As well as boosting market share and profits, it also provided the momentum for transforming Motorola from a technology to a lifestyle-driven company. Jim Wicks, vice president of consumer experience design, remembers consumers likening its products to "some Cadillac that nobody wants"[7] when he joined the company in 2001.

However, the RAZR's success and Motorola's subsequent rejuvenation around it is no textbook case of grand top-down strategy. It emerged at a time of cultural change at the top of the company and then became the catalyst around which the company reinvented itself.

The late Jeffrey Frost was a key pathfinder for the new Motorola. He left Nike to join the company as chief marketing officer in 2001, and he pioneered the Hello Moto campaign in 2002. Frost had grasped the start of a big-picture market shift from features to fashion. At this point, the brand's communications had been given much-needed fizz, but the company didn't have products that could deliver on the promise.

The Motorola RAZR's huge success provided a catalyst and template for the company's design renaissance. The KRZR is a slimmed-down, exquisitely finished, and premium-priced evolution of the RAZR platform.

## THE RAZR AS CATALYST FOR MOTOROLA'S STRATEGIC RENEWAL

In 2003, the genesis of such a product was spotted roaming the Advanced Development Department in the form of a mocked-up super-thin phone, which had been achieved by reconfiguring internal components. Motorola assembled a skunkworks team of designers and engineers, some of whom had recently been pulled off another high-end phone project. Project Razor Clam was given the objective of developing and launching a low-volume "statement product" within the year.

The pressure was on to produce a knockout phone with the goal of building more buzz than sales, and therefore normal rules would not apply. In the tradeoff between thinness and functionality, the team would lean toward the former—focus was the name of the game. Time constraints meant that corners were cut and rules broken. For example, the usual consumer tests and network operator consultations were bypassed. Also, the lack of the usual constraints associated with a mass product, and the singular pursuit of the Wow! factor, allowed for the use of high-end materials and usability tradeoffs. One such compromise was going with a handset width that the usability team advised was four millimeters too wide.

Another cornerstone of the story is Ed Zander, who joined as CEO midway through the RAZR's development. As well as encouraging the project, he instigated a bonus structure to focus the whole company on the end consumer and to reduce interdepartmental wrangling.

The initial marketing plan was to label the phone the V3, in line with Motorola's naming convention. However, Frost, who had been tracking the project, did not like the idea of such an elegant phone having such a pedestrian name. Inspired by the project code name, he championed the four-letter RAZR and got behind the project with a strong communications campaign.

The RAZR V3 was released in November 2004 as an exclusive fashion phone, with a high price of $500, along with a service agreement in the United States, and the unsubsidized price of $2,000 in Russia. It was an instant hit, generated buzz in all the right circles, and sold a very respectable 0.75 million units in the final quarter of 2004. In the fast-moving world of mobile phones, and particularly in an era of restless design studios, the natural reaction would have been self-congratulation and a move to begin work on the next killer product—but not this time.

## THE RAZR AS CATALYST FOR MOTOROLA'S STRATEGIC RENEWAL

The 2005 budget that had planned around selling 2 million RAZRs was revised upward by the new head of the cell phone division to a target of 20 million. This threw the gauntlet down to the marketing and design departments to extend the product's success well outside the original market niche. The iconic success of the RAZR made the job of developing a design language extension platform easier, since the usual competing views were largely absent, replaced by enthusiasm for building on a success story.

A black variant found its way into the 77th Academy Awards gift bags and was released in early May 2005; the price of the standard V3 was lowered to a mid price point around the same time. The pink version became a legendary Christmas success in the U.K. in the same year. Early 2006 saw the launch of the lower priced SLVR family—an articulation of the RAZR design language into a candy-bar format. The three different SLVR models share a similar appearance but are equipped with feature sets to hit different price points. In July 2006, the company announced two more RAZR offspring—the narrower, taller, and exquisitely finished KRZR K1 clamshell and a slider format called the RIZR.

SLVR represented an extension of the RAZR design language to a candy-bar format and cheaper price points.

## THE RAZR AS CATALYST FOR MOTOROLA'S STRATEGIC RENEWAL

While critics have accused Motorola of milking one idea and not having a follow-up, a counter point of view is that the company has pioneered a more mature way of managing a product lifecycle. Its focus on a small number of cell-phone product platforms, such as the RAZR and the PEBL, is analogous to the automotive industry, in which marketing resources promote the platform sub-brand rather than individual models. Advertising features the top-of-the-range "hero" product, under whose halo the cheaper variants bask. Not only does this platform approach make for effective marketing, but it also allows designers to focus on doing a few things well and helps reduce the total number of component variants to be engineered, sourced, and managed.

Germade makes it clear that the long-term success of the RAZR should be firmly laid at the feet of senior management and their vision: "They saw more sales potential than perhaps the design team did, and really showed leadership through pricing and communications." And he emphasizes the importance of "designing the right culture" in the company if strategy is to remain alive and relevant. "We have themes and hypotheses that we use as guides—until they are proved wrong." One such guideline is that consumers should be able to identify a Motorola phone from three meters away. Annual strategy reviews also ensure that the design department remains aligned with the corporate and marketing objectives. "Branding from the inside out" is the phrase Germade uses to underline this new product-driven approach; when the product is the brand, "consistency of implementation is really important."

Jim Wicks sums up the joined-up way in which his company is now able to build strategy: "What really defines our design group's positioning now versus three years ago is that it's really tightly woven into the way we plan our products, our strategies, our marketing, and how we prioritize which technologies we go after."[8]

The RAZR story provides a strong case of an emergent, learning, and responsive strategy. It was not drawn up in glorious isolation and handed down to the implementers. Its authors knew the market was changing and that Motorola had to change too, and they thought RAZR could contribute to the changing perceptions of an elite. At the same time, through intervening in the market, Motorola discovered potential far outside this fashion niche. This traditionally technology-driven company was open enough

**THE RAZR AS CATALYST FOR MOTOROLA'S STRATEGIC RENEWAL**

to realize that it had underestimated consumer demand for high style, astute enough to spot the long-term potential of an initial success, and agile enough to rapidly shift its priorities from technology toward lifestyle. Most impressive, to those familiar with corporate life, it rapidly aligned its design, marketing, and technology strategies around a platform approach and reaped the rewards.

It is also instructive to note that such success was achieved with a notoriously weak user interface. This suggests two lessons: first, do not underestimate the power of the blink factor[9] of product identity in the consumer experience; and second, think what Motorola could do if it fixes its UI, which it seems more than capable of doing.

## *Endnotes*

1. Bruce Nussbaum, "Design Gets Its Due in Davos," *BusinessWeek*, January 11, 2006.

2. A few innovative education establishments, such as IIT Institute of Design, in Chicago, D-School at Stanford University's Joint Program in Design, and the International Design Business Management program in Helsinki, are now addressing this gap.

3. All the quotes in this chapter (unless noted otherwise) are from personal conversations.

4. Gary Hamel, *Leading the Revolution: How to Thrive in Turbulent Times by Making Innovation a Way of Life* (Boston: Harvard Business School Press, 2000).

5. Design & Art Direction's 2005 President's Lectures, London, December 7, 2005.

6. Walter Kiechel, "Snipping at Strategic Planning," *Planning Review*, May 1984.

7. Jim Wicks, "Weaving Design into Motorola's Fabric," IIT Institute of Design Conference, May 2006 (*www.id.iit.edu/events/strategyconference/2006/perspectives_wicks.php*).

8. Wicks, ibid.

9. For an excellent exploration of the influence of snap judgments on all walks of life, see Malcolm Gladwell's *Blink: The Power of Thinking Without Thinking* (New York: Little, Brown: 2005).

# Chapter 8

# Developing Tangible Strategies

by Laura Weiss

*As businesses ponder where to put their resources to ensure future suc-
cess, they are increasingly turning to innovation firms to help sort out
the options related to their long-term decisions. Laura Weiss presents
a framework consultants can use to lead clients from "discovery" to
"delivery," a design-grounded process that becomes a pragmatic "innovation engine" by combining expertise in human, technical, and
business factors.*

TODAY, ALMOST EVERYONE is familiar with the now-famous statement made in the
late 1950s by former IBM CEO Thomas Watson, Jr., that "Good design is good business."
That concept, a breakthrough in the post–World War II industrial era, was grounded in
the belief that a commitment to design would help a good product to reach its full potential, presumably through increased sales of a more functionally robust and aesthetically pleasing object.

Today, Watson's philosophy has proven sustainable, if no longer novel, and there
is much contemporary evidence to that fact. The Polaroid I-Zone, with its creative reinterpretation of the simplest camera, has made instant photography relevant to a whole
new generation of users (and became the number-one-selling camera within months
of its introduction).[1] Similarly, the Palm V, with its elegant reinterpretation of the Palm
Pilot, made the high-tech functionality of its predecessor appealing to a much wider
and more mainstream audience. Both products are strong examples of design making

a difference to a company's top-line growth. And yet, for every Palm V, there's an Apple Power Mac G4 Cube or 3Com Audrey—products whose design boldness failed to save them from a marketplace failure due to either an inadequate understanding of target users, a poor business plan, or both. Good design, it seems, is not always good business if it is not pursued as an integral part of a wider set of activities that together enable the most successful innovations to happen.

But if Tom Watson's statement does not tell the entire story, it at least signals the beginning of a burgeoning design awareness that some 40 years later has been propagated by management evangelists such as Tom Peters, Gary Hamel, and many others. Design is now firmly part of the lexicon of innovation—the ultimate expression of applied technology, design, and business sensibilities. In a special 1999 issue dedicated to the topic of innovation in industry, *The Economist* proclaimed, "Innovation has become the industrial religion of the late 20th century."[2] The article goes on to point out that innovation can manifest itself in ways that are not just limited to the production of a consumable product. Today's companies and organizations, driven by market dynamics, social and environmental issues, technological developments, and even government deregulation, view innovation as the perpetual "next frontier" and the key to achieving a competitive or operational advantage. As such, everything is now subject to innovation—not just physical objects, but also political systems, economic policy, ways in which medical research is conducted, and even complete "user experiences" (for example, a passenger's journey with Amtrak's new Acela service). It is no surprise, then, that the application of design sensibilities and skills now extends to innovations as varied as online interactions (Amazon.com's One-Click feature) and improved business processes (the application that enables that same feature). Both of these connect consumers and providers in ways that ultimately contribute to larger industry innovations.

## EVIDENCE OF BROADER NEEDS

As the quest for breakthrough innovation has increased, so too has the demand for consulting services that can provide expertise and a fresh perspective. If these services are to provide value by delivering meaningful results, what exactly do their clients need in addition to superior design? The requirements are no longer limited to the "well-defined problem," in which a project brief addresses a fairly well-understood and presumably stable business context. Today, much bigger questions are being asked, which move beyond product specifications to broader, more challenging issues. Instead of asking the consultant to "design this new widget for me," where the widget is already identified, a client might ask, "Should we be designing a new widget, a new widget and service bundle, or something else altogether?" The following is a basic typology of innovation challenges a provider of innovation services might typically encounter today.

The loosely defined problem: The client presents a preliminary business plan or a nascent product idea, without a clear business case. The client might ask, "Where, and how, should we be looking for breakthrough opportunities that address customer needs and meet our business objectives?"

The too-many-options problem: The client lacks effective tools to select and implement the most promising option(s). The client might ask, "If we already know where we want to focus our business, how do we generate and select product or service concepts that will get us there?"

The technology investment problem: The client is seeking commercialization options or validation for investing in a new technology, new applications for an existing technology, or knowledge of external technology threats. The client might ask, "What is the impact of future technology on this product/service?"

The innovation void problem: The client would like to develop a more innovative and sustainable approach to its internal product development process. The client might ask, "How can we develop a vision of the future for our products so that we can plan and guide continued innovation efforts?"

Regardless of which challenge (or hybrid version) has been articulated, the client's most immediate need is to identify an appropriate direction for the innovation effort before it can actually embark on it. Thus the demand for consulting services is increasingly focused on turnkey solutions that incorporate additional upstream and downstream activities that facilitate critical decision-making associated with the earliest stages of new product and service development. Whereas traditional core services offered by design consultancies and others focus on helping clients do things the right way in terms of design, engineering, and manufacturing, now they are being engaged for "strategic services" to help them choose to do the right things in the first place (Figure 1).

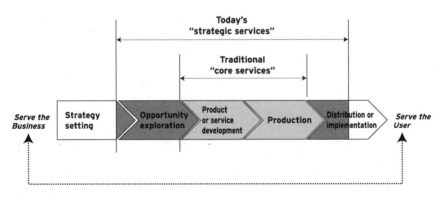

Figure 1. Extending core services to strengthen the connection between business needs and user needs.

## ENABLING DISCOVERY, DECISIONS, AND DELIVERY

Because innovation programs today are increasingly strategic, traditional design services must grow and develop the additional capabilities needed not only to serve clients more effectively but also to increase the likelihood that the results of their engagement will be a product or service that eventually gets to market as a truly successful innovation. In the summer 1999 *Design Management Journal*, IDEO's Tom Kelley argued that designers are well positioned to help companies seeking to unlock their capacity for innovation because they naturally take an inductive approach to the problem-solving process and employ powerful visualization tools to communicate the results.[3] Today, that theory is put into practice at consultancies like IDEO, whose industrial design and engineering activities (along with the substantially critical roles of human factors and interaction design) are being expanded even further to incorporate the investigation of business factors. As discussed earlier, business issues have long been part of the innovation equation, but they have often been pursued in isolation and independently from the creative side. A more powerful approach, it can be argued, involves the concurrent exploration of issues associated with user desirability, technical feasibility, and business viability by an interdisciplinary team that utilizes design-based processes and communication tools.

## THE INNOVATION ENGINE

By leveraging expertise in each of the interrelated areas of human factors, technical factors, and business factors to address the client's innovation problem, the consultant can help lower the functional barriers that often restrict, rather than inform, breakthrough in-

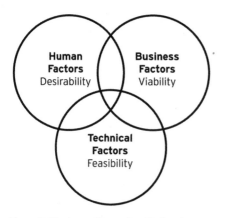

Figure 2. The innovation engine: Design sits at the intersection, as an enabler and the result of integrated capabilities.

novation within a typical business organization. For example, the elusive issue of desirability (or what motivates consumer behavior) demands an understanding of how people interpret and interact with the things they encounter in the world— including new technologies or even new business models. Exploring feasibility means understanding how those new technologies can be harnessed to make a nascent product or service concept come to life in a way that is meaningful for users. Finally, assessing viability means understanding whether embracing a new technology or supporting a particular user need is truly aligned with the organization's strategic objectives and competitive positioning. Undertaken together, these interdisciplinary activities fuel the engine that powers early-stage innovation in an equitable and mutually inspirational way (Figure 2).

## DESIGN AS INTERFACE

This kind of interdisciplinary approach starts to bridge a common gap between the client's own business analyses of these very topics and the consultant's innovation and design processes. Even so, successful client-consultant collaboration is often undermined by the lack of a common platform for effectively communicating during concept identification and development (Figure 3). Driven by the innovation engine and leveraging design-based tools and processes, innovation initiatives can go beyond the discovery of new ideas to knowledge of how or whether to implement them.

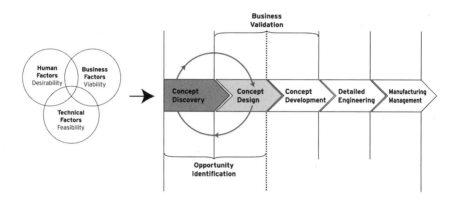

Figure 3. Early-stage conceptualization driven by the innovation engine.

IDEO's recent work with a leading computer technology company is a good example of these ideas in action. The client's primary objective was to develop a strategic vision for its future Internet presence that was less reflective of its internal business structure and more reflective of user needs and goals. The desire to optimize the online user experience (and in the process increase revenues) is the subject of much "best practices" discussion today, as Internet technology continues to have a profound effect on the development and delivery of products and services. But it was the client's secondary objectives that provided some much larger and perhaps more significant challenges—the requirement that the creative vision also be aligned with business and brand objectives and that it be a catalyst for cross-company evangelism and action (specifically the prioritization and planning of future development investments to make the vision a reality). The goal of making the client's business objectives relevant to the end-user, and enabling the user's needs to influence the development of the client's business objectives, is particularly difficult for a traditional "technology push" enterprise. But it represents an opportunity to demonstrate the power of integrating business, human, and technology factors at the earliest stages of an innovation program. A close collaboration with the client throughout the iterative cycle of discovery, decisions, and delivery activities was enabled by the deployment of design-based processes and tools (Figure 4).

**Discovery:** The earliest stages of any innovation program involve contextual research. In this case, the client's program required the exploration of user groups (and the characteristics of their unique needs and goals), business objectives and systems (and the key

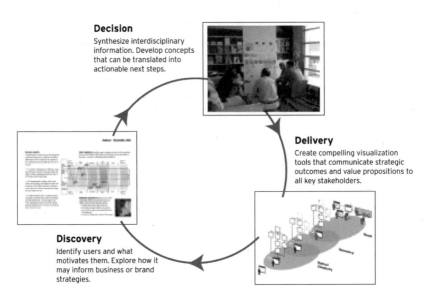

**Decision**
Synthesize interdisciplinary information. Develop concepts that can be translated into actionable next steps.

**Delivery**
Create compelling visualization tools that communicate strategic outcomes and value propositions to all key stakeholders.

**Discovery**
Identify users and what motivates them. Explore how it may inform business or brand strategies.

Figure 4. Design as interface: processes and tools.

stakeholders responsible for them), and industry and technical trends (and their impact on new products and services). An organic but highly collaborative process enabled the simultaneous consideration of the problem from these various points of view. The organization and synthesis of disparate user, business, and technical information was also stimulated by the development of visual frameworks within a shared team room (a dedicated project space that visibly displays all forms of work in progress) that mapped user personas onto various business constructs (for example, examining stages of the "total customer experience"). Compared with the more data-oriented analyses of traditional customer and business research, the collective results of these discovery activities provided a visually rich catalyst for collaboratively setting the conceptual direction of the client's Internet strategy.

**Decision:** Making good use of the outputs of the discovery process in a way that establishes a strategic anchor and migration path for evolving the client's Internet presence was the next challenge. Because critical decision-making is often a cross-company activity, it must transcend functional silos and different stakeholder agendas. The deployment of design-based processes and tools in a collaborative setting (such as a workshop) proved to be useful in generating ideas about, and gaining agreement on, the principles for the vision. In developing visual tools and interactive exercises for such activities, it is important to consider the style, format, language, and comprehensiveness of the ideas communicated. Compared with more static decision-making methods, the tools used in this context became a common foundation for better informed discussion and debate.

**Delivery:** Building on initial principles that set the direction for development, the vision was articulated in the form of a singularly simple graphic that compressed multiple, related concepts onto a single page. This kind of design iconography serves as a critical tool for evangelizing the program results. To be sustainable, it must also be easy to reference (that is, take up residence in the client's briefcase for impromptu discussion) and easy to comprehend (that is, speak to a variety of audiences). Compared with more-traditional analytical deliverables, design-oriented deliverables help continue the discovery process as the program undergoes more focused development and refinement.

## TANGIBLE STRATEGIES

The result of leveraging interdisciplinary capabilities with design processes and tools as interface is the client's ability to gain focus and move forward, convincingly, with a new product or service development program. It is too often the case that new innovation activities stall, in the words of a colleague, in the "Bermuda Triangle" that frequently seems to exist between the concept design phase and continued concept development. This juncture is typically where the greatest amount of internal selling must occur within the client's organization or where the client's inability to determine an actionable next step becomes evident, resulting in a loss of momentum, haphazard choices, or the actual suspension of the entire innovation effort. Because innovation by definition is an activity that results in some kind of value-added change (organizational, operational, or experiential), making the transition from ideation to implementation is crucial.

In the case of the technology client described earlier, there had been two prior consulting engagements focused on developing a future vision for its Internet presence. The first was led by a top management consulting firm that delivered a substantial report that was analytically thorough but which lacked a compelling user-oriented story or enough creative expression of the proposed results to build momentum for further investment. The second was led by a design consultancy that delivered the creative big idea but at a level of abstraction that didn't readily translate into actionable initiatives and which didn't transcend disciplinary or functional boundaries. As suggested in this chapter, design can manifest itself in ways that go beyond product styling. And as a greater range of consultancies offer "strategic" services, design capabilities can be a differentiator in the discovery, decision-making, and delivery challenges associated with an integrated innovation effort. The transformation of broadly creative concepts into "tangible strategies" grounded in the realities of a business enterprise can help migrate the best new ideas into the development pipeline and onto the market more successfully by demonstrating benefits to both users and the company that provides those benefits.

Find related articles on *www.dmi.org* with these keywords: consulting, innovation, interdisciplinary product development, Internet, strategy

### Suggested Reading

Hamel, Gary. *Leading the Revolution* (Boston: Harvard Business School Press, 2000).

Kelley, Tom. "Designing for Business, Consulting for Innovation." *Design Management Journal*, vol. 10, no. 3 (Summer 1999).

Pine, B. Joseph II, and Gilmore, James H. "Welcome to the Experience Economy." *Harvard Business Review*, July-August 1998.

Porter, Michael E. "Strategy and the Internet." *Harvard Business Review*, March 2001.

## *Endnotes*

1. The I-Zone leveraged Polaroid's instant-film technology, which contributed to its success. Yet, the company was disastrously late in joining the digital revolution—proving once again that good design is not always good business, if larger strategic issues aren't being taken into account when new products are developed.

2. Valery, Nicholas. "A Survey of Innovation in Industry." *The Economist*, February 20, 1999.

3. Tom Kelley, "Designing for Business, Consulting for Innovation," *Design Management Journal*, vol. 10, no. 3 (Summer 1999), p. 30.

# Chapter 9

# Managing the Evolution of Microsoft's Hardware Business

by Andy Cargile and Ken Fry

*Over its twenty-five-year history, the hardware division of Microsoft Corp. has delivered innovative products that delight customers and contribute revenue to the company. Andy Cargile and Ken Fry describe how a growing emphasis on the user experience and the application of several key business principles have helped their division create compelling designs that simultaneously respond to advances in technology, the demands of the marketplace, and the human spirit.*

WHEN MOST PEOPLE think of Microsoft, they don't think of hardware. And truly, being a hardware product team in the world's largest software company makes for a unique set of challenges, as well as opportunities. The Microsoft Hardware Division was founded in 1982 on the principle of deep integration of hardware with software. The division was originally charged with creating the company's first mouse compatible with Microsoft Word. Subsequent releases of the Microsoft Mouse led in market share, consumer popularity, and industry awards. The 1990s saw an expanding variety of products, including PC keyboards, gaming joysticks and gamepads, a cordless telephone system, PC audio speakers, and trackball devices.

In 1992, the Microsoft Hardware team hired its first industrial designer. Today, the hardware user experience (UX) team is composed of more than twenty-five UX professionals, including industrial designers, interaction designers, model makers, user researchers, ergonomists, and copywriters. The team works within a community of more than 550 UX professionals across Microsoft and helps develop products as core members of the two hundred-person hardware division.

User experience design and research has played an essential part in the evolution of Microsoft Hardware's business strategy. The tight integration of UX with our technology and business strategy has served as a powerful accelerant for rapid revenue growth.

Business strategy evolution can occur by accident, coincidence, or intent; it can also result from a changing competitive environment. Clearly, the preferred way to accelerate business evolution is by intent. However, changes to business strategy without a focus on integrating user, market, and technology factors can result in stagnation.

## FOUR STAGES OF BUSINESS STRATEGY EVOLUTION IN MICROSOFT HARDWARE

Microsoft has been a technology leader in the mouse and keyboard business for many years. However, when we branched out into other hardware products, such as interactive toys, gaming peripherals, and broadband networking equipment, we were met with limited success. Some products were too early to market; some were too late. Some products were too broadly focused; others were too narrowly focused. Many products provided great value to customers but didn't balance their focus on the user with a focus on the business or technology aspects of the products. Innovation was focused solely on the product and tended to be driven primarily by technology innovation. Although we were recognized for technology innovation and recorded a number of firsts, we barely stayed ahead of the competition.

Microsoft Hardware has always been profitable and has experienced major success with some products. However, the failure of a few individual efforts made that success inconsistent and less predictable. We've gained momentum in recent years by adopting business strategies that focus more deeply on the customer experience. We have returned hardware to its roots of tightly integrating hardware and software. Each business strategy has led to an increase in revenue across the hardware business.

## STAGE 1: COMMODITY STRATEGY

Visit any consumer electronics store and, in the PC peripherals aisle, you will find rows of products differentiated by a wide range of features, shapes, and prices. In the late 1990s, Microsoft Hardware was not equipped to compete across the board in such a broad and deeply competitive market. We were accustomed to developing and launching a mouse or keyboard product every year or so. Things changed when we started framing our success within the context of the broader competitive landscape. We knew we had to change how we developed and launched products if we wanted to be successful in the world of "commodity" products.

After the release of the industry's first optical mouse in 1999, Microsoft Hardware moved from launching a few products a year to launching multiple products across mouse, keyboard, and other product categories. This new product line strategy required that we consider how our products compete with other hardware manufacturers in a

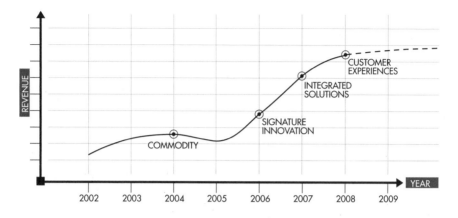

Figure 1. Microsoft Hardware revenue growth across four stages of business strategy evolution. Each stage begins at the moment revenue is realized from a particular business strategy.

growing market with increasing competitive pressures, such as product development strategy, cost to develop and manufacture hardware, time to market, and relentless competition based on price, features, and design. We evolved in each of these areas (Figure 1).

Microsoft Hardware revenue and profit remained strong at this stage. However, we tended to prioritize revenue over customer value and lost traction as a technology innovation leader.

## STAGE 2: SIGNATURE INNOVATION STRATEGY

To regain our reputation for thought leadership, we evolved our "signature" innovation strategy. This was to focus on developing high-end products featuring the latest technology advances. Over time, these technology features trickled down to other products in the line and fed our revenue-focused products. Our signature innovation strategy was essential to sustain our leadership position in a computer peripheral market that valued commodity products.

A high-end product that resulted from an early effort to define a signature innovation strategy was our Optical Desktop Elite for Bluetooth (Figure 2). In 2001, we saw an opportunity to take advantage of the Bluetooth technology and to use it in a wireless keyboard. Bluetooth

Figure 2. Microsoft Optical Desktop Elite for Bluetooth.

technology was originally developed to enable people to use wireless headsets with their cellular phones. However, the technology evolved to enable a variety of peripheral devices to connect wirelessly to the PC. As a result, this keyboard combined the latest in technology with a variety of new features.

Both the commodity and signature innovation strategies were based on customer research. We invented several new technologies and features to address user needs and then performed customer research that helped us to understand which of these innovations people found most desirable. Although some observational research approaches were in place, our product planning relied heavily on asking customers to tell us what they wanted. This practice of defining opportunistic needs based on technology innovation, and stated needs based on a specific approach to customer research, was a good start to staying competitive. However, we had room to improve and evolve.

The Microsoft Hardware business grew in this stage. However, we tended to equate innovation with technology and to overemphasize technology innovation as a product differentiator that customers valued.

## STAGE 3: INTEGRATED SOLUTIONS STRATEGY

Up to this point, conventional wisdom held that people would not pay for software integrated into hardware peripherals. It was technology and feature innovation together with great industrial design that drove purchase decisions. But innovative software features, such as the Magnifier feature on our mouse products, started to generate excitement in the market. The Magnifier is like a magnifying glass held up to your computer screen, enlarging the area of your screen that fits inside the lens. The feature is useful for detailed tasks like touching-up photos (Figure 3).

Emerging from this new focus on value-added software, we evolved our original business strategy to include hardware and software integration as a core principle. In the landscape of customer needs and emerging opportunities, we began to see an entirely new dimension of innovation.

While we continued to value opportunistic and stated-needs research to inform our integrated solutions business strategy, we were perfecting another way of understanding the customer. It wasn't enough to listen to what customers said they wanted. We needed to better understand their behaviors, motivations, needs, and frustrations. We focused more on observing people's behavior within the context of their experience: not just what people said, but how they behaved. This helped us understand their unarticulated—or latent—needs. Also, the last five years have seen dramatic changes to the computing environment at home, prompting us to understand user behavior at a deeper level. As a result, observational field research emerged as a core practice within Microsoft Hardware.

This additional focus on latent needs became an important accelerant for the business strategy of integrating hardware with software. Features such as the Magnifier and our integrated solutions strategy are the result of this research approach. The integrated solutions strategy helped us grow revenue and thrive in the market.

Figure 3. The Magnifier on Microsoft mouse products is like a magnifying glass that is held up to your computer screen. With a press and hold motion, the Magnifier enlarges the area of your screen that fits inside the lens.

## STAGE 4: CUSTOMER EXPERIENCES STRATEGY

Our current stage of evolution puts the customer experience at the center of our business strategy while building on the strengths of each previous stage. The goal of our customer experiences strategy is more than hardware and software integration. For our key products, we design for complete and seamless end-to-end experiences. An end-to-end experience considers other integration opportunities with ancillary hardware and software, and it enforces consistency from point-of-purchase through product use.

First released in 2006, the Microsoft Web cam product line is an example of this business strategy (Figure 4). Web cams are portable cameras that record video or still images on a PC for distribution over the Internet. Most Web cams are inexpensive to purchase, although the quality of the video is often low. We could have competed on price, features, technology, and design, but that would have missed the larger opportunity: connecting families to each other across the Internet.

In our research, we found that users new to video communication were not drawn to technology and features. They just wanted to set up a conversation easily and reliably. They wanted to emotionally connect with their loved ones who lived far away.

Figure 4. Microsoft LifeCam VX-1000.

Our focus on balancing stated, opportunistic, and latent needs enabled us to antici-pate what customers wanted. These anticipated needs guided our strategy as we created a new Web cam product category and business. For example, customers told us they just wanted something simple. We watched them and learned that many of their chal-lenges with existing cameras were less a matter of operating the camera hardware and more about the camera setup process, the initiation of a call, and the reliability of the connection. Anticipating customer needs, we extended these simple observations into the design of the end–to-end hardware/software video communication experience. Our goal was to make video communication as simple and reliable as a phone call. We iden-tified hardware and software integration opportunities with Windows Live Messenger, contact lists, and with the creation of a seamless connection, and we were able to focus on the experience.

Had we applied a commodity strategy to our Web cam business, it is likely the prod-uct would have had only moderate success competing on technology innovations and features. Because we care about creating great customer experiences, we were able to change how the market perceives and adopts products like this and to grow the entire product category. To underscore the value of customer experience, several companies in this market have followed our lead by focusing more on the end-to-end customer experience.

## THE RIGHT TRAITS FOR ACCELERATING EVOLUTION

Microsoft Hardware business evolution has not relied on a silver bullet to ensure suc-cess. Instead, we have identified five traits that accelerate our evolution and growth, namely: involving the right people, balancing competing factors, focusing on holistic needs, using a disciplined approach, and playing "chords of innovation." We explicitly weave these traits into the DNA of the organization so that we can build on them and evolve further.

Today our business results are stronger than they've ever been in our twenty-five-year history and position us to experience new levels of success in the future.

## GET THE RIGHT PEOPLE ON THE BUS

Microsoft Hardware is a relatively small group of two hundred people. We consistently earn the highest revenue per employee in the company. We could not deliver this level of business performance if we did not take Jim Collins' advice in Good to Great: Why Some Companies Make the Leap . . . and Others Don't to heart: Get the right people on the bus. We have no single visionary or superstar. Instead, we have developed a very strong interdisciplinary team of leaders who collaborate effectively to drive our business. This team is composed of leaders from market, technology (both hardware and software engineering), and user-experience-oriented teams, aligned with business leaders of each of our product lines. Each leader possesses customer focus, technical savvy, and business acumen. As we grow and find new opportunities, we work tightly as a team to deliver the right products to drive the business.

Having the right people on the bus means that we are flexible enough to evaluate new opportunities regardless of where they come from. We are empowered to collaborate closely and make decisions in a similar way at both the business and product level.

## BALANCE MARKET FACTORS, TECHNOLOGY FACTORS, AND USER FACTORS

We define what the hardware organization delivers by focusing equally on the market, technology, and user factors that lead to business success (Figure 5). Even though each factor represents a different area of focus for the hardware organization, they all must work together seamlessly. We've found that when we overemphasize one factor over the others, we experience less consistent and predictable results. To accelerate evolution, we keep the three factors in balance without a single one dominating.

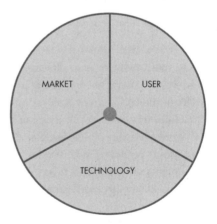

Figure 5. The integration of market, technology, and user factors is core to Microsoft Hardware's business strategy.

## FOCUS ON HOLISTIC NEEDS

Each of the market, technology, and user-oriented teams relies on insight generated by three distinct approaches to research.

1. Teams that are focused on market factors seek to understand what customers, retailers, and salespeople say they want (that is, their stated needs) to inform business strategy decisions.

2. Teams that are focused on technology factors create technology opportunities that link to defined user needs (that is, opportunistic needs).

3. Teams that are focused on user factors rely on ethnographic and observational research to expose unarticulated user needs (that is, latent needs).

Figure 6. Market, technology, and user factors are informed by stated, opportunistic, and latent needs research data. The integration of these data sets helps define anticipated needs.

Combining all three approaches holistically helps us anticipate customer needs within the context of the business landscape and enabling technologies (that is, anticipated needs—see Figure 6). In the past, we relied heavily on stated and opportunistic needs, but our evolving focus on latent and anticipated needs has accelerated the evolution of this business strategy.

## ENGAGE IN A DISCIPLINED PROCESS

Because problems are identified and eliminated early, every dollar spent on research and iterative prototyping at the beginning of a software development project saves you $100 at product launch. Hardware development cost savings can be more dramatic than software development efforts. Because hardware has high downstream costs in tooling and manufacturing, what you save is actually more like $1,000 per dollar spent. Our ability to accelerate the evolution of our business relies on a disciplined process across all phases of hardware product definition and development.

A key advantage of this disciplined process is that it allows us to have repeatable successes in product development while driving down costs. It also allows us to learn from missteps as we try new things. As with the other traits, we push this into our organizational DNA so that each project member continually looks for ways to improve our process.

## PLAY "CHORDS OF INNOVATION"

Larry Keeley of the Doblin Group has proposed a model for innovation strategy that recognizes ten types of innovation. These include product, process, channel, customer experience, and business model innovation. A company that is very good at one type of innovation can be easily copied or bested by a competitor. But if a company is focused on multiple types of innovation at the same time (that is, a chord of innovation), competitors have a tougher time being successful.

Microsoft Hardware used to focus on a single "note" of product innovation. As we have evolved a customer experience strategy over the past several years, we have begun to develop multiple notes—a chord—of innovation within a product or line. The trait that accelerates growth for us is not any particular chord of innovation. We've adopted the innovation framework and recognize that we must be flexible with how we express multiple types of innovation simultaneously. Customer experience is an innovation type that is expressed in all the chords that Microsoft Hardware plays. Like other traits, the organization has incorporated this framework into our DNA, and it is regularly expressed at the individual team level as part of our product development process.

## A FUTURE IN PROGRESS

Looking at this chapter as a case study, you will see a work in progress. It describes how Microsoft Hardware—a large business within a very large software corporation—has evolved and grown by integrating our focus on the user experience with business and technology strategies.

Last year marked our best year across every business metric, including year-over-year growth. What is particularly exciting is that these results are based on a year of products that are primarily the outcome of our integrated solutions strategy. The products that are the result of our customer experience strategy are only beginning to enter the market. Our business strategy is not based on a single focus on revenue, technology, features, or design. Instead, our products rely on the strong integration of the user experience with business focus and technology leadership to accelerate our business growth. We are hopeful that our upward trajectory will continue under this new strategy.

What's the next stage of our evolution? We have yet to discover the answer to this question. We already know that our business success will continue to rely on traits that have accelerated our evolution to this point. And we will continue to explore and discover new traits as we evolve our business strategy.

### Suggested Reading

Christensen, Clayton M., and Michael E. Raynor. *The Innovator's Solution: Creating and Sustaining Successful Growth* (Boston: Harvard Business School Press, 2003).

Collins, Jim. *Good to Great: Why Some Companies Make the Leap . . . and Others Don't* (New York: Collins, 2001).

Doblin Inc. "The Ten Types of Innovation." *www.doblin.com/ideas/TenTypesOverview. html.*

Kim, W. Chan, and Renée Mauborgne. *Blue Ocean Strategy: How to Create Uncontested Market Space and Make Competition Irrelevant* (Boston: Harvard Business School Press, 2005).

Pine, B. Joseph, and James H. Gilmore. *The Experience Economy: Work Is Theater & Every Business a Stage* (Boston: Harvard Business School Press, 1999).

*Chapter 10*

# The Best Strategy Is the Right Strategy

by Sohrab Vossoughi

*The "right strategy" enables brands to meaningfully connect with target customers across a breadth of products or services. A project to redesign KitchenAid's line of appliances allowed Sohrab Vossoughi to examine how his firm achieves this connection by creating a consistent brand experience through a pyramid of rational steps that move from a grounding in brand core values to visual position-mapping to design principles to signature elements.*

IN THE LATE 1990s, Whirlpool Corporation and Ziba Design entered into a collaborative partnership to solve a typical business problem: The white-goods manufacturer was having difficulty in the marketplace because its entire value proposition was based on either cost or quality—price point or product attributes. Producing between 70 and 80 million units a year, Whirlpool tended to conceive and design its numerous brands (including Whirlpool, Roper, and KitchenAid) and product lines as categories—as if they were refrigeration businesses or fabric care businesses or microwave businesses—rather than as individual brands with stories to tell. The only thing that truly differentiated the product in the marketplace was the logo it had on it.

Chuck Jones, vice president of global consumer design for Whirlpool, described it this way: "There was a feeling that we were at a stalemate. We would come out with a fin on a washing-machine agitator and we would say, 'Buy Whirlpool because we've got this hyper-efficient fin on this agitator that will get your clothes 20 percent cleaner.'

Then, within twelve to eighteen months, all our competitors had a fin. To use the analogy of chess, every time we would check someone, they would checkmate us."

There was an added layer of complexity to the problem. Whirlpool had been using demographic data to understand its target customers, and this essentially differentiated them by details like salary and geographic location. The data placed Whirlpool customers in broad categories but did not provide the level of detail necessary to truly understand what they desired from their experiences with their home appliances.

At Ziba, clients come to us with this type of dilemma on an almost daily basis. In a rush to keep up with the competition or maintain market share, there seems to be a pervasive, almost knee-jerk reaction in product and service brands alike—companies try to match their competition feature for feature or, alternatively, they try to strike out and "be different." While new stylistic elements, color palettes, logo placement, and even a new product may emerge from the repositioning process, neither strategy digs deep enough to actually solve the problem. At best, companies can temporarily check the competition, but that doesn't get them any closer to establishing a relevant brand that connects with their target customers and creates a loyal bond.

Whirlpool Corporation was at a crossroads and planned to shift away from a category-focused approach to a brand-focused approach. Jones recognized that the only way to step away from what he calls random acts of design was to establish a comprehensive design strategy, and he engaged Ziba to lend thought leadership and rigor to the process.

## WHAT DESIGN STRATEGY IS AND WHAT IT IS NOT

Too often, the word "strategy" is applied to design solutions that only scratch the surface of a business challenge. More often than not, these strategies are an exercise in form and color consistency or a trends-informed, flavor-of-the-month approach, or a designer's stylistic bias that is used over and over again, no matter what the product is. In fact, these are simply examples of a design language. Design language is just one of many components that comprise a design strategy.

At Ziba, design strategy is informed by three essential elements: a deep understanding of the values, attitudes, and behavior of the target customer; the nature of the company's values, essence, and character (also known as the DNA); and the time-based trends that serve as the backdrop to the product or service experience. We want to create the right brand language for that unique brand and its target customer at that specific point in time. Without these elements as a foundation, any design language is merely opinion or an exercise in making pretty things. The understanding of customers' desires, brand DNA, and timeliness creates relevancy. Relevancy establishes meaning and is the backbone of a design strategy that is flexible and can be leveraged over time.

Ziba's strategic design model (see Figure 1) is a strategy pyramid that consists of four layers: core values, visual position mapping, design principles, and signature elements. Core values, along with essence and character, are the basic tenets by which a company conducts business and presents itself to the market. Together, these attributes form the

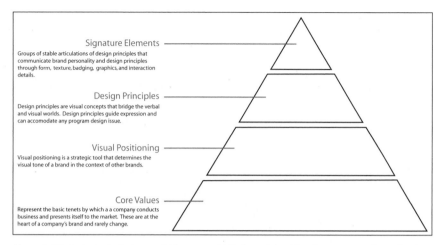

Figure 1. Ziba's strategic design model is a pyramid that consists of four layers: core values, visual position mapping, design principles, and signature elements. Design strategy must begin with establishing core values and build from there. The result is a visual brand language that is iterative and flexible enough to evolve with time.

DNA of the brand and rarely change. Visual position mapping is a strategic tool that determines the visual tone of a brand in the context of other brands. Design principles are visual concepts that create the bridge between the verbal and visual worlds. They define the visual characteristics of the brand; they guide expression and inform design decisions for all of its strategic touch-points—what Ziba calls the 360-degree experience. Signature elements are groups of elemental embodiments of design principles that communicate brand personality through form, texture, logo badging, color, surface, and interaction details. A comprehensive design strategy builds on each preceding layer in the pyramid. The result is a rock-solid visual brand language that is iterative and flexible enough to evolve with time.

## KITCHENAID'S CORE VALUES

When Whirlpool partnered with Ziba to help revitalize its brands, it had already been engaged in an internal process to develop a brand strategy. Whirlpool, Roper, and KitchenAid—what were they as individual brands, what did they stand for, what was their value proposition, why should consumers care about them? The company had also begun to shift its focus away from demographic customer data to psychographic data, and it had completed research that created rich profiles of its target customers. Essentially, Whirlpool had been successful in establishing the first level in the strategy pyramid—its core values—and shared this data with Ziba to inform the discovery process.

Whirlpool's research revealed that KitchenAid's essence was "The passionate pursuit of epicurious." The psychographic profile of KitchenAid users was as the home enthusiast—a passionate cook who takes deep satisfaction from tools that respect and leverage his knowledge, experience, and skills. The brand's core values were profession-alism, passion, heritage, and fit/feel/finish. KitchenAid's stand mixer, for example, had become an icon—the heavy, almost industrial, cast metal had become a symbol of the hard-working, dedicated homemaker. Details like these, however, had gotten glossed over in the rush to add features or drive the price down to compete. KitchenAid's new products lacked the features that deeply resonated with its customers and were the very foundation of the company's heritage. KitchenAid needed to re-establish that heritage.

What Whirlpool needed next was to mine its data, translate its brands' DNA, and harness its design expertise to create a design strategy that served its customers' deep-seated desires. Moving forward, the resulting visual brand language would inform every design choice for each brand. Although Ziba engaged in this process for each of Whirl-pool's brands, this chapter will focus on our work with KitchenAid.

## BUILDING THE STRATEGY PYRAMID

To translate KitchenAid's brand equities into a long-term, innovative visual brand lan-guage that would inspire cooking enthusiasts and provide a competitive advantage, we employed Ziba's strategic design process, which is known as VIBE™—visual and interac-tive brand equity. VIBE translates consumer perceptions of brand attributes into con-sistent, three-dimensional brand experiences through a four-step process: perceptual mapping, reference designs, perceptual evaluation, and design strategy creation. This process creates the three remaining layers in the strategy pyramid: visual position map-ping, design principles, and signature elements.

## VISUAL POSITION MAPPING

The VIBE process begins with perceptual mapping exercises with target customers. The perceptual map is the cornerstone of the process. It is used to determine the visual tone and characteristics of a brand in the context of other brands. Our team worked with Whirlpool branding specialists to create and refine Whirlpool's perceptual map through literature scans, cross-functional brainstorms, and a review of internal brand docu-ments. The final perceptual map was formed by two axes that are both exclusive and differentiated: extroverted vs. introverted and thinking vs. feeling.

To validate the verbal descriptions of each axis, we conducted a study. Out of 120 personality characteristics gleaned from Myers-Briggs and other personality assays, as well as Whirlpool's own brand attributes list, we drew eight, which were assigned to each axis descriptor and validated for use in customer interviews.

We also conducted cross-functional brainstorms to develop discrete categories of images that would be used to determine the visual qualities of each axis. We selected three categories—architecture, products, and textiles/graphics—and selected and cropped sixty images to represent a range of formal principles and visual characteristics, while avoiding any associative prejudice.

We conducted image and adjective sorting exercises with 106 customers in four U.S. cities—New York (n=20), Denver (n=30), San Francisco (n=30), and Atlanta (n=26).

First, participants were presented with the logos of Whirlpool brands and their corresponding competitors. Participants were given thirty-two personality characteristics (eight for each axis descriptor), listed in random order on index cards. Customers were told they could apply as many characteristics as they wanted to each brand and could use the same characteristics to describe up to three brands if they wished. Following a brief description of each brand's personality traits, participants were asked to describe their ideal brand of home appliances using the thirty-two personality characteristics. Image sorting helped to uncover which shapes, colors, textures, and materials consumers associate with each brand attribute.

In the last exercise, participants were then asked to sort the aforementioned Whirlpool stack of sixty 3"×3" image cards. Each stack contained two of each image. Cards were rearranged to avoid order bias and fraternizing. Participants were instructed to place each image on two of the four axis descriptors, which were listed across the top of a large sheet of paper. For example, the same image could be placed on extroverted and feeling or extroverted and thinking. By placing two of each image, customers indirectly identified the quadrant of the perceptual map to which the image belongs.

We compiled, plotted, and analyzed the personality characteristics each participant assigned to the four brands, removing extreme outliers, in order to determine the final shape of each brand personality. The location and perimeter of each shape defined the brand's personality; the area and volume of the shapes indicated consistency of brand message. We performed a similar process for image sorting. All in all, 6,360 image placements from 106 customers were captured and analyzed.

The mapping process resulted in a visual map of KitchenAid's current brand position and its desired brand position (Figure 2). Next, after extensive cross-functional

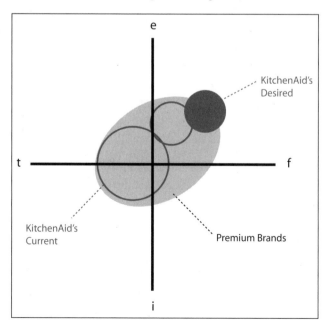

Figure 2. Ziba and Whirlpool branding specialists created a perceptual map formed by two axes that are both exclusive and differentiated: extroverted vs. introverted and thinking vs. feeling. The map was used in conjunction with a visual sorting exercise to plot customer perception of KitchenAid's previous and desired brand position.

brainstorms, we arrived at an abstraction of visual tones (Figure 3) for each quadrant of the perceptual map and to the creation of a preliminary design palette for KitchenAid's desired brand position. KitchenAid needed to follow the precedent-setting, emotional, high-involvement associations generated by heritage products like the stand mixer in order to establish a clear, unified, and relevant brand personality that served the attitudes and values of its target user: the home enthusiast.

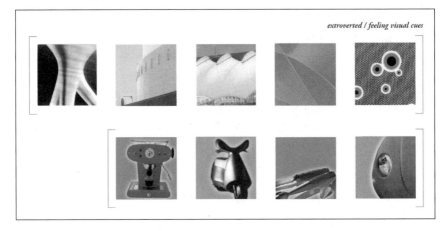

Figure 3. An abstraction of visual tones for each quadrant of the perceptual map shown in Figure 2 was created to serve as the preliminary design palette for KitchenAid's desired brand position.

## DESIGN PRINCIPLES

The third layer of the strategic pyramid is responsible for establishing the visual character of the brand and building a bridge between the verbal and the visual worlds. Abstracted from visual positioning imagery, design principles provide the underlying subtext of a brand's visual expression and are used across the 360-degree experience of a brand. They are infinitely flexible, providing designers the freedom to be creative in a multitude of contexts. KitchenAid's design principles included exaggerated scale, fusion, natural order, and resonance.

With this added level of preliminary detail, we created theme boards to unite the findings from the visual mapping and design principles studies in a visual presentation of the desired brand position. Together these elements would serve as the guide for testing hypotheses in the next phase of the VIBE process: creating reference designs.

Reference designs translate theme boards into designs for concept exploration. We applied the design principles to renderings of a cooktop stove, dishwasher, washing machine, double oven, and refrigerator. Each rendering expressed visual themes from the perceptual mapping exercises in slightly different ways.

Next, perceptual evaluation allowed us to determine the effectiveness of each design concept. We asked customers to evaluate the product concepts based on their effectiveness in communicating key attributes. Using the renderings, we had them circle elements of the designs that were influencing their opinions and cross out things that were conflicting with their perceptions. The result was an understanding of each concept's ability to communicate KitchenAid's brand attributes and of which elements were contributing to this perception. After this consumer evaluation, a single design language was refined and visual themes were translated into principle guidelines and possible signature elements. We applied these to full-size products and tested them an additional time with consumers to finally establish the relevant visual brand language for KitchenAid.

## SIGNATURE ELEMENTS

With customer research complete, final signature elements could be refined. Signature elements are the most highly specified elements of the strategy pyramid. Although they respond and change with market and user needs, they should be applied consistently within their brand family. The KitchenAid design strategy contained a palette of eight signature elements that were further broken down into four categories: body, details, user interface, and logo placement (Figure 4).

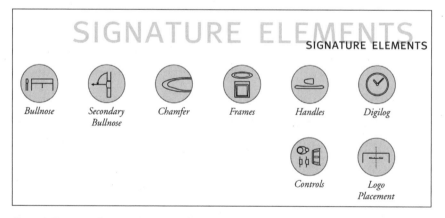

Figure 4. Signature elements are groups of elemental embodiments of design principles that communicate brand personality through form, texture, logo badging, color, surface, and interaction details.

Not every element of a product is controlled with the constraints of a signature element. Expression zones are visual elements on the product within which designers can improvise, with appropriate combinations of signature elements and design principles, to solve program-specific design problems. Whirlpool worked together with Ziba to create a strategic toolkit that identified the areas of each product concept that were to be treated as expression zones, as well as the visual brand language elements that contributed to particular design solution (Figure 5).

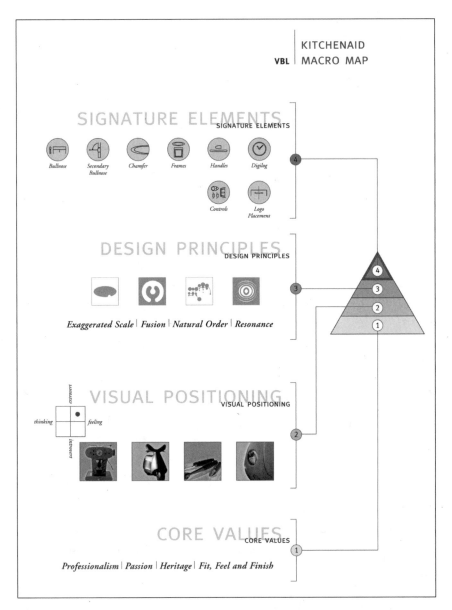

Figure 5. An overlay of Ziba's strategy pyramid with its strategic design process, known as VIBE—visual and interactive brand equity.

## KITCHENAID SUCCESS STORY

The result of the strategic design process was KitchenAid's ProLine—a line of major home appliances based on KitchenAid's core values of professionalism, passion, heritage, and fit/feel/finish. ProLine leveraged the inherent properties of materials and processes (Figure 6) to reinforce KitchenAid's warm, commercial look and feel and to improve the appliances' durability and extend their longevity. Commercial-grade materials were used judiciously to have impact as long-distance signifiers (significant details noticed from at least 10 feet away), as well as to enhance touch-points and connections—for example, heavy cast metals and stainless steel to communicate commercial durability. Plated zinc die-casting, formed stainless steel, formed carbon steel, porcelain cast iron, and extruded aluminum were used for structural components; we used brushed stainless steel as a cosmetic wrap. Handles were made of cast aluminum for strength and durability. The KitchenAid logo was boldly embossed into the centerline of significant signature elements to emphasize qualities of permanence, longevity, and durability.

Creating the KitchenAid ProLine visual brand language accomplished two key objectives. First, it provided KitchenAid with a strong point of view that reestablished the

Figure 6. The finished product: KitchenAid's ProLine major appliances.

brand's heritage and allowed it to compete with European manufacturers that were eroding its core market share. Second, it reduced development cost and time. As a result, product placement grew exponentially with KitchenAid's strongest retail partner. ProLine allowed KitchenAid to secure exclusive distribution with some of its key trade partners and strengthen its channel partner relationships. It also created a halo effect for its other products.

Perhaps even more important than the initial success of a visual brand language, however, is the test of how it survives future iterations and application across product lines. After working together to create the visual brand language for KitchenAid major appliances, Whirlpool asked Ziba to apply the language to its portables line, which included a waffle iron, a hand mixer, and a food processor (Figure 7). The language was robust and flexible enough to accommodate that product line. Chuck Jones described the impact: "In the first couple of years after introducing that language, we were basically making as much money from waffle makers as we were from top-mount refrigerators. The margin impact for Whirlpool was incredible. The language was a market success. Trade partners all the way from Williams-Sonoma to Target really embraced it."

Figure 7. Whirlpool asked Ziba to apply the visual brand language to its portables line. The products were a market success and were embraced by trade partners from Williams-Sonoma to Target.

## DESIGN STRATEGY MAKES GOOD BUSINESS SENSE

There are so many reasons why a comprehensive design strategy makes good business sense. First, the already-defined visual brand language reduces the product development cycle time of future design challenges because it allows development to jump ahead on a timeline. It cuts costs and increases ROI by streamlining and focusing product development and, in some cases, parts of the concept refinement process. As development teams become more familiar with a strategic toolkit, they become more time-efficient. This does not mean they are forced to sacrifice quality. On the contrary, quality is enhanced because experience is leveraged from one product to the next. Together, the company's products assume a consistent, brand-rich experience. Products reach the market cheaper and faster.

In addition to its direct effect on the bottom line, a design strategy also influences companies' ROI by building brand equity through appearance and interaction details. Consistent product look-and-feel has a real and material impact on a company's brand equity—and subsequently on sales figures.

Design strategy benefits companies internally, as well. A comprehensive design strategy makes the design process transparent and inclusive. Jones found that the process his group engaged in with Ziba created organization pull instead of organizational selling. "Essentially, we could 'show the math' of how we moved from a brand position to a visual position. It was not just a bunch of designers sitting in a corner magically making the transformation in their heads. There was a solid research foundation under it," he says.

Jones also found that being able to involve marketing, engineering, and manufacturing in the research and design process enabled his group to do a bit of change management along the way. "We were so open with sharing exactly how we were using consumer data to lead us to a visual position. It completely eliminated the traditional barriers that design organizations often run into with other functions inside an enterprise. They were able to move right along with us as we were developing this visual language. At the end, people understood why the KitchenAid product looked the way it did, why the Whirlpool products looked the way they did, and why the signature elements were the way they were. It was a great thing."

Jones surmises that strategic design is responsible for moving Whirlpool Corporation out of its business stalemate. "I would say that whether it is our annual growth in the intervening years, market share, profitability, stock price—pick your metric—while you can't attribute all the success to design, I'd submit that design was a key driver."

# SECTION 3

## METHODS AND INTEGRATION
## OF DESIGN STRATEGY

Now that this anthology has presented information about creating corporate strategy and creating design strategy in section one, and implementing design strategy in section two, the next step is to better understand the tools and techniques to integrate design strategy within an organization. To this end, as with the preceding chapters, we present a set of diverse opinions from experts.

If one is to create and build design strategy, first one has to develop an imperative for design in the organization. Claudia Kotchka was given just this assignment at P&G, and it wasn't easy. Her chapter tells a story of integrating new thinking about design into the corporate culture. Mark Dziersk explores the move from linear to visual thinking and shows how design and creativity are at the heart of innovation. Jeremy Alexis demonstrates design strategy's role in building customer loyalty, while EunSook Kwon and her colleagues express the importance of design in the workspace for boosting employee creativity, communication, and productivity. Protecting design's proprietary intellectual properties is almost as important as creating them in the first place, and Joshua Cohen explains the ins and outs of these processes. Gert Koostra and Jos Vink present specific methods to measure the effect of graphic design on brand perceptions. All these ideas lead to new methods and techniques with which to integrate design and corporate strategy.

Here too we discover several very important key points. Bear in mind that we're not talking about traditional strategy, supported with volumes of quantitative research and little true insight, but rather about using design thinking and methods in the ideation and development of corporate strategy and the design of artifacts and services to make corporate strategy come to life. The goal is to create that which is meaningful to a company's customers and prospects, and there is no better way to do so than through design strategy.

**Integrate design into an organization by embracing corporate culture.** The simple fact is that corporate culture drives every organization. To be effective at building design strategy, one must integrate design into that culture by embracing its key elements. The techniques will vary from company to company, because each organization has its own particular culture; however, it is most important to recognize what the organization values most and to create design strategies to support these internal values, whether they center around customer satisfaction, innovation, time to market, or teamwork. Recognize the ability of design and design thinking to adapt to any given situation and improve it. This can become a synergetic situation, and with time it can empower the design function to help drive strategy and organizational success.

**Trust qualitative research, and think in visual terms.** One of the biggest challenges design leaders must overcome is the lack of hard data about design performance. All too often business executives rely on quantitative data; after all, isn't all business run on numbers? But today we are beginning to recognize the value of intuition, as we realize that some of our greatest business successes have been based on gut instinct. Consider Microsoft, FedEx, Dell, Apple, and Facebook—all businesses started by college dropouts. Design, too, is very much a part of intuition and instinct. As we saw in section one, it is possible to measure the values of design; but if the rise of the creative class is key to successful organizations of the future, as social and economic theorist Richard Florida would have it, design and design strategy will play a key a role. Thus, observational research, mind maps, visual thinking, and fast prototypes will be more influential, and may be more effective, than traditional methods.

**Design leads to customer delight.** There is no doubt that every company aspires to have satisfied customers, and it seems that every organization is fixed on what drives customer loyalty. The argument we present here is that design can take customers from simple product satisfaction and some measure of loyalty to a perception of meaning, relevance, and value in their lives. Becoming meaningful and relevant to your customers goes a long way toward securing loyalty. Traditionally, businesses focus on the first "moment of truth" (the purchase decision) and the second (the repeat purchase). But today it's a customer's market, choices abound, and consumers are not responding as well to traditional "push" marketing as they have in the past; they perceive their decisions to be self-driven, and that drive is based on personal meaning. Design can have a profound effect on customer choice, satisfaction, loyalty, relevance, and meaning. Indeed, design can have a tremendous influence on the "triple bottom line"—i.e., at economic, social, and environmental levels.

*Chapter 11*

# The Design Imperative in Consumer Goods

by Claudia Kotchka

*Procter & Gamble is undergoing a transformation. Cutting-edge technologies and mass-marketing have long been the company's approach to leveraging sales of many of the world's most well-known and respected brands. Claudia Kotchka discusses how design is being added to that strategic mix today to help strengthen customer loyalty and to reach increasingly segmented markets.*

IN A SURVEY recently conducted by the Boston Consulting Group among about 950 executives, 90 percent of the respondents said organic innovation was absolutely essential to their industries—they could not survive without it. By "organic," they meant grown from inside rather than through acquiring companies. But the most telling part was that more than half of those executives were not satisfied with the financial returns they were getting on their investments in innovation. So there is a lot of room for improvement out there, and it is my belief that design is one of the great solutions to the challenge.

Here at Procter & Gamble, innovation has always been an imperative. To me, innovation is also a design imperative. But that's not the tradition at P&G where, when you use the word "innovation," it tends to translate as technology.

Not that P&G doesn't care about design—far from it. From the start, we felt design was important because we were interested in branding. If you are going to brand something, you have to design it. Consider the design of Ivory soap. In addition to having a logo and a package that stood out, the product was white; it was pure; it had a light fragrance; it floated.

Ivory soap was the product of conscious design even at the beginning. If you're going to brand something, you have to design it.

Tide was P&G's first detergent. Now, in the age of consumer choice, there are nineteen variants of liquid Tide alone.

But in spite of that auspicious beginning, somehow along the way we turned into more of a technology company. We launched new brands, all based on technology—Tide being the first detergent. The launches of Pampers, Crest, Always, and others were all based on technology.

Then we discovered the power of advertising, and print ads turned into radio turned into TV, and all of a sudden, we were a mass-market company. We developed a great model: technology plus scale plus TV equals success. And that worked for years. We had a great formula—and we followed it consistently.

Technology and scale ruled. You start with the science, then scale it by making one thing fast. Manufacturing loves nothing better than to see bottles of Tide running so fast on the lines that they're just a blur of orange. It is very efficient and helps us deliver high-quality products at a reasonable cost.

So in this context, what was the role of design? Making things pretty. Start with science, put it in a package that runs fast down the manufacturing line, and make it pretty. This actually caused one of our design managers to claim, "Design is the last decoration station on the way to the market." And, in fact, it often was.

Indeed, in our zeal to be efficient, and believing that the only thing that mattered was the technology inside, we actually put three of our shampoos and four of our body washes in identical packages. Only the label changed. This was an infamous moment at P&G. It prompted one of our designers to propose an even more efficient idea—just use one label and then check off whatever product is inside. He was trying to make a point, but not everyone got it.

Then the market changed. Consumers didn't really want to be "mass" anymore; they wanted to be treated as individuals with unique needs and desires. So Crest, which was very simple in 1980, exploded into eighty-seven variants and eight hundred SKUs. I can't even keep track of them. Even Tide—also very simple in 1980—exploded. We have nineteen variants of liquid Tide and more than four hundred SKUs. But consumers didn't just want new technology. Unfortunately, some of our brands had to learn this the hard way.

For example, in the early 1990s we developed a new Pert shampoo formula for kids. And, of course, we had great technology in it. We launched it in the same package as the rest of the Pert lineup, differentiated only by a pale yellow color and a new label featuring a little star on the bottom. This star actually proved to be quite controversial because it didn't really match the rest of the line, but we put it on there anyway to communicate that it was for kids.

We expected the product to be very successful. After all, we had great technology. But the competition recognized technology alone would not win. L'Oreal launched a very distinctive line for kids—it had a great fragrance and fun package shapes—at a premium price. So what happened? That product grew to a 3.2 market share, while Pert languished at .1. That was a great lesson for us.

Then, in 2001, our CEO declared, "We cannot compete on technology alone." I know this may sound like a no-brainer, but at the time it was a somewhat radical statement at P&G. We were selling cans of coffee; Starbucks was providing an experience. We needed a new model.

## DESIGN TO DELIGHT

Our new model includes design. What does that mean? One thing it means is using design to transform great technology into an engaging consumer experience—something that tells a story, something consumers would love to have in their home. Design to delight. It's not just a matter of putting things in the same package and writing "New and Improved" on it. We want to take those new technologies and transform them into experiences. We want to build loyalty by having consumers fall in love with our brands.

Another way to use design is to identify new ideas. We already have great technologies; we don't always have to invent new ones to find ways to excite consumers and build loyalty.

One example is Kandoo, a line specifically designed to empower little kids, who are always saying, "I can do it myself." A huge hit in Europe, it was recently launched in the United States.

The first product was for potty training. They are wipes that pop up one at a time. Kids love them, and they don't waste an entire roll of toilet paper. We also designed a soap dispenser kids can use with one hand. You push the top and foam comes out. Moms were happy because the kids loved it, it didn't waste soap, and it also helped teach them good habits.

Little kids are always saying, "I can do it myself." The Kandoo line of products (seen here, Kandoo wipes and soap dispenser) were designed specifically for them.

Another design opportunity relates to the explosion in consumer choices. Consumers want to be respected as unique individuals, and so the business response has been more choices—more products, five hundred television stations, magazines for every interest, so many websites you can't find them all, and more services. There's just more of everything out there. So now consumers are screaming, "But I want it simple. Make my life simple." This is a big dilemma. In fact, consumers don't actually want choices—they just want what they want. They just don't want to have to deal with what other people want.

That's a design problem. It certainly hasn't been solved yet, and the design community is uniquely equipped to tackle it. It's clear that market segmentation is critical—for P&G and, I think, any other company. Design plays a very important role in helping us to understand those segments and then in understanding how to delight people in those segments.

## INSEPARABLE DESIGN

So if our new model integrates design in all our work, then all we have to do is build design into the DNA of P&G. That was my charge in 2001, and it sounds easy enough. But it's not. It's a big culture change—a bigger culture change, I think, than people actually expected. Culture change in any company is hard, and why is that?

According to Roger Martin, dean of the Rotman School of Management at the University of Toronto, "Organizations resist change because they are made up of individuals who are working at what has always worked." And at P&G our old model had worked. But we had to change.

So what did we need to be successful? Step one: a great CEO as an advocate for design. It's got to start at the top, and if you don't have the CEO lined up, forget it.

But at P&G, as with any large corporation, we need more advocates than the CEO alone. We need the business unit presidents' support, as well. Without senior management lined up and passionate about design, we cannot get out of the starting blocks.

Great design talent is also a must. But our needs go beyond design mastery. Our designers also have to inspire, teach, and lead the business to great design. We once had a consultant assess our design organization, and she asked, "Don't you have any designers who are sheltered—doing actual design work, hidden away?" The answer is no. Our design managers are on the front lines every single day. They're co-located with the business units and they have to motivate, educate, and lead in addition to being great designers. They have to be able to get people to listen. It's a challenge.

Next—and this, again, should be pretty obvious but is not—get design integrated early. If we don't want to be the last decoration station on the way to the market, we need to start any new initiative with design already on the team. This is an area in which we are making huge progress. It makes a difference. It shows. It's pretty easy to look at our product launches and know which ones included design from the very beginning.

Then, of course, at P&G, we need measurement tools. As I once heard Bruce Nussbaum, assistant managing editor of *BusinessWeek*, say: "Corporations can't get away from measurements." Let me tell you, that's P&G to the T. We love to measure everything. So we're always looking for new ways to measure the power and the impact of design. We haven't cracked this yet, but we're always looking for new tools.

## CALLING IT DESIGN

It's clear to me that businesses need designers, but they don't always know it. If you ask a business leader what she needs, what she wants, you will get these kinds of responses: "I want emotional connections with my consumer. I want better overall experiences for my consumer. I want passionately loyal consumers. And I want more innovation that delights." You and I know that's what designers do, but it doesn't always translate that way to business leaders.

Remember the Boston Consulting Group study mentioned at the beginning of this chapter? Well, BCG also asked those executives which companies they most admired for innovation. And which company do you think they named? You got it: Apple. So you would think they would make the connection between Apple and design.

In fact, what did these business leaders say about Apple? Here are some quotes: "The company focuses on ease of use, successfully extending the uses of technology in everyday life." Sounds like design. "They understand that aesthetics and image are important elements for consumer adoption." "They package and market complex technologies in a very simple and attractive way." That's beautiful design.

The good news is that business leaders want design, but they don't always call it that. So how do we help them understand that design is what they're asking for? That brings up a key lesson for me: Don't try to explain design. Actually, we tried for a long time. We had so many definitions of design, none of which really worked, that I figured, "All right, I give up. I'm not going to try to explain it. Instead, I'm going to show it." And I came up with two examples.

In the first example, I would walk into a business leader's office and say, "Here's a measuring cup. I bought this at Wal-Mart. How would you improve it?" A typical reply was "But you can't really make it any better. It functions. It pours. It works. What's there to improve?"

Oxo's new measuring cup lets you see how much liquid you're pouring in without stooping or holding the cup in the air. Why didn't anyone think of that before?

Then I pulled out Oxo's measuring cup. It was just wonderful to see the light bulbs go off. The response was usually, "Oh, why didn't anyone think of that before?" Then I explained that designers watch how people use things and then use their skills to make those things better. With the Oxo cup, you can see how much liquid you're pouring in without stooping or holding the cup in the air. It's easy to hold. It actually pours better. It's stable.

That's design. It's not just about making it pretty (not that making it pretty is bad, by the way). It's about adding value.

The next example I use is Altoids. I explain that what's exciting about this product is that it's made with pure peppermint oil. And to really communicate that this is pure peppermint oil, the company put the mints in a very old fashioned tin to give them a feeling of authenticity. Inside they've put this really nice paper—again, very old-fashioned. The mints themselves aren't perfectly round, so they look handmade. They're not packed evenly, so they look hand-packed. All this detail has made Altoids very successful. They became the number-one brand in this category—at a significant price premium to the next competitor—and they did it in just a few years.

"Now," I would say, "pretend that Procter & Gamble buys this brand. What are we likely to do with it?" I usually got the same answer every time, which was: "The first thing we're going to do is cost-save this tin. There's absolutely no need for it. And we're going to get rid of this stupid piece of paper. It serves no functional value whatsoever. And we're going to pack it evenly and full." To which I say, "Exactly. And this is what you get—Proctoids. And we'll put these mints in cheap plastic, make each mint uniform, and pack it full."

We still have the same outstanding, pure peppermint taste. But do you want to buy it? Do you even want to eat it? Would you pay as much for it?" "No," comes the answer. And I say, "That's design." Again, an example of just showing design rather than trying to explain it.

Similarly, we use internal and external case studies that demonstrate the power of design. They're very effective because they translate into a language that business understands: Design builds business; design generates consumer loyalty. All these things resonate with business leaders.

I could go on and probably name fifty more things we have learned. A lot of them we learned the hard way. There's a quote that goes, "Learn from someone else's mistakes, because you won't live long enough to make them all yourself."

The exciting news is that we are making huge progress at P&G. Design is on people's radar screens. Business leaders are beginning to understand the power of design to build passionately loyal consumers.

# Chapter 12

# Visual Thinking: A Leadership Strategy

by Mark Dziersk

*Mark Dziersk is convinced that "design" and "strategy" traditionally reflect two very disparate realms within the world of business. He urges designers to communicate with those responsible for strategy by using their talent for visualization and storytelling—"languages" that can powerfully convey content in such arenas as the DNA of the consumer experience, innovation options, and approaches to decision-making.*

ABOUT TEN YEARS ago, I quit balancing my checkbook. During a particularly challenging sequence of addition and subtraction, frustrated beyond recovery, I gave up. Just stopped. It had simply become too much. "Perhaps not the best way to build wealth," you say. "That's crazy!" you might be thinking. But, you know what? It's worked out okay for me.

Every month I take in so much, and so much goes out. I sort of keep track in my head. Kind of do things that I know I can afford and get a little aggressive with the spending every now and then. Imagine running a business that way. Hard to picture, right? Now imagine the freedom, the amazing number of resources that would be diverted and focused differently, like creativity and innovation, if we eliminated accounting altogether. Never happen?

Creativity is the key to innovation. And if innovation is the Midas touch of businesses' success today, well, let's just say innovation doesn't happen by adding columns of numbers. Most businesses are run and led by finance-focused business managers, armed with . . . strategies. If creativity is the fuel by which innovation comes to life, then strategy is the mirror equivalent for business and for those business managers.

The truth is that very few designers understand strategy, much less leverage it in their work. But the design world is trying and is making inroads. Dealing with and converting ambiguity to a clearly focused strategy is key and gives design thinking the leverage for running competitive businesses in the post-dot.com, post-"distribution dictates direction" business world we live in. (Distribution—think Wal-mart—has had a huge impact on why and how things have been designed. That impact is waning.) The real trick is not to get designers to think and act like business people—it's exactly the opposite. Let's face it: Design and strategy start from completely different places. If business management in general sees design and strategy as two completely different concepts and protocols, then design managers and designers need to do a better job of communicating design thinking and strategy.

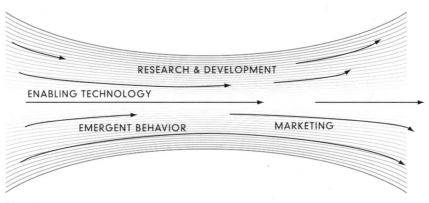

RESEARCH & DEVELOPMENT

ENABLING TECHNOLOGY

EMERGENT BEHAVIOR          MARKETING

Figure 1

Consider for a moment the two charts below. The chart above (Figure 1) describes a classic, controlled business model. Data input and ideas are funneled in through a tight "controlled environment," and products, services, and all other revenue-generating results are exhausted out the far end. Everything belongs to the company, and little is shared outside its boundaries. The second chart (Figure 2) describes the companies that are succeeding today by means of a model commonly referred to as open innovation. Porous borders and products, projects, technology, licensing arrangements, are all part of the mix.

Let's consider the open innovation model in Figure 2. Is it too grand to say the world of product and brand creation has been turned on its head? Consumers have changed. They are hyper-informed, do their own research, and have global access to information, products, and an almost infinite number of choices. In contrast, many agencies and marketers think and behave as if it's still 1980. Figure 3 outlines this mindset. The idea that products can be pushed at consumers through clever advertising and traditional

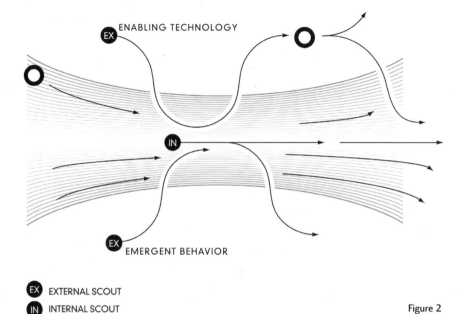

EX EXTERNAL SCOUT
IN INTERNAL SCOUT

Figure 2

selling techniques and fed down a funnel of investment—only to be compromised at the execution phase when it is "thrown over the wall" to the place where design and production meet—is no longer valid. In the end, the company winds up delivering a compromised result. Just consider for a moment how many new product launches fail today; some suggest the percentage is as high as 80 percent.

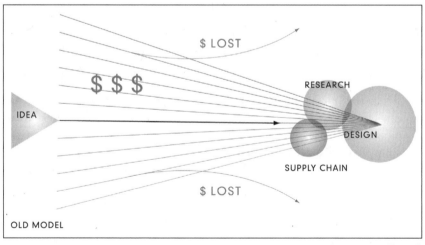

Figure 3

Figure 4 outlines a new view. It suggests uncompromised delivery of consumer experiences—to borrow from Apple CEO Steve Jobs, "insanely great products," which

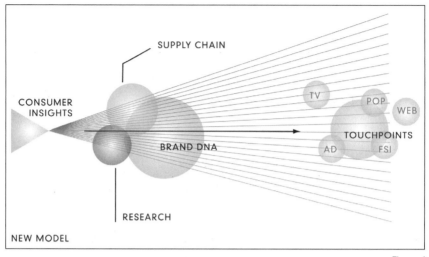

SUPPLY CHAIN

CONSUMER
INSIGHTS

TV

POP

WEB

TOUCHPOINTS

BRAND DNA

AD          FSI

RESEARCH

NEW MODEL

Figure 4

are based on a core DNA from which strategies are developed. Experiences that never disappoint and messaging that's inspired by those experiences. Think Dyson or Dove.

The new model suggests the use of cross-functional teams, led by people with strategic outlooks, as well as phenomenal interpersonal and deep analytical skills. You know—designers.

Excuse me?

## DESIGN STRATEGY: AN OXYMORON

Strategy, leadership, and process classes are common in most MBA programs. They are not commonly a part of design training. Let's define strategy, in the context of this chapter, as the careful planning of next steps and actions based on the expected outcomes of previous actions. Doesn't sound at all like design school, does it? Designers are more likely to find insight and meaning from, say, the Jackson Pollock painting presented in Figure 5.

The meaning in an image like the Pollock painting is implicit—defined by emotional response. Understanding this kind of meaning has become a very valuable tool in developing products and brands that are must-haves. These insights cannot be easily articulated; they defy rational, logical examination. That's where designers come in. Careful, methodical analysis is simply not the way most creative people are disposed to think and act. Yes, of course, there are exceptions. But, whether through nature or nurture, most creatives do not have the strategic tools that are expected of MBA graduates. And as many designers have noticed, we fall victim to ourselves and to this lack of self-knowledge in many business situations.

The typical design process begins with some sort of survey of the situation and the problem to be solved (often called an overview and objective statement) and the execution of a visual tool known as a lifestyle board, mood board, or emotional study (Figure 6). The purpose of these boards, in most cases, is to help the designer inform and visually

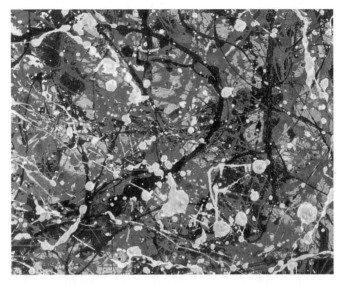

Figure 5

Figure 6

articulate the brand or product character. Two designers in front of this kind of board could talk for hours about the emotions evoked by the imagery, the semiotic cues, or the meaning conveyed by the intersection of seemingly disparate images that connect them intuitively, albeit invisibly. (It helps if a cappuccino or espresso is involved.)

To nondesigners in the business world, something like this makes about as much sense, and is interpreted about as effectively, as your average Jackson Pollock work. An MBA's depiction of a strategy might look something like what we see in Figure 6 and, really, is likely to present as much of a mystery to a designer as a lifestyle board would to a business manager.

The matrix format is a relatively simple methodology and results in boards that are rich in meaning but that also suggest some level of analysis. This is a step in the right direction.

Now, it's clear that some kind of visual articulation is necessary in order to get to the distillation of a brand character: Words are easily misinterpreted. This is especially challenging when the visual language must also work hard to telegraph product attributes and benefits to the consumer. But visual articulation is also important when solving a problem that involves strategic goals and initiatives. At its core, design is a problem-solving process, and if it is to truly help bridge the problem or opportunity with the solution, easier and better visualization methods are needed. However, where business managers are concerned, design as a profession needs to be more adept about visualizing thinking.

There is a good chance that in the near future, especially in design-driven companies, marketers will report into design. However, as a profession, design is completely unprepared for this to happen. Most designers, using design speak, could not keep the CEO of a major company interested for more than twenty minutes. Visualizing strategic design thinking is the key to effectively communicating. Below is an example. Let's say we want to make an argument about investing money into a major design effort in order to create an innovation pipeline.

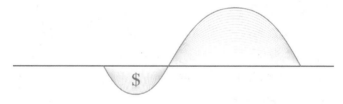

The figure above illustrates a business that invests money in a project, looking for a return. Now, consider the figure below.

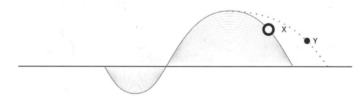

The X in this diagram represents the point in a project at which the designer is most often called in—the point I like to call the "'my hair's on fire' project imperative," when the brand or product is in decline. Usually, in a highly competitive business climate, the best that can be done is Y.

Smart companies are more likely to look like this:

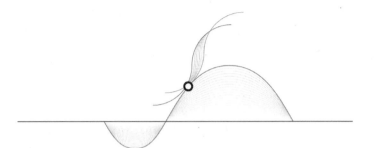

Smart companies divert resources from successful launch teams to start new initiatives—to compete with themselves. Truly visionary companies look more like this:

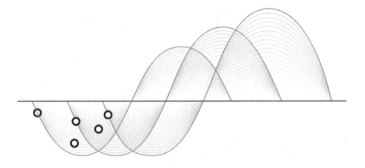

Visionary companies invest in the DNA around a brand or product, leveraging creativity to create a continuous pipeline of innovation—without reinventing the wheel each time out.

## CAN YOU SEE WHAT I SEE?

The four charts above are an example of using simple graphs to communicate big ideas and strategy. In fact, the presentation above is most effective if it's sketched in real time in an interactive way. Graphs like these pin ideas down, give them credibility, and demonstrate that these theories can be measured.

There is a clear difference between a designer's perspective and that of a marketing or brand manager, or an R&D or supply chain professional, for that matter. Business managers are charged with being quantitatively predictive. No wonder so many concept options are required, and there is such a heavy dependence on validation research. Business managers often view the conventional creative process as soft and weakly speculative.

The creative process can in fact be an extremely powerful tool, especially when combined with a strong and highly developed company DNA. This DNA directs the core of strategic design thinking and the creation of all company, brand, product, and visual paths to customers. It is best described as "implicit meanings" captured in nonprescriptive, visual interactions. It also helps if these visual interactions are set to music. This tends to enhance the expression of the emotions that underpin the visual storytelling. (I'm right back to the lifestyle board's example, aren't I? Many people reading this article are probably thinking, "What did he just say . . .?")

A strategy based around a tool—let's call it the DNA around which the consumer's experience and interaction with the device, package, or service is centered—must be at the core of every go-to-market effort. This DNA is an important strategic tool, developed by synthesizing consumer insights, brand insights, R&D, and manufacturing requirements in a meaningful, implicit way. Methods for visualizing DNA are many and varied. What is new here is the idea that designers create the vision. In the past, this has been the responsibility of an ad agency or an internal marketing function.

The strength of the DNA is that it is a free-standing storytelling device to guide all future efforts toward the confluence of media points and the development of pipeline ideas. Alternatively, it becomes an effective tool that allows designers to defend the relevance and resonance of their work. It tells a story.

At Pixar, the animation giant, no matter how much technological expertise and innovation is brought to bear in the field, the story is always king. Stories are memorable; storytelling is effective. It creates links between disparate notions, and requires emotion to run parallel to ideas. Everybody likes and remembers a good story.

Here's a visual story borrowed from a friend and colleague, designer Richard Seymour. When describing that difficult-to-picture innovation process, Richard asks his listeners to imagine a building being imploded, coming down through controlled explosive charges (Figure 7). The debris cloud that results is a metaphor for the beginning of the design process, a time in which interesting, unpredictable connections are made and ambiguity is prevalent. Now, visualize running the film backward and constructing the building: controlled chaos leading to a clear and finalized end point. It's a compelling analogy for the process of design. Without the risk of letting go in the debris cloud, original ideas and connections will not be made. With the understanding that the film can be run backward, and with faith in the process, business minds can be convinced to come along.

Here is another story that gives us a memorable example of strategy and the use of 3D tools for visualization. A 1934 article on design published in *Fortune* magazine out-

Figure 7

lines an interaction between iconic designer Norman Bel Geddes and W. Frank Roberts, then president of the Standard Gas Equipment Corp, a company that produced cooking ranges. Bel Geddes wanted to sell Standard a modular platform strategy for building all Standard products. Roberts wasn't convinced that was the right approach. To win the president over, Bel Geddes had his staff build every single module and part used to make the ranges as cardboard boxes that were true to size. He then arranged the boxes from the door of the elevator to the door of his office, requiring the CEO on his next visit to, literally, crawl over hundreds of the cardboard simulations to reach Bel Geddes in his office. There, Bel Geddes displayed a much smaller handful of modular and integrated components that represented Standard Gas's world as it could be. The strategic importance of the modular approach, as well as the business implications, was inescapable.

Stories are important ways to communicate all kinds of ideas and processes. Earlier, I mentioned that at its core, design is a problem-solving process, and that we need better ways to describe these processes. Rather than follow the typical observe-differentiate-refine-execute model we often cite, designers must allow others to participate in the design process, creating a chart that looks something like Figure 8.

And that's on a good day. Because it suggests the often messy and nonlinear activities that surround the typical protocol.

Figure 8

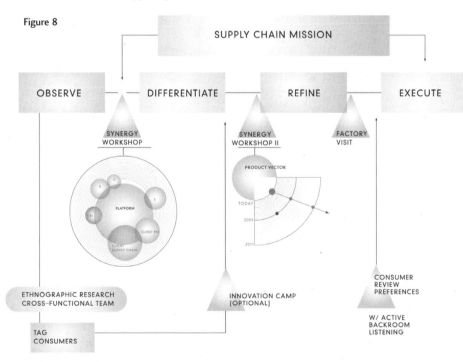

## YOU DRAW THE BOX; I'LL BREAK OUT OF IT . . .

Innovation is usually associated with disparate or unexpected associations, typically drawn from the right brain, the creative side. This is why innovation is often regarded as coming from out-of-the-box thinking. It's certainly a counterintuitive notion that to innovate quickly, one must think strategically. But the simple truth is that continuous innovation requires one to see and think long distances into the future. In most industries, investment capital and distribution channels need to be anticipated well in advance of execution.

There are many effective ways to think and to communicate in this way (see Figure 9). Process charts, for instance, are a way to depict strategies that are being executed.

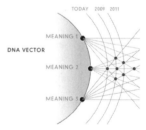

Figure 9

The key here, however, is not which chart to use but to visualize in a way that allows your thinking to be seen and understood. Design strategy means thinking past the project into the needs and longer-term goals of the brand, of R&D, of bringing products or services to market. It requires understanding the space that can be addressed and the boundaries of that space. Where does the reason to believe in that space begin and end for the consumer? It also requires understanding and participating in planning for capital expenditures and manufacturing investments. This is new territory for design—demonstrating business and brand leadership by creating and visualizing company strategies inspired from a design point of view.

The reality is that the creative process, the manifestation of design strategy, is often not linear, regimented, easily measured, or even described successfully. This complicates design's ability to communicate and draw others toward it as a leadership model. It is also why design strategy can often be seen as a contradiction in terms and a difficult parallel to other, more readily described processes and strategy roadmaps. It can be a leap of faith to invest money and resources in a cloud of debris. It can appear risky. But without risk and creativity as ingredients, we wind up in the same place again and again.

Design and strategy need to work together, but they originate from very different kinds of experience. Business is hungry for design thinking and needs strategy to have a reason to believe. Designers have to understand their role in the business imperative. The opportunity is too big to let slip by or to let others lead. Designers revel in ambiguity, the thrill of not knowing how much money is in the account, the acceptance of risk, nonlinear paths to results. However, to expect business to share these traits is expecting too much. To many business managers, the whole idea of design strategy doesn't compute. Business needs to increase its understanding of design—but the truth is, the vehicles for that to happen are few and slow to be developed.

Visualizing, storytelling, DNA, and adaptable processes all help enormously. For designers today, a good understanding of the comfort zone others have with ideas and concepts is a tool as powerful as any Alias rendering or beautifully executed prototype. Creativity is the currency, but the strategic foundation is equally important. It frames the work in a way that is understood and leads to other successes. Success leads to growth, and growth to increased share. So maybe it's crazy to think in extremes—crazy like not counting your money. Unless, of course, the more you count, the less creative the whole thing becomes.

**ACKNOWLEDGMENT**

I would like to thank Michael Colton, Associate Creative Director, laga/One80 Design, for his many contributions to this chapter.

# Chapter 13

# From Lock-in to Lock-out: Using Design to Create Fiercely Loyal Customers

by Jeremy Alexis

*With Wal-Mart and Apple as exemplars, Jeremy Alexis analyzes how a focus on distinctive solutions, emotional connections, and favorable economics are design levers that position organizations to maximize loyalty and lock out competition. Alexis also explains how success in this arena links understanding the profitability of various customer segments with an integrated approach to marketing, sales, product development, and business strategy.*

IT IS A common observation: As soon as the plane lands, at least half the passengers quick-draw their Blackberries to check their e-mail and voicemail. The device responsible for this behavior is sometimes mocked as a "crackberry" or "an extra appendage." Some may see this as a sad commentary on modern business life, but it is also evidence of fiercely loyal customers.

Most of the quick-draw artists on the plane will also likely be members of the airline's frequent-flier program. Whereas the Blackberry derives loyalty from an easy-to-use interface, consistent service, and a robust device design, the airline derives loyalty from a complex and expensive reward program that includes call centers, free product giveaways, and sophisticated accounting practices. A recent study reported in *Brandweek* shows that offerings such as the Blackberry (along with similar products from Samsung and Palm) and Google have the most-loyal customers, while companies such as, for example, American Airlines have increasingly less-loyal customers.[1]

The companies at the top of this survey share a set of common factors—they offer products and services that are easy to use and address a holistic set of customer needs. In other words, they are well designed. This evidence suggests that traditional levers for creating loyalty (reward programs and contracts) are easy to copy and increasingly less effective, and that those companies should look to new, more-powerful levers to build better relationships with their customers.

## THE NEVER-ENDING SEARCH FOR LOYAL CUSTOMERS

Creating loyal customers remains a goal (often articulated as the most important goal)[2] of most companies. Estimates put the number of books on customer loyalty in the thousands.[3] In North America alone, companies spent $1.2 billion on loyalty programs in 2003, and this number is increasing, according to Gartner analyst Adam Sarner.[4] There are more than 8,600 supermarkets, fifty airlines, thirty phone companies, twenty hotel chains, and dozens of credit cards that offer loyalty programs.[5] However, according to McKinsey & Company, organizations often underestimate the full cost of setting up loyalty programs, and then, even if sales increase, the program may actually result in losses.[6]

In addition, companies spend a great deal on technology to help them manage their customers—with less than stellar results. In 2004, North American companies spent $10.9 billion on customer relationship management systems.[7] However, only 28 percent of companies that implemented a CRM system last year believed it led to any improvements.[8]

Despite these efforts, and not including customers of outliers like Google and Samsung, consumers are increasingly less loyal to brands and products. For example, food retailers will lose up to 40 percent of their new customers in three months,[9] and only about 10 percent of customers are 100 percent loyal to certain consumer products.[10]

In a nutshell, customers are less loyal, and loyal customers are less profitable than most companies estimate.[11] Much of this can be attributed to increased choice and availability of information. However, we should not overlook the fact that many organizations have incomplete and old beliefs about loyal customers (see Figure 1). This evidence begs the question: Should companies be concerned about creating loyal customers, and if so, what tools can a thoughtful design manager employ to build more sustained and mutually beneficial customer relationships?

| Old logic: loyal customers . . . | In reality: loyal customers . . . |
|---|---|
| Cost less to serve | Have higher expectations from your organization and your offering |
| Will pay more for your offering | Get the best price from your organization helped by their experiences |
| Are receptive to cross selling | Are very sensitive about your organization taking advantage of their loyalty for marketing and price increases |
| Will create positive word of mouth buzz for your brand: they will market it for you | Are not reliable marketers, and do not always present accurate and positive messages |

Figure 1. Rethinking beliefs about loyal customers.

## THE RANGE OF STRATEGIES FOR CREATING CUSTOMER LOYALTY

The answer is deceptively simple. A company's goal should be to create completely satisfied customers through a more thorough understanding of their needs and through distinctive offerings. According to research conducted for Harvard Business School by Thomas O. Jones and W. Earl Sasser, "To a much greater extent than most managers think, completely satisfied customers are more loyal than just satisfied customers."[12] Traditional loyalty efforts produce customers who are only marginally loyal, and they make it easy for customers to switch to competitors. In contrast, completely satisfied customers become fiercely loyal customers, exhibiting the qualities that were once assumed common for all loyal customers. But this class of customer loyalty can be difficult to cultivate; it requires an integrated approach of design, development, sales, and marketing, and it cannot be achieved with a standalone program.

Figure 2 details the six available levers for creating customer loyalty. The three levers on the left are the more common strategies. Customers (both consumer and B2B) are becoming more adept at avoiding lock-in; it is not a desirable condition from a customer's point of view. These levers operate under the false assumption that programs can change and control customer behavior. Although the programs may see initial success, customers will soon learn how to extract the maximum value from them while contributing limited value and loyalty.

| Lever | Loyalty programs | Contracts | Limited choice | Distinctive solution | Emotional connection | Favorable economics |
|---|---|---|---|---|---|---|
| Source of loyalty | Repeat purchase builds rewards | Obligated, early termination results in fee | Other choice is nothing | Solve best for customer needs | Customers are aligned with/buy into brand | Best economic proposition |
| Example | AA advantage | Cell phone contacts | Utilities | Total Merrill from Merrill Lynch | Apple | Wal-Mart |
| Challenges | > Expensive<br>> Easy to copy<br>> Customer loyal to program, not brand | > Can create adversarial relationship with customers<br>> Can lead to complex accounting | > Subject to privatization and monopoly regulation | > Complex to manage<br>> Requires constant updating | > Requires deep customer knowledge | > Hard to manage<br>> Can lead to low profits |
| These levers: | • Modify customer behavior<br>• Can easily be copied<br>• Create marginal, temporary loyalty | | | • Build on/leverage existing behavior<br>• Are difficult to copy<br>• Create sustained loyalty | | |

Figure 2. The six levers for building customer loyalty.

The three levers on the right create more-sustained, fiercer loyalty, and they reinforce and enhance customer behaviors. Not surprisingly, the three levers on the right benefit the most from integrated design efforts, which suggests that design managers have a more important role in building customer loyalty than is generally accepted.

To create fiercely loyal customers, companies will often employ several levers simultaneously. To illustrate this point, we'll look at two examples: Wal-Mart and Apple.

## WAL-MART: FAVORABLE ECONOMICS AND EMOTIONAL CONNECTION

Among retailers, Wal-Mart's customer base is second in loyalty only to that of Target.[13]

The company has created a sophisticated system of partner relationships and logistics that provide its customers with consistently low prices. Customers are loyal to Wal-Mart because of the favorable economics created by these systems. In addition to price, Wal-Mart has created a close emotional connection with its customers. Despite recent stories of labor and sourcing issues, most of them are fiercely loyal to the brand. Wal-Mart uses design strategically, creating a brand and a store environment that is aligned with the beliefs and values of its core audience. That audience is attracted to simple, uncomplicated signage and merchandising and a store look that embodies economy. It remains to be seen how recent efforts to add more upscale elements to the store will affect the core audience.

### APPLE: EMOTIONAL CONNECTION AND DISTINCTIVE SOLUTIONS

Apple is commonly mentioned when discussing customer loyalty, and it is especially instructive in this case; it would be difficult to identify a brand with more-loyal customers. This high degree of loyalty results from the application of multiple, but well-integrated, levers. Apple has honed and strengthened this emotional connection over the years. The company also offers its customers unique solutions, such as the iTunes/iPod system. Customers are loyal to the iPod because it made digital music easy to use. Other digital music systems required users to understand a dizzying array of file extensions, to log on and establish accounts with several service providers, and ultimately to live with a device that was not an attractive or desirable object.

### A DESIGN MANAGER'S GUIDE FOR CREATING FIERCELY LOYAL CUSTOMERS

As noted above, design and design thinking (both within the internal team and with consultants) can play a critical role in customer loyalty efforts. A design team's core value lies in developing economical and user-centered solutions and/or creating emotive and meaningful brand experiences, which ultimately are responsible for creating the most loyal customers. Figure 3 details how design efforts can be employed as part of the three most powerful levers.

So far, we have shown that traditional loyalty efforts will not create completely satisfied, and thus fiercely loyal, customers. We have also argued that design is well positioned to create this new class of loyalty. The challenge remains for design managers to articulate this argument within their companies and then to build an integrated approach to employ more-effective loyalty levers. When implemented properly, these efforts will create customers who:

▲ Are more accepting and accommodating of product launches that require further iteration and refinement

| Lever | Potential design interventions |
|---|---|
| *Distinctive solutions* | • Conduct design research to understand unarticulated and unmet needs.<br>• Develop product platforms that address a comprehensive needs set.<br>• Conduct usability testing to ensure offerings are best in class for usability and usefulness. |
| *Emotional connections* | • Conduct design research to understand customer values, aspirations, and passions.<br>• Develop brands that communicate emotion and feeling, not just functional value.<br>• Develop products and communications that customers covet and desire. |
| *Favorable economics* | • Conduct usability design studies to understand which elements of the current offering can be shifted to customers.<br>• Seek innovative fabrication and sourcing models.<br>• Assess product and service design with intent to reduce unnecessary components and complexity. |

Figure 3. Design interventions that can build customer loyalty.

Note: The interventions in Figure 3 are intended to be illustrative, not exhaustive.

▲ Will be instrumental in moving your offerings from early adopter to early majority markets

▲ Can become partners in your innovation and development efforts

Although implementation at your company will vary based on culture and industry, the following guide outlines a four-step process for defining the appropriate levers, design interventions, and organizational strategy for creating fiercely loyal customers.

1. Shift mindset from "lock in" to "lock out."

2. Diagnose the current level of customer loyalty.

3. Identify the appropriate levers and interventions.

4. Collaborate on an implementation strategy.

## SHIFT MINDSET FROM "LOCK IN" TO "LOCK OUT"

The first step is both the most important and the most challenging. It requires you, the design manager, to immediately shift the focus, first of your team, and eventually of your future collaborators, to the correct path for achieving customer loyalty. Most loyalty programs are based on a company-centered point of view, and they attempt to lock customers in to services and offerings.

When a company takes a customer-centered point of view, which is ultimately required if you intend to create completely satisfied customers, the corporate focus needs to change. The goal of the loyalty efforts should be to provide products, services, and communications that are so compelling and distinctive that customers do not even consider switching, essentially "locking out" competitors and substitutes.

Although initially challenging, this change in focus will be liberating. Most of the people in your organization will not disagree with this suggested change (few companies do not give at least lip service to "putting the customer first"). However, despite their agreement in principle, many of your colleagues will not be converted until they begin to see change and results. It is critical for the design team to remain vigilant, positive, and dedicated to the effort during the uncomfortable period between initial agreement and full buy-in based on results.

## DIAGNOSE THE SITUATION

Once your colleagues agree in principle, the design team should begin an analysis of the current situation. The team should gather data to help answer the following questions:

- ▲ How loyal are our current customers?
- ▲ What levers do we employ to build their loyalty?
- ▲ How effective are these levers?
- ▲ How loyal are our competitor's customers?
- ▲ What levers do they employ?
- ▲ Do our competitors do anything related to loyalty that we wish we did or wish we could do?
- ▲ What can we learn from companies in other industries?

Much of the loyalty data may already exist. However, it is important to understand the methods used to collect the data and the objectives of each study. Loyalty studies, like any good piece of research, need to limit bias. Often, these studies can be biased to show loyalty stronger than it actually is. Ideally, you want to be able to identify customers who are not satisfied, somewhat satisfied, and highly satisfied, and the drivers behind each segment's current state.

## CHOOSE THE RIGHT LEVERS

Your situation diagnosis will help your team to understand what gaps need to be filled in order to create more-loyal customers. Your study will also likely reveal opportunities created by your competitor's myopia or company-centered focus on loyalty. Now, your team can select and then detail the appropriate levers.

- ▲ Set realistic and appropriate goals. Your team should be sensitive to the presenting condition and position of your customers. If you have identified that the majority of your customers fall in the lower range of somewhat satisfied or even not satisfied, it may be difficult to move all the way to fully satisfied with one set of interventions. In fact, these customers may prefer your organization to focus on getting the basics right before they will become more loyal. It is critical to set goals that are appropriate for your customers and that can be achieved by your team. This is truly a case where it is smarter to under-promise and over-deliver.

- ▲ Identify existing and new organizational capabilities. Your selection of levers should be aligned with your organization's capabilities. So, if your company does not have the sourcing and logistics capabilities to deliver low-cost offerings, selecting favorable economics as a lever may not be the appropriate choice. There may be some instances in which the team identifies new capabilities that need to be developed or nurtured. This will require additional collaboration and resources; developing a new capability is a strategic decision.

▲ Use multiple levers simultaneously. As noted earlier, several levers should be employed for maximum impact. Ideally, these levers will be mutually reinforcing. For example, if you choose to deliver the lowest price to achieve favorable economics, you should also be able to create an emotional connection with your customers based on offering them a low price—this should be a key benefit for your customers.

## DEVELOP AN INTEGRATED APPROACH

With a set of interventions defined, your team can now begin to plan the implementation with other disciplines and functions. To the extent it is possible, you can include a broader coalition during development, but at this point it is critical to move efforts to a larger, more cross-functional team.

At the core of this integrated approach is the idea that customer loyalty is not created by a standalone program but is the result of orchestrated efforts of marketing, sales, product development, and strategy.

It is critical at this point to create a coherent business argument for loyalty. Despite the common sense and clear benefits of creating completely satisfied customers, there will no doubt be individuals in your organization that still require convincing. A tool for making this argument and for engaging skeptics is the profit/satisfaction matrix illustrated in Figure 4. This tool integrates your design-focused research, which segmented customers according to loyalty, with research that likely lives in the finance department and details which segments of customers are most profitable.

|  | Not satisfied | Somewhat satisfied | Highly satisfied |
|---|---|---|---|
| Profitable customer | Start by getting the basics right to build initial loyalty. | Conduct research and apply appropriate levers to build satisfaction and loyalty. | Monitor and adjust efficacy of levers to ensure ongoing satisfaction and profitability. |
| Break-even customers | Provide incentives for customers to become more profitable and satisfied or to exit. | Apply appropriate levers and pilot alternative business models. | Shift cost/service burden to customers. |
| Unprofitable customers | Develop incentives to steer these customers to different offerings and services. | Prototype and pilot alternative business models. | Shift cost/service burden to customers. |

Figure 4. The profit satisfaction matrix.

Combining these data into a single model will require some cleaning and modification, but it will create a common tool to help guide and shape a robust strategy. This model also will force a much-needed collaboration among design, marketing, sales, and finance. What is important is that this model will move the customer loyalty conversation to a strategic level of the same rank as profitability. Although not always acknowledged, profitability and customer loyalty have a mutually reinforcing relationship:

▲ If you just focus on creating profitable customers, without trying to make them completely satisfied, your competitors can easily poach these highly valued customers.

▲ If you just focus on creating "completely satisfied" customers, without understanding profitability, you may rack up losses serving them.

Depending on the nature of your business, it may be possible to put individual customers (likely in a B2B environment) or customer segments in each cell in the model. Figure 4 lists strategies as appropriate for customers or customer segments in each cell.

## SUMMARY THOUGHTS

Companies should strive to create fiercely loyal, profitable customers. This can be achieved only through rethinking existing logic about customer loyalty and loyal customers, integrating loyalty efforts with offering development, marketing, and sales, and close collaboration between the strategy and design functions within the organization. Cultivating fiercely loyal customers requires ambition and risk-taking but will ultimately provide your company with a valuable and sustained relationship.

## *Endnotes*

1. Kenneth Hein, "High Tech=Loyalty," *Brandweek*, 10/31/2005, vol. 46, no. 39.

2. Ibid.

3. Timothy L. Keiningham, *Loyalty Myths: Hyped Strategies That Will Put You Out of Business and Proven Tactics That Really Work* (New York: Wiley, 2005).

4. Margaret L. Young and Marcia Stepanek, "Trends: Loyalty Programs," *CIO Insight*, December 1, 2003.

5. *www.businessweek.com/adsections/extravel/frequent/flyer/miles/flyer_index.htm.*

6. James Cigliano, "The Price of Loyalty," *The McKinsey Quarterly*, no. 4, 2000.

7. *CRM Magazine*, vol. 9, no. 11, November 2005, p. 23.

8. Julia Chang, "Embracing CRM," *Sales & Marketing Management*, vol. 157, no. 11, November 2005.

9. Brian Woolf, *Loyalty Marketing: The Second Act* (Greenville, SC: Teal Books, 2001).

10. A.S.C. Ehrenberg, *Repeat Buying: Facts, Theory, and Applications*, second ed. (London: Charles Griffin and Co., 1988).

11. Werner Reinartz and V. Kumar, "The Mismanagement of Customer Loyalty," *Harvard Business Review*, July 2002.

12. Thomas O. Jones and W. Earl Sasser, "Why Satisfied Customers Defect," *Harvard Business Review,* November–December 1995.

13. Kenneth Hein, op. cit.

# Chapter 14

# Law Meets Design: Transforming Valuable Designs into Powerful Assets

by Joshua Cohen

*Ownership is critical to leveraging the long-term value of innovations. Joshua Cohen recommends a spectrum of legal tools design managers should exploit to maximize the return on creativity. A compelling theme of his advice is that these strategies should not be put off until a design is complete. They should be initiated during planning and development and continue through the full lifecycle of a venture.*

IT IS WITHOUT question that value is added by innovative design. But the full commercial value of design is unrealized if it can be copied by competitors, without consequences. While it is true that being first to market will nose a design innovator ahead of its competition, that commercial advantage becomes robust with the benefit of exclusive design rights.

It is therefore incumbent upon companies to transform design into a protected asset. By doing so, companies can secure design ownership—the enviable position of being both free to use an innovative design without infringing the rights of others and armed to prevent others from using that design. Like a real estate deed that provides both the freedom to occupy land and the right to exclude others, design ownership provides an exclusive design domain.

But achieving design ownership requires strategic planning. Uniquely positioned to support this effort, design managers are best prepared to do so when they recognize design as a potential asset and employ strategies to secure design ownership throughout a design's lifecycle.

## PROTECTED DESIGN = COMMERCIAL ASSET

Commercial assets fall within one of two categories: physical assets, like buildings and machinery, and intangible assets, like inventions, brands, designs, and the other forms of intellectual property (IP) that are the fruits of innovation. As an intangible IP asset, a protected design is as much an asset as is capital equipment. And in today's economy, a company's IP assets are often more valuable than its physical assets.

Put simply, IP assets increasingly take center stage. Though Caroline Davidson created Nike's swoosh design in 1971 for a mere $35, that iconic symbol has evolved into a prime asset for Nike. And an hourglass-shaped bottle, designed by the Root Glass Company in 1916, became and remains an immensely valuable asset for Coca-Cola.

Various mechanisms for protecting designs are provided under U.S. law (see sidebar below), making IP rights available for design innovations that advance aesthetics, performance, manufacturability, and brand identity. These IP rights extend to innovative consumer products, packaging, graphics, and purely technical innovations ranging from computer software and chemical compositions to machinery. Design innovations (and their respective IP protections) include:

▲ Ornamental product and packaging designs (design patents)

▲ Functional aspects of products and processes (utility patents)

▲ Source-identifying symbols (trademarks and trade dress)

▲ Artistic and literary works, including computer software (copyright)

▲ Valuable commercial secrets (trade secrets)

| Design Protections | | | | |
|---|---|---|---|---|
| | Patents | Trademarks | Copyrights | Trade Secrets |
| Subject Matter | **Utility patents:** any new, nonobvious, and useful process, machine, manufacture, or composition of matter.<br><br>**Design patents:** any new, nonobvious, and ornamental design for an article of manufacture. | Mark by which the goods or services of one source may be distinguished from other goods or services. | Original works of authorship fixed in a tangible medium—including literary, pictorial, graphic, sculptural, architectural, and software works. | Any secret formula, pattern, device, program, method, process, technique, or compilation of information that gives a business an advantage over competitors. |
| Scope of Protection | Right to exclude others from making, using, offering to sell, selling, or importing the patented invention. | Protection against other designations that are likely to cause confusion, cause mistake, or to deceive. | Exclusive right to reproduce, prepare derivatives, distribute copies, publicly perform, and display the work. | Protection is afforded against misappropriation by wrongful means and use of the subject matter by another. |
| Duration | **Utility patents:** 20 years from effective filing date.<br><br>**Design patents:** 14 years from issue date. | As long as qualified use continues. Federal registration is granted for 10 years with 10-year renewals available. | Life of author plus 70 years. For corporations, shorter of 95 years from first publication or 120 years from creation. | Potentially unlimited duration provided proper precautions against disclosure are maintained. |
| Transfer of Rights | Rights can be assigned by an instrument in writing. | Assignment must include the goodwill associated with the mark. Can be licensed with owner control over the quality of goods or services provided under the mark. | Copyright rights can be assigned by an instrument in writing. Copyright rights may also be licensed. | Rights can be licensed or sold as business know-how. |
| Infringement | Anyone who makes, uses, offers to sell, sells, or imports the patented invention without authorization. | Use of a designation with goods or services in a manner likely to cause confusion. | Anyone who reproduces, prepares derivatives, distributes copies, publicly performs, or displays the work without permission. | Misappropriation occurs through acquisition, disclosure, or use of a trade secret obtained by improper means. |

Because any single product may (and often does) embody features providing brand identity or aesthetics alongside features relating to performance and manufacturing advantages, comprehensive IP protection often calls for separate protections covering various aspects of the same product. A product or package can enjoy utility patent or trade secret protection for its functional features, while the aesthetic elements of the same product or package can enjoy protection through design patents, copyright, and potentially long-lasting trademark and trade dress protections.

## PROTECTED DESIGN = POTENTIAL ICON

### Apple's iPod: Comprehensive IP Protection

The wild success of Apple's iPod stems not only from the way it works but also the way it looks. The intuitive functionality provided by the iPod's unique user interface is matched by the style and image evoked by its elegantly monolithic aesthetic. Whether its style outweighs its functionality in the eyes of consumers or vice versa, the combination unquestionably drives consumer purchase decisions.

The value to consumers provided by the functional and aesthetic features of the iPod is reflected directly in the IP protection sought by Apple, which includes a collage of utility patent, design patent, and trademark protections (see sidebar below). The iPod therefore exemplifies the use of various modes of IP protection to cover a single product comprehensively.

Design managers and IP counsel should therefore collaborate to consider all applicable modes of IP protection. As with the iPod, IP counsel can pursue utility patents to

### Apple's iPod®: Comprehensive IP Protection

With staggering sales of more than 22 million iPods in Apple's 2005 fiscal year and 14 million in Apple's first quarter of 2006 alone (a 207 percent increase over the first quarter of 2005), the considerable value of Apple's iPod design and brand image is worthy of aggressive protection. Predictably, these efforts include trademark, utility patent, and design patent protections, and it would not be surprising to learn that trade secret protections are also in place.

Before the iPod was introduced in 2001, Apple applied to register IPOD for products including "portable and handheld digital electronic devices." As peripheral products for the wildly successful iPod came to the market, Apple applied to register MADE FOR IPOD for "a full line of electronic and mechanical accessories and computer software ..."

Apple also secured design patent protection for ornamental features of the iPod, including:

- US Patent No. D469,109: MEDIA PLAYER
- US Patent No. D506,476: MEDIA DEVICE
- US Patent No. D516,576: MEDIA DEVICE

To protect functional aspects of the iPod, Apple also pursued utility patent protection, including:

- US Patent Application Publication No. 2004/0055446: GRAPHICAL USER INTERFACE AND METHODS OF USE THEREOF IN A MULTIMEDIA PLAYER

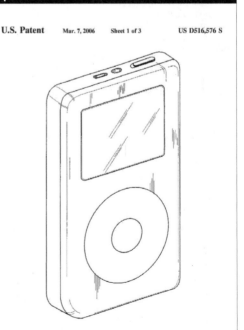

U.S. Patent   Mar. 7, 2006   Sheet 1 of 3   US D516,576 S

US Patent No. D516,576.

exclude competitors from using important functional aspects of a design. And IP counsel employs the exclusive rights afforded by a design patent to help secure the brand identity needed for trade dress protection. With a thoughtful strategy, the comprehensive protection afforded by utility patent, design patent, and long-lasting trade dress protections can help a product like the iPod achieve iconic status.

### Eames Lounge Chair: Enforcing IP Rights

The famous Eames Lounge Chair is synonymous with furniture design innovation. It is also linked in the minds of furniture buyers with its maker, Herman Miller. Trade dress protection for the Eames design simultaneously guards the commercial advantage enjoyed by Herman Miller and protects consumers from purchasing knock-off products. The trade dress and trademark rights secured by Herman Miller for the Eames Lounge Chair (and the Eames name) illustrate the power afforded by securing and enforcing design rights (see sidebar, below).

To retain them, IP rights must therefore be policed and perhaps enforced to exclude competitors. It is therefore incumbent upon design managers and IP counsel to monitor the activities of competitors and to challenge those activities when they infringe IP rights.

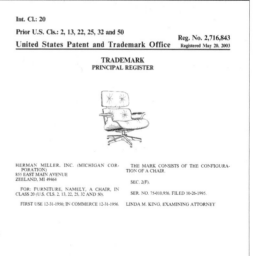

#### Eames® Lounge Chair: Enforcing IP Rights

The Eames Lounge Chair made by Herman Miller is a design icon. Celebrating its fiftieth anniversary at the time of this publication, the Eames Lounge Chair was introduced in 1956 on the set of NBC Studios' TV Home Show, when Arlene Francis interviewed Charles and Ray Eames about their new approach to furniture design.

Challenged by knock-offs of the Eames Lounge Chair over the years, Herman Miller successfully sued furniture-seller Palazzetti Imports and Exports, Inc. In the words of Henry Gowin, secretary of the Foundation for Design Integrity, "The public is becoming increasingly aware of intellectual property protection (patents, trademarks, trade dress, and copyrights) and the importance of supporting original design, while the knock-off producers are learning the consequences of infringement." Herman Miller was ultimately awarded US Trademark Registration No. 2,716,843 for the three-dimensional design of the Eames Lounge Chair. Herman Miller also owns US Trademark Registration No. 1,187,673 for the mark EAMES for furniture for home, office, and commercial use.

Herman Miller recently launched its Get Real awareness and education campaign. It alerts consumers to the ethical and economic implications of buying design knock-offs rather than supporting original designs and their designers. This impressive campaign for authenticity reinforces the value of the Eames design, as well as the designs of other innovative products.

Int. Cl.: 20

Prior U.S. Cls.: 2, 13, 22, 25, 32 and 50

Reg. No. 2,716,843

**United States Patent and Trademark Office**   Registered May 20, 2003

**TRADEMARK**
**PRINCIPAL REGISTER**

HERMAN MILLER, INC. (MICHIGAN CORPORATION)
855 EAST MAIN AVENUE
ZEELAND, MI 49464

FOR: FURNITURE, NAMELY, A CHAIR, IN CLASS 20 (U.S. CLS. 2, 13, 22, 25, 32 AND 50).

FIRST USE 12-31-1956; IN COMMERCE 12-31-1956.

THE MARK CONSISTS OF THE CONFIGURATION OF A CHAIR.

SEC. 2(F).

SER. NO. 75-010,956. FILED 10-26-1995.

LINDA M. KING, EXAMINING ATTORNEY

US Trademark Reg. No. 2,716,843.

### Post-it Notes: Protecting Improvements

To call the expansion of 3M's Post-it Notes product prolific is a serious understatement. Post-it Notes exemplify successful efforts to broaden the value of a brand (see sidebar, following page). By securing IP rights for new uses of (and markets for) the original Post-it technology, 3M extends and expands a strong competitive advantage.

By seeking IP protection for innovative extensions of an original product, design managers and IP counsel coordinate their efforts to expand the competitive advantage provided by the original product. And doing so throughout the life of a design

## Post-it® Notes: Protecting Improvements

3M's ubiquitous Post-it Notes illustrate the value of protecting product improvements. The original Post-it product was the result of a 1968 3M discovery of a releasable adhesive, and the idea for repositionable notes using that adhesive came to another 3M scientist much later, in 1974, when a bookmark fell out of his church hymnal.

Though they were not introduced into the marketplace until 1980, Post-it Notes are now available in 8 standard sizes, 25 shapes, and 62 colors, and more than 600 Post-it products are sold in more than 100 countries.

3M has sought new competitive advantages, expanding and protecting its Post-it product offering by pursuing trademark, design patent, and utility patent protections:

- US Trademark Registration No. 1,046,353: POST-IT
- US Patent No. D496,964: ORNAMENTAL DESIGN FOR A SHEET DISPENSER
- US Patent No. 6,722,501: PACKAGE ASSEMBLIES WITH ATTACHMENT STRIPS
- US Patent No. 6,669,992: STACK OF SHEETS WITH REPOSITIONABLE ADHESIVE ALTERNATING BETWEEN OPPOSITE EDGES ...

Int. Cl.: 16

Prior U.S. Cls.: 2, 5, 22, 23, 29, 37, 38, and 50

**United States Patent and Trademark Office**  Reg. No. 2,402,722  Registered Nov. 7, 2000

**TRADEMARK**
**PRINCIPAL REGISTER**

MINNESOTA MINING AND MANUFACTURING COMPANY (DELAWARE CORPORATION), AKA 3M,
3M CENTER
2501 HUDSON ROAD
SAINT PAUL, MN 551441000

FOR: STATIONERY NOTES AND NOTE PADS CONTAINING ADHESIVE ON ONE SIDE OF THE SHEETS FOR ATTACHMENT TO SURFACES; ADHESIVE TAPE FOR STATIONERY OR OFFICE USE; COVER-UP TAPE FOR PAPER; TAPE FLAGS; PRINTED NOTE FORMS; PRINTED NOTES FEATURING MESSAGES, PICTURES OR ORNAMENTAL DESIGNS; ADHESIVE-BACKED EASEL PAPER AND EASEL PADS; BULLETIN BOARDS; GLUE STICKS

FOR STATIONERY OR OFFICE USE; AND PAPER AND CARDBOARD SHEET MATERIAL HAVING ADHESIVE COATINGS ON BOTH SIDES FOR ATTACHMENT TO WALLS OR OTHER VERTICAL SURFACES TO HOLD DISPLAYS OR OTHER MESSAGES IN PLACE, IN CLASS 16 (U.S. CLS. 2, 5, 22, 23, 29, 37, 38 AND 50).

FIRST USE 8–27–1999; IN COMMERCE 8–27–1999.
OWNER OF U.S. REG. NOS. 1,046,353, 1,718,114, AND OTHERS.
THE DRAWING IS LINED FOR THE COLOR YELLOW.

SN 75–610,586, FILED 12–22–1998.

TRICIA SONNEBORN, EXAMINING ATTORNEY

US Trademark Reg. No. 2,402,722.

maximizes profits. Conversely, the failure to seek new competitive advantages forfeits potential IP assets.

### DESIGN PROTECTION TAKES PLANNING

Recognizing design as a potential asset is a strong start, but careful planning is needed to secure design ownership. And because strategies for design protection should be employed throughout the lifecycle of a design, it is important to consider the phases of that lifecycle, the processes by which designs are developed, and the structure of design development teams.

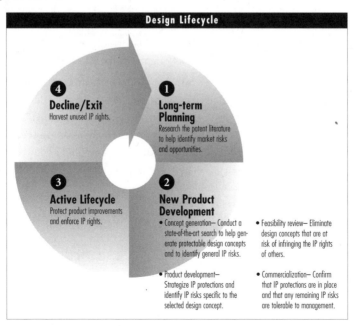

**Design Lifecycle**

**4 Decline/Exit**
Harvest unused IP rights.

**1 Long-term Planning**
Research the patent literature to help identify market risks and opportunities.

**3 Active Lifecycle**
Protect product improvements and enforce IP rights.

**2 New Product Development**
- Concept generation— Conduct a state-of-the-art search to help generate protectable design concepts and to identify general IP risks.
- Feasibility review— Eliminate design concepts that are at risk of infringing the IP rights of others.
- Product development— Strategize IP protections and identify IP risks specific to the selected design concept.
- Commercialization— Confirm that IP protections are in place and that any remaining IP risks are tolerable to management.

As a member of a design development team (and together with representatives of the design, engineering, and marketing disciplines), IP counsel employs strategies to optimize IP protections and reduce infringement risks. IP considerations are thus integrated into the design process. And in the staged new product development processes now implemented by many companies, IP "deliverables" are met at strategic junctures throughout the design process.

Though it is during the new product development phase of the design lifecycle that the value of design is transformed into a commercial asset, IP strategies should also be implemented in the phases that precede and follow the new product development phase. IP considerations are indeed important in the long-term planning phase that precedes new product development and in the active lifecycle and decline/exit phases that follow new product development.

Strategies for pursing design ownership are ideally timed and tailored to meet specific goals:

- ▲ Generate ownable designs—Research prior solutions to the design challenge early in the long-term planning phase and in the concept generation stage of new product development. This general research includes a state-of-the-art search of patent literature (patents and published patent applications), which is analyzed by IP counsel and shared with the development team to spark design innovation. Just as the iPod design team would have looked to Sony's 1979 Walkman and related patents for inspiration, design development teams benefit from studying past design efforts.

- ▲ Avoid designs owned by others—Identify IP risks associated with proposed design concepts—ideally, in the feasibility stage of new product development—so that risky design concepts can be screened out early. Once a design concept is selected for further development, a targeted search looks for patents relevant to that design concept. As needed, IP counsel facilitates a "design around" to place the final design outside the scope of IP rights of others.

- ▲ Secure IP rights—IP counsel leads the development team's efforts to protect selected design concepts in the feasibility stage of new product development. IP protection is sought not only for the preferred design concept but also for alternative concepts that may later be preferred by the company or the company's competitors. Before product launch, IP counsel ensures that IP protections are in place, including foreign protection when a product will be sold or licensed overseas. And upon product launch, IP counsel establishes procedures for monitoring the activities of competitors to police IP rights.

- ▲ Enforce and expand design assets—Even after design protection has been secured, steps should be taken in the active lifecycle phase to enforce IP rights. New competitive advantages can also be sought during the active lifecycle phase in connection with design improvements.

▲ Harvest design assets—In the decline or exit phase in which a design reaches its sunset, IP counsel can help extract value from IP assets. Instead of allowing them to go unused, IP assets can be harvested at this final phase by licensing or selling IP assets to other companies or by using those assets as leverage to settle disputes with other companies.

## IP ASSETS REALIZE THE FULL VALUE OF DESIGN

The full commercial value of design is realized only after steps are taken to transform valuable designs into IP assets, and design managers are uniquely positioned to oversee this transformation. To do so effectively, design managers first recognize design as a potential asset and team with IP counsel to set strategies for design protection throughout the design lifecycle. True design ownership and powerful IP assets are then within reach.

*Chapter 15*

# Measuring the Future Brand Effect of Graphic Design

by Gert Kootstra and Jos Vink

*In evaluations based on five criteria—identification, differentiation, saliency, the transfer of functional brand meanings, and the transfer of emotional brand meanings—Gert Kootstra and Jos Vink are able to quantify the brand impact of specific designs. Amplifying their analysis with a range of illustrations, they review projects that support (and a couple that fail to support) the objectives of their respective organizations.*

PROVING RETURN ON investment has become something of an obsession for designers, who by nature are more attuned to qualitative than to quantitative measures. As design takes a more significant role in business and designers seek to improve the stature of their profession, methods to validate design as a source of added value become more important. Happily, the Dutch Designers Association, or BNO as it is called in the Netherlands, has developed a quantitative research instrument that is proving its merit in a variety of companies.

Qualitative research can offer insights into which opinions, associations, or ideas certain designs conjure up. Quantitative research, on the other hand, maps the extent to which these opinions, associations, and ideas exist in certain target groups.

Qualitative research may well provide a reliable indication of design effectiveness, but because observations cannot be reflected numerically, that reliability is sometimes disputed. Quantitative research uses a far more extensive survey, which adds to its reliability and leads to greater certainty regarding the effects of some designs. Another advantage of quantitative measurements is that numerical reflection of research data enables statistical analysis. In this way, the results of the research can be compared at different times or places. Keep in mind that comparisons to previous research or competitor performance do require an accurate score profile—preferably within a standardized research instrument. This preference is also fueled by the need to keep research expenses low, and by the desire to be able to build a database for benchmarking purposes.

The BNO brings together more than 2,500 individual designers, as well as two hundred design agencies and design departments within companies. It represents them and promotes their business, social, and cultural interests. In 2003, the BNO surveyed its members to find out if any of them undertook measurements of design effectiveness in their organizations. One of the things the survey uncovered was that design ROI was researched only on a small scale and then mainly on the initiative of clients. What measurement there was mainly took the form of concept testing—through in-depth individual interviews or focus sessions. All of it was qualitative; quantitative research was rarely undertaken. In fact, there didn't seem to be any research instrument available to carry out quantitative research. And since such an instrument could not be found in any of the literature either, the BNO study group decided to develop one itself.

## A TOOL FOR BRAND BUILDING

BNO/DesignEffect aims to chart the effect that design has on the creation and maintenance of brands. The tool can be deployed in research into brand symbols (logos), as well as in brand communications, such as Web sites, packaging, brochures, ads, and magazines. It measures the influence design has on consumer valuation; it also measures design effects in relation to brand effects—design effects being the intended and desired consumer valuations of a design stimulus, and brand effects being the distinctive results of these valuations. After all, a design strategy is not isolated but something that follows naturally from the brand strategy.

Pinpointing and tracking the role of design in the consumer process can, in our opinion, best be done using the concept of the brand. This approach to effectiveness research is based on insights from psychology, and it links visual observation to the consumers' choice process. The aim is to find out whether the design objectives, expressed in intended changes in consumer and user valuation or perception, have been achieved. The process of assigning meaning and associations used in the brand concept is the design process at issue here.

In Figure 1, we present the theoretical model on which BNO/DesignEffect is based. The model reflects the tensions between the brand owner's design intentions and the design valuations of the intended target group. Design intentions relate to corporate objectives and are partly inspired by brand identity, brand concept, and other brand strategic considerations, such as current or desired positioning.

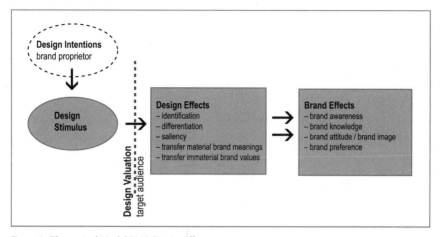

Figure 1. Theoretical Model BNO/DesignEffect

In an ideal situation, the formulated intentions and the intended effects on the target group will also constitute the core of the creative brief for the design work. We are working on the assumption here that the chosen design intentions will subsequently be incorporated into the design by the designer.

The perceptions of the intended target group are directly reflected in design valuations: the extent to which an item is deemed to apply to the stimulus. These perceptions are indirectly reflected in the brand awareness, brand knowledge, brand attitude, and brand preference of consumers and users. By analyzing the scores on the different items, we can predict which brand effects will occur and to what degree. The performance scores can also be compared with those of other stimuli, which have been researched using the same items.

The model is based on the following assumptions:

▲ Attributes and aspects of a design have certain effects on observers.

▲ Design effects can be subdivided into five dimensions: identification, differentiation, saliency, conveying of material brand meanings, and conveying of immaterial brand values.

▲ As a result of these five effects, the design has a demonstrable influence on brand effects in terms of awareness, knowledge, attitude/image, and behavior.

▲ Perceiving the design over a short period of time has the same influence as when the design is perceived by the target group for a longer period of time. The intensity (power) of the valuation will vary greatly, but the contents (the nature of the associations) and direction (positive or negative) will vary to a lesser degree.

With respect to consumer behavior, the research model will be limited to purchase intention, commitment, and loyalty. Experience in the area of advertising effectiveness research has shown that behavioral criteria, such as actual purchase, are affected to a large extent by factors that cannot be controlled within a research setting.

## DRAWING UP AND VALIDATION OF AN ITEMS LIST

A good items list is needed to measure to what degree a stimulus has a positive effect. Items are meanings or attributes based on which stimulus is researched. This list should not be too long; that would cause the research to be too lengthy and expensive, and it would also make it repetitive, leading the respondents to have difficulty focusing. A second criterion is that the items list has to be validated using statistical research.

The two market research firms of Ruigrok MC and Blauw Research were involved in the development of the DesignEffect items list. Extensive qualitative preliminary research uncovered around 140 items, which through statistical analysis and follow-up research were reduced to eighty, then to forty, and eventually to twenty-eight items, divided over seven dimensions. These dimensions are subdivided into values, personal attributes, and emotions. In Figure 2, we provide an overview.[1]

This division was made by defining which items are interlinked. Their mutual coherence is determined using a factor analysis. These factors are subsequently tested for their unambiguousness using a reliability analysis; they were then checked to see to what extent they accounted for the general valuation of the design. This relevance is established using a regression analysis.

The quantitative validation research[2] was carried out by way of an online survey of 880 respondents, using six different designs. This survey led to the conclusion that the BNO/DesignEffect instrument shows the statistically significant discrepancies in the brand effect of different designs.

| Item | Factor | Character |
|------|--------|-----------|
| Progressive | Progressive | Value |
| Modern | Progressive | Value |
| Innovative | Progressive | Value |
| Trend-setting | Progressive | Value |
| Traditional | Traditional | Value |
| Serious | Traditional | Value |
| Formal | Traditional | Value |
| Classic | Traditional | Value |
| Social | Social | Value |
| Human | Social | Value |
| Personal | Social | Value |
| Optimistic | Social | Value |
| Daring | Daring | Personal attribute |
| Imaginative | Daring | Personal attribute |
| Creative | Daring | Personal attribute |
| Original | Daring | Personal attribute |
| Reliable | Reliable | Personal attribute |
| Accurate | Reliable | Personal attribute |
| Self-confident | Reliable | Personal attribute |
| Efficient | Reliable | Personal attribute |
| Happy | Happy | Personal attribute |
| Cheerful | Happy | Personal attribute |
| Lively | Happy | Personal attribute |
| Sociable | Happy | Personal attribute |
| Enjoyment | Enjoyment | Emotion |
| Inspiring | Enjoyment | Emotion |
| Surprising | Enjoyment | Emotion |
| Satisfying | Enjoyment | Emotion |

Figure 2. Items List BNO/DesignEffect

## WHAT DOES BNO/DESIGNEFFECT MEASURE?

DesignEffect predicts brand effects of a design by measuring design effects. The five design effects are defined as follows:

### Design Effects

1. *Identification.* The owner, producer, or sender of the brand article or message becomes known through design. Another function of design is categorization. This effect can be assessed by the extent to which the design provides pointers toward the sender and/or the respective category.

2. *Differentiation.* Design contributes to the way a brand article or message stands out in relation to the competition in the eyes of consumers. This design effect can be assessed by the extent of perceived difference (uniqueness) within a specific category.

3. *Saliency.* Design can contribute to a brand by its level of strikingness, or attracting the attention of consumers by being different.

4. *Transfer of material (functional) brand meanings.* Through physical aspects, such as shape, size, color, material, structure, and imagery, design actively contributes to the perceived performance of the brand. The design effect can be assessed by the extent to which the design contributes to the perceived performance of the brand.

5. *Transfer of immaterial (emotional) brand meanings.* Through visual expression, design contributes to the psychosocial meaning of the brand, leading to the attribution of certain values, character traits, or emotions to it. The design effect can be assessed by the extent to which the symbolic brand meaning (expressed by the design) is perceived by the observer.

This last design effect can be subdivided into the following attributes:

▲ Values: The extent to which the design facilitates the perception of the symbolic (psychological) brand values

▲ Personal attributes: The extent to which specific personal attributes are attributed to the brand by the design through visual expression

▲ Emotions: The extent to which the design reaches out to emotions ascribed to the brand

### Brand Effects

The five effects described above give a design a demonstrable influence on the awareness, attitude, and behavior of consumers. This influence includes a distinction between four brand effects: namely, brand awareness, brand knowledge, brand attitude and image, and brand preference. We know these effects from classical theoretical models such as AIDA or DAGMAR that explain how marketing communications works. These models suppose a hierarchy (order) of effects that is passed through when confronted with a stimulus; awareness will lead to the development of knowledge about the brand, and this knowledge in turn will lead to developing an attitude toward the brand. Subsequently, preference will result from a well-developed attitude. The stages follow the three main effect categories: knowledge (cognitive), attitude (affective), and behavior (conative).

The brand effects in our instrument coincide with four stages in the working process as presented in these models. A fifth and sixth stage—namely, intention and purchase—are omitted, as we explained earlier in the text. Now, if we believe design can have an effect in the various stages of the working process mentioned above, we have to make a theoretical connection between the five distinctive design effects as proposed and the four brand effects.

Brand awareness is the extent to which the target group can recognize the brand within a certain product class. The design effect can be determined on the basis of the degree to which design contributes to recognition, remembering (memory value), and strikingness (saliency) of the brand. It can be important for effectiveness that the design provide some pointers to the category in question—in particular, for new brand introductions or drastic changes to a brand design.

Brand knowledge refers to both brand awareness and knowledge of the attributes (the attributes and advantages linked to the brand article). This is therefore a much broader concept than brand awareness. The added value of a brand depends on, among other things, a great level of familiarity with and clear expectation of the performance (on a more concrete instrumental level). The design effect can be charted on the basis of the degree to which design contributes to the perception of product attributes and the perception of the advantages of using the product. We specify product-related meaning as material brand meanings; the design effect can be determined on the basis of the perception and valuation of these brand meanings in relation to the research stimulus.

When the design is intended to convey material brand meanings or immaterial brand values, customers will better understand what is meant and assume a more open mind with regard to the brand. Material brand meanings will sooner lead to cognitive evaluation (knowledge-oriented), while immaterial values will lead to affective evaluation (attitude-oriented).

The brand image is the sum of all the impressions consumers have of a brand (or brand article), which can, in turn, influence their behavior with respect to that brand (article). All attributes that are attributed to the brand are part of the brand image, but so are the more abstract attributes and advantages that are associated with the product, and therefore rub off on the product. (Attributes and advantages can also be simply thoughts or perceptions.)

Apart from that, the brand values, personal attributes, and emotions attributed to the brand also play a decisive role. We refer to these as the immaterial brand values.

Brand owners can try to influence the brand image to develop into their desired direction by publishing the values chosen for the brand—its personal attributes and emotions—as recognizably and unequivocally as possible. The design effect can be charted on the basis of the attractiveness of the design (likeability): Does it appeal; is it original; does one have an affinity for it; does one feel a connection with it? But it can also be measured on the basis of the extent to which design contributes to the saliency of the brand, and the perception of personal attributes, emotions, or values that go with the brand.

Brand preference occurs when the brand occupies a prominent place in the consumer's awareness set. When design is deployed to differentiate (that is, to contribute to consumers' perceptions of the brand article as different from that of other providers), this will also add to brand preference.

Final valuations of the design can, in principle, lead to brand preference formation—for example, on the basis of visual preference: "This design has the greatest appeal to me," or "This design suits me the best." The degree of consumer brand preference gives us a clue regarding purchase intention and possibly also regarding actual purchasing behavior.

A number of factors influence this—for example, the extent to which the design is perceived as unique, distinctive, and attractive. The perception of the price/quality ratio is also important. Moreover, the design effect can also be charted on the basis of the extent to which design contributes to brand commitment and brand loyalty. Especially through the conveyance of immaterial brand values, consumers can gain insight into the brand and assess to what extent it is convincing, authentic, and in keeping with their personal orientations. Mind you, not all brands are concerned with this aspect, which tends to apply to those for which a certain ideology or brand personality is at the forefront (think Ben & Jerry's ice cream or Apple Computer). The creative expression of that ideology or personality through design influences perception and valuation.

Figure 3 summarizes the design effects that can be used to determine various brand effects. Not all design effects lead to the same brand effect; a clear distinction can be made here. Identification and saliency can both have a positive effect on brand awareness (when signaling the brand clearly) but are unlikely to influence other brand effects.

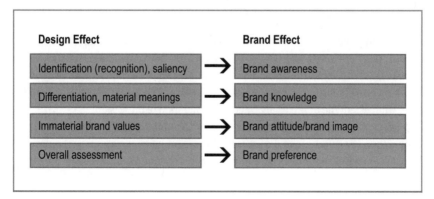

Figure 3. Related Effects

And the conveyance of material (functional) brand meanings more likely result in brand knowledge as an effect, whereas conveying immaterial brand values—a more attitude-oriented design effect—tends to affect the brand image.

Design effects and brand effects need to be congruent to prove effectiveness. When, for instance, the design strategy is aimed at creating a brand image but the only design effect that can be found is identification, the brand effect of design will be limited to brand awareness. After all, the ability to contribute to a brand image necessitates the transfer of immaterial brand values as a design effect. Therefore it can be argued that in this case the effectiveness of the current design strategy—referring to the measured stimulus—is doubtful.

## HOW TO USE THE INSTRUMENT

Prior to use, the client company or brand owner provides a questionnaire with a check-list indicating what it is looking to achieve with the design. This should include a se-lection from the standard items list. On some occasions, this means having the brand values adapted to the items that best suit them. The client can, however, still add a num-ber of additional items it would like to see measured.

The design in question is subsequently presented to at least three hundred respon-dents from the intended target group, using the standardized questionnaire. All ques-tions are—barring one—multiple choice; in this way, processing the answers is kept simple, and expenses can be limited. (The one open question asks for spontaneous as-sociations.) Respondents answer the questions while continuously viewing the design on the screen. They can enlarge the image by clicking on it.

The client receives an extensive report, including a handy score card. Blauw Re-search and Ruigrok MC are building a joint database so that the results of the survey can be offset against earlier scores of other designs within a certain sector or a specific com-pany. This is useful because it gives a score—for example, the score for trend-setting—a clearer profile. If the benchmark score for that value is 4.7, a score of 5.7 (which is in itself not very high) will still be considered relatively good.

When you want to check or find out to what extent an existing brand image possibly influences the valuation of a design, you have the option to go for a so-called split-run setup. By this, we mean the possibility that established brand associations can positively or negatively affect the valuation of the design object. When researching a design, you can then carry out random checks, where half the research population views the design without the brand image (and brand name), and the other half views the design with the brand image. By subsequently comparing the scores of both spot checks, you can find out to what extent the brand image affects the valuation of the design.

Another option is to compare an existing or revamped design to that of some of the competitors. The effect of the design is then determined by the scores of the design in question, as well as the comparison with the scores of competing designs.

## WHERE IT IS USED

BNO/Design Effect can be deployed for a number of research projects:

- ▲ Testing existing designs that may require revamping (due to decision-making/ investment decisions or to obtain input for the design brief)

- ▲ Testing of existing versus new design (certainty regarding the return on the renewal)

- ▲ Pretesting concepts and design tendencies (selection of the best concept; well-founded decision)

- ▲ Post-testing of launched designs (identifying market effect)

- ▲ Benchmark testing (own design versus competition's)

- ▲ Testing for one or several target groups. This could occur when different versions of a design are developed for one brand in order to target different groups. The client may want to gauge the effectiveness of this strategy.

## BNO/DESIGNEFFECT IN ACTION

- ▲ DesignEffect was used to assess the current brand design of the largest chain of independent mortgage advisors in The Netherlands. The marketing department felt revamping was necessary but had no clear evidence. The goal was to realize a sound and objective basis for the decision-making process and to gain more insights for the direction in which redesign should take place. However, the scores on all the design effects were very low, indicating no brand effect at all. In short, the existing brand design added zero value to the brand. The research resulted in the advice to start a drastic redesign project.

- ▲ The Hague University is working on repositioning itself, with quality, market leadership (regional), and challenge (international) as the core elements. Based on the new positioning, the university had a new logo designed. It then wanted to pretest the design concept to see to what extent it contributed to attaining the repositioning objective. Research was conducted among The Hague University's international relations, among Polish students, and among the parents of Polish students. The report compared the results from these groups. First the spontaneous associations evoked by the design were defined. These associations were subdivided into positive and negative ones. The designs were subsequently assessed on attractiveness, appeal, suitability, distinctiveness, and strikingness. The research also charted the degree to which the respondents considered a number of aspects applicable to the logo of The Hague University and in comparison with those of its competing educational institutions. This included a closer look at the seven brand values the organization wanted to attribute to the design. Benchmark figures from previous DesignEffect studies were used to point out to what extent a score was below or above average.

- ▲ In 2007, TPG Post, the Dutch national postal company, was rebranded and renamed TNT Post. The new company hoped to investigate the brand image effects of the alteration by means of two studies using the same instrument. It identified brand image effects with regard to no fewer than ten specific design intentions, all related to immaterial brand values. The result of both studies has to prove if, and to what level, the new TNT brand design contributes to the desired TNT Post brand image, in comparison with the contribution of the former TPG design to the TPG brand image.

▲ For the first TPG study, two samples were taken, one from a business and one from a general audience. Both samples were at random confronted with two out of six design applications, varying from the bags and clothing of postal workers to the postal car fleet, Web site, advertisements, and brochures. The TPG study showed high scores on identification and saliency, but its score for differentiation was only average. The design clearly contributed to the TPG brand image, based on a transfer of immaterial brand values. However, three of the ten intended design aspects could not be found at all. Apparently, the task for the new TNT brand design would be to convey these three missing aspects. It also became clear which of the distinctive brand design applications could be improved. In fact, a number of conclusions were drawn that served as input for the final efforts of the designers working on the new brand.

▲ Rabobank hoped to visually separate its advertising for its retail and wholesale segments through the use of photography and customized layouts. The idea was to address distinctive values targeted to the two audiences while retaining a high level of identification and differentiation. For both audiences, the bank identified three brand values: close, concerned, and trendsetting. However, it also identified specific design values (intended design aspects) for each segment. For retail, for example, the values were described as warm, human, and powerful; for wholesale, professional, surprising, and innovative. DesignEffect was used to gauge the effectiveness of this approach. The two photography styles and two layouts were presented in four mutual combinations to both target groups, along with text elements.

The results clearly indicated the effectiveness of the design with regard to the four brand effects. However, it is difficult to predict the level of intensity of these effects, since this strongly depends on the way the design will be used (for example, the choice of media involved), and on the frequency with which it will be used. DesignEffect also found that the designs were likely to have little impact on brand awareness because they received a fairly average score on saliency and on distinctiveness in comparison to the benchmark. The designs also did not convey any knowledge about the use of the brand or any new knowledge concerning the brand. On the plus side, based on the overall scores, the researchers felt the redesign would affect Rabobank's brand image positively. The combination of the retail photo and layout seemed to convey a strong effect with regard to two specific brand values and two intended design aspects. Therefore, it would seem that there will also be a positive effect on brand preference, even if the level of differentiation is fairly average.

## AN ILLUSTRATION OF THE USE OF BNO/DESIGNEFFECT

One of the participants in the development of DesignEffect is Informatie Beheer Groep (Information Management Group), the government organization in charge of student grants in The Netherlands. With several million clients, communication is a critical success factor for customer satisfaction and for building a reputation. However, research showed that the current image was stale and weak. During a brand revamp in 2004, Information Management Group decided to introduce a systematic approach based on a new communications strategy that focused on a more effective and more personal target group approach.

This new strategy centered on a clear differentiation of functional information on the product level (regarding the "what": the content of specific regulations) and motivational information at business-process level (the "how to": interaction with clients). This resulted in a separation of brand meanings that gave direction to the design policy.

Information at the product level was intended to be clear, simple, and spot-on. At this level, it had to address functional product features and related functional benefits, such as, for instance, no interest, or a flexible redeem schedule. Information at the motivational level had to express the softer benefits of the products, such as reliability, freedom, and safety. In terms of design effects, the first level was about identification, saliency, and conveying functional meanings, while the second was about differentiation and conveying more-abstract concepts.

During the development of tactical communications, such as brochures, magazines, and Web sites, the designers worked with clearly defined design values and guidelines, but up to this point no tests had been conducted. Theoretically, it seemed that functional information would drive brand awareness and brand knowledge, while motivational information would drive brand attitude and brand image.

Two brochures were tested during rollout and implementation, and the results were in line with what had actually been planned. Even though the scores were more or less satisfying, it was felt they could be improved. Design at this tactical level of communications is a continuous and cyclical process leading to renewal every two to three years. Using DesignEffect enables the organization to monitor this process in a very accurate and structured way.

## CONCLUSIONS TO BE DRAWN

The results of BNO/DesignEffect are promising, and clients are happy to work with it. But it is still used only on a small scale, and it has not yet found its way to SMEs (small and medium-size enterprises). DesignEffect is particularly suitable for organizations pursuing an active brand policy closely tied in with their design policy.

We are cautiously optimistic about this instrument's future prospects. After all, design is still a neglected area of market research, and it cannot be expected to suddenly come to the fore. There is a lack of market research tradition, and the concept of design effectiveness and how it can be measured is still uncharted territory.

A second reason is that formulated design objectives make or break the assessment of design effectiveness, and unfortunately these design objectives are often formulated too loosely. Design specialists point out that the quality of the design brief is often poor because of this.

The determination of this type of design effectiveness requires a clear analysis on the basis of the knowledge of design as a branding instrument. That is probably where the complexity of this approach of effectiveness research lies. There seems to be a distinct lack of knowledge of design effects and their relation to brand performance, which is a void that BNO/DesignEffect can help to fill.

## ACKNOWLEDGMENTS

The development of a method to predict design effects was conducted in close collaboration with Dr. Edward Groenland, research director of Blauw Research and professor at Nyenrode Business University in The Netherlands. We would furthermore like to extend our gratitude to all who have contributed to the development of this instrument, in particular to Wout van der Wijk, Marja Ruigrok, and Pieter van Ginkel.

### Suggested Reading

Kootstra, Gert L. "The Role of Design in Brand Development," in: Rik Riezebos (ed.), *Brand Management, A Theoretical and Practical Approach* (Harlow, U.K.: FT/Prentice Hall: Pearson Education, 2002).

# Chapter 16

# Design Managers as Company Strategists: The Power of the Eighth S

by EunSook Kwon, Michael Cooper, and Joe Synan

*Across the spectrum of design management issues, the workplace is often overlooked. In a thoughtful analysis and case study, EunSook Kwon, Michael Cooper, and Joe Synan indicate how a fine-tuned office layout can improve communications and business processes, complement an organization's structure and strategies, promote adaptability and facilitate change, and enhance performance and job satisfaction.*

IN MANY ORGANIZATIONS, the capabilities of the design manager are often overlooked by corporate strategists as they plan the company's future direction. That's a shame, because design managers can play a critical role in helping a company improve its performance.

But how are designers to get this across to their business counterparts? We are often told that designers must learn to speak the language of business if they want to secure a place at the strategy table. We suggest they take a look at the 7S model.

Corporate strategists have long used this model as a planning and management tool. The seven S's refer to superordinate goals, strategy, structure, systems, skills, staffing, and style. We suggest that design managers, who understand the importance of workplace design, incorporate an eighth S: space.

## THE 7S MODEL

In the early 1980s, Thomas J. Peters and Robert H. Waterman Jr. identified the 7S model for use in analyzing and planning for organizations. Their work was described in their landmark book *In Search of Excellence.* Stephen R. Covey used a similar framework in his book *Principle-Centered Leadership.* The theory advanced by these authors was that an organization is best managed, and therefore best changed and improved, by understanding these seven dimensions:

- ▲ Superordinate goals—The business's long-term goals
- ▲ Strategy—The business's focus and approach to products and markets
- ▲ Structure—Organizational charts, reporting relationships, job descriptions, and individual responsibilities
- ▲ Skills—The degree of capability and expertise in the company's workforce
- ▲ Systems—Business processes
- ▲ Staffing—Compensation and motivation of the workforce
- ▲ Style—The values and behaviors of the workforce

Figure 1. The 7S model.

Key to this theory is the understanding that the most important aspect driving a company's success is organizational balance (see Figure 1). A successful company is not necessarily one with the best strategy. If the organization doesn't have the skills to execute that strategy, success will be hard to come by. In other words, all seven dimensions need to be supportive of each other and in balance.

## WORKPLACE DESIGN AS THE EIGHTH DIMENSION

The physical design of the office environment came into consideration as early as 1939, when Frank Lloyd Wright conceived the first modern open-office environment in his design of the Johnson Wax Building: one large room, filled with clerks seated at row upon row of desks (Figure 2).

After World War II, America's economy began to grow at an unprecedented rate, and with it came the white-collar worker—as well as the need for more office space and for the efficient use of that space. What developed was the first truly modern office block with the design of the Lever House in 1952, followed by the Seagram's Building in 1956, both located in New York City. What differentiated these buildings from previous high-rise towers built from 1900 to 1950 was the development of the planning grid as a design tool to modularize, standardize, and optimize the floor plan for each floor in the building. Now workplace designers could repeat Frank Lloyd Wright's 1939 single-floor open-office concept on multiple floors to improve company efficiency. The

Figure 2. The Johnson Wax building: Frank Lloyd Wright, architect.

result was the modularization and standardization of the corporate office from Tokyo to New York.

In the mid 1960s, office-furniture manufacturers introduced another innovation: the low moveable wall system, placed around a desk. This marked the introduction of the ubiquitous office cubicle as the key component used in open-office planning and found in corporate workplaces of all sizes today, as illustrated in Figure 3. The open-office design concept, with multiple cubicles in repetitive formation, fit more people into less space and reduced costs for the organization. It also spawned many detractors, the most popular being Scott Adams and his Dilbert cartoons. The manufacturers of these cubicles have made many technological, ergonomic, and aesthetic improvements in the past five decades; however, the need for varying amounts of space depending on specific job functions was often ignored in the push to achieve the highest density possible.

Recently, the emphasis in workspace design has begun to shift from high-density efficiency to meeting a more-complex range of corporate and individual worker needs. Organizations continue to experience pressure to reduce costs, so the first instinct for many of them has been to continue with the high-density open-office concept. But design managers still ask that critical question: At what point do high-density and open-office environments become counterproductive to the organization's performance?

Figure 3. The ubiquitous open office.

Perhaps the most compelling reason organizations have continued with high-density and open-office design for the past fifty years is the fact that there has been little published data linking workplace density to organizational and worker performance. Deciphering the point at which high density and open office intersect with reduced performance, higher turnover, increased absenteeism, job satisfaction, and so on, is still a work in progress.

New digital technologies and network systems also encourage organizations and design managers to look more closely at the work environment to find better and more creative design solutions that balance organizational needs with those of the individual. It is for this reason that we believe an opportunity exists to use the eighth S to help balance these changing needs; the 8S Model (Figure 4) can be a key variable in improving organizational performance and catalyzing organizational transformation, as well as worker satisfaction.

Figure 4. The 8S model.

## THE 8S MODEL

Our premise is that corporate strategists cannot afford to overlook the transforming effect of the work environment and its role in supporting all seven S's. Space is not about real estate; rather, it is about the socio-behavioral dynamics (that is, adjacencies, space utilization, openness and privacy, standards, and so on) that occur within that space, creating human interactions and social settings within the workplace. Design managers are uniquely adapted to share their insights into the work environment and how it relates to the seven other dimensions.

Table 1 lists some important workplace design tools that affect these dynamics. Using these tools, design managers can develop and implement a workplace design that supports the other seven dimensions of the organization.

| Table 1: The Eighth S and Its Relationship with the Other Seven | | |
|---|---|---|
| **The Original Seven Dimensions** | **The Eighth Dimension: Major Tools for Designing Space** | **How These Design Tools Affect the Other Seven Dimensions** |
| Structure & Systems | **Adjacencies** (how people and job functions are physically positioned relative to each other) | To assure effective communications and flow of business processes in the organizational structure and systems |
| Skills & Style | **Space utilization** (the overall and specific density of people and offices) | To match the skills and the style of the organization |
| Structure, Strategy, Staffing & Style | **Openness and privacy** (the application of open-office and private-office designs)<br><br>**Standards** (selection and application of rules relating to type, size, and other features of furniture, equipment, and related amenities) | To create workplace standards to complement organizational structure, strategy, staffing, and style |
| Strategy & Superordinate goals | **Flexibility and adaptability** (the built-in capacity for easily rearranging, moving, and reconfiguring the physical features) | To assure that space can easily support the changing strategy and superordinate goals of the company |
| Staffing & Style | **"Five-sensing" the environment** (conscious application of light, color, scent, sound, and texture in the environment) | To address all aspects of staffing (human behavior) and style |
| Superordinate goals & Strategy | **Symbols and branding** (placement of design features selectively throughout the workspaces to reinforce philosophies, ideas, and concepts) | To assure continuous reminders of the organization's superordinate goals and strategy |

## THE 8S MODEL: A CASE STUDY

To illustrate and support the position that the 8S model can be critical to the transformation of an organization, we offer this case study.

In 1991, Texas Eastern, an energy conglomerate and Fortune 100 company later to become Panhandle Eastern and finally Duke Energy, decided to spin off its petroleum products pipeline division as a separate company, TEPPCO (Texas Eastern Products Pipeline Company). TEPPCO set out to identify itself as a standalone company with its own mission statement and corporate culture. One of its primary goals was to become a world-class, best-of-breed pipeline enterprise. TEPPCO initially engaged McKinsey & Company to assist in establishing its business strategies using the 7S model. The company also engaged two of the authors of this chapter to assist in the design of its new workspace. It was in this process that we discovered firsthand the opportunity to use the eighth S as an additional tool in transforming the organization. By understanding the interplay among all eight dimensions, the design manager, along with the company strategists, was able to achieve a successful outcome, with improved organizational performance and organizational transformation (Table 2).

| Table 2: TEPPCO Transformation | | |
|---|---|---|
| 8S Dimensions | Before | After |
| Superordinate Goals | Profitable regulated pipeline | A world-class pipeline company: best of breed |
| Strategy | Operating efficiency | Diversity of products moved; key relationships with customers |
| Structure | Division of an energy conglomerate, operations focused | Stand-alone company, separately traded; balance of operations and marketing/customer relations |
| Systems | Operations optimization, based on historic best practices | Economic analysis of all decisions |
| Skills | Operations | Operations, marketing, and customer relations; environmental protection |
| Staffing | "You are lucky to have a job" | Performance pay; emphasis on career development |
| Style | Conservative and closed; low disclosure | Thoughtful, analytical, smart, open; high disclosure |
| Space | Traditional departmental office assignments; 100% closed, private offices; separation of executives within all departments | Team neighborhood assignments related to business processes; 80 percent open environment, with very high visual transparency; attractive, open group work areas |

To become a world-class pipeline company required TEPPCO to make a dramatic transformation in its business model, resulting in changes in all seven dimensions of the organization. Some of these business changes included enhancing the company's product lines through its pipeline. Initially, TEPPCO primarily shipped LPGs (liquefied petroleum gases), NGLs (natural gas liquids), and other refined petroleum products, such as jet fuels. One result of the business transformation was new product lines, as the company began to ship new fuels and fuel mixtures through its pipelines. This particular change required enormous contributions of time and effort in brainstorming and generating ideas from all levels of the organization. In addition, successfully implementing this change affected TEPPCO's work flows and business processes, which in turn necessitated a reorganization of the company's business units, as well as reassignment of employees from a departmental organizational structure to a team-based (or project-based) structure.

Other business changes were driven by the company's need to improve its operational safety and efficiencies in shipping products, its desire to significantly improve its customer service, and, perhaps most important for its shareholders, its goal to enhance bottom-line profitability. All of these objectives profoundly changed TEPPCO's way of doing business and affected every employee. Indeed, TEPPCO leadership knew from the start that without the support, hard work, and commitment of all the employees, the company would be setting a course for failure. Buy-in had to come from all, and this meant giving employees the best technologies, the best business tools, the best leadership structure, and the best compensation and incentive plans possible. At least for the designers, it was only logical that the company now needed the best possible work environment if it were to achieve success (even though TEPPCO leadership, initially, saw no reason to change the existing work environment). The responsibility fell on the designers to demonstrate that a new, innovative work environment—the eighth S—could play a key role in TEPPCO's transformation.

The implications of this responsibility emboldened the designers to request their participation in the leadership strategy meetings, focusing on the implementation of TEPPCO's business changes. Their active participation in these meetings made possible two critical breakthroughs. First, the designers were able to fully grasp the magnitude of the changes in store and the ramifications they posed for the company work environment; and second, the designers, armed with the insight gained from their participation in the leadership meetings, were able to convince the leadership in a relatively short time that they should be looking at examples of innovative design concepts in other parts of the country.

After witnessing some of these design ideas firsthand, in one case including a trip to Epcot Center in Orlando (which seemed an unlikely connection at the time but proved most valuable in turning the leadership around), company leaders agreed to look at some new design ideas for TEPPCO. In response to this challenge, the designers set forth to develop a bold new workplace design that, when first experienced by the employees, would convince them that they "were not in Kansas anymore." (This was a favorite quote of Mike Burke, then company CEO of TEPPCO.) From the moment an employee stepped off the elevator, he would see and feel a distinct change from the old, traditional, mundane, TEPPCO look.

The bold new workplace design addressed each of the business changes by providing a large degree of openness, along with built-in flexibility to take advantage of future changes to the workspace. Work areas had abundant natural light and generous pathways for travel and group gathering spots for impromptu meetings (Figure 5); they were also organized in small clusters to humanize (that is, de-Dilbertize) employees' individual work spaces (Figure 6). Meeting areas were centrally located on every level around a three-story open atrium (Figure 7) and adjoined by a three-story central stair for ease of vertical travel from floor to floor (Figure 8). And a control room (Figure 9), the 24/7/365 operations center for the three thousand-mile pipeline, was located immediately off the reception area (Figure 10) for open viewing by customers and employees alike. The control room viewing area was intentionally located by the reception area to serve as a reminder to employees that TEPPCO's business was (and still is) about the pipeline and the customers it serves. (In TEPPCO's old offices, the control room was tucked away in a dark, obscure interior room, with access limited to operators. Most TEPPCO employees didn't know where it was located.)

Every design feature throughout the workplace served a dual purpose; one was obviously functional, but the second was symbolic. For instance, the three-story atrium adjoining stair and meeting areas was symbolic of TEPPCO's team approach. The individual work areas were symbolic of the importance the company placed on the individual. The control room served as the heartbeat of the entire company. These examples

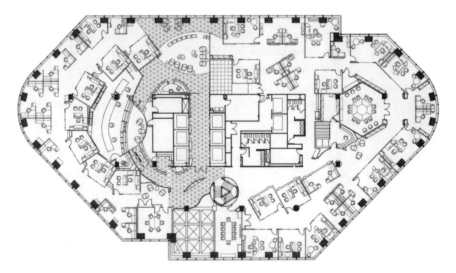

Figure 5. The floor plan of TEPPCO's 32nd floor, showing the greeting and visitor center. Glass-walled offices maximize natural light in the interior; this plan also illustrates the concept of creating an exciting and creative work environment designed specifically to facilitate functional rather than status-based needs.

Figure 6. Typical work area, showing the combination of office with glass wall and small clusters of workspaces with ample natural light and privacy.

Figure 7. Meeting areas congregate around a three-story open atrium and are open, vibrant in color and materials, and intended to be viewed by all.

Figure 8. The three-story interconnecting stairway, which is surrounded by a three-story team area center serving multiple teams of varying sizes, all of which are visually connected to promote a corporate culture of oneness and togetherness.

Figure 9. TEPPCO's control room viewing platform adjoins the company's main reception area. The intent is to allow employees and customers alike to view TEPPCO's most critical operation: a three thousand-mile pipeline that runs from Baytown, Texas, to Albany, New York.

Figure 10. At TEPPCO's greeting and visitor center, the visitor is not only met by a greeter but is also introduced to TEPPCO via a nine-screen viewing wall that gives an overview of the company and its operations, as well as the daily flow through the pipeline.

and others were to be symbolic and visual reminders to TEPPCO employees that the organizational transformation was a point of fact. There would be no turning back to the old ways in doing business. The employees were now part of a grand plan to make TEPPCO a world-class pipeline company, unlike any other.

TEPPCO continued with its transformation through the 1990s and 2000s, employing the 8S model; with each successive expansion in 1997, 1999, and 2002, the design managers were asked to use the same workplace design tools used in 1991 to ensure design continuity and to restate TEPPCO's commitment to improve organizational performance. From 1991 through 2006 (at which time it was bought by Enterprise), TEPPCO outperformed its competition and maintained it's preeminence as a world-class pipeline company.

## SUMMARY

Companies today are taking the critical steps to improve and transform their business models with the rise of new management theory, technological innovation, and economic shifts; however, the workplace design concept introduced in the 1960s still prevails today. Workplace design can support a company's working philosophy, but it remains a challenge to convince organizations of its efficacy in improving organizational performance. The 8S model is a design management tool that can simultaneously improve company performance and create a desirable work environment.

From the perspective of the design industry, shaping a company's culture to enhance knowledge management is becoming the pre-eminent issue in achieving design competitiveness. As the work of creating and harnessing knowledge within the organization continues, companies will turn their focus from efficient working environments to a more creative learning and working environment.

In this knowledge-based paradigm shift, the design management profession has the opportunity to profoundly shape the future of companies by sharpening and deploying the eighth S in strategic visioning, planning, and management. Collaboration between design managers and corporate strategists in planning for this transformation will improve the chances for successful outcomes and will improve organizational performance, as well. Because of its tangible, multimodal, and interactive design features, the eighth S signifies the design manager's role as a visionary interlocutor, catalyst, and strategic planner.

The design manager's perspective will give strategists the opportunity to inspire workers with exciting workspaces. The key lever of knowledge worker creativity will be deployed in a wide variety of workspace design options. Workspace will be consciously and intentionally chosen to help drive the new strategic direction, utilizing new options for openness, connectivity, and teamwork.

### Suggested Reading

Becker, Franklin. *Offices That Work: Balancing Communication, Flexibility, and Cost* (Ithaca, NY: International Workplace Studies Program, Cornell University, 2001).

Pfeffer, Jeffrey, and Sutton, Robert I. *The Knowing-Doing Gap: How Smart Companies Turn Knowledge into Action* (Boston: Harvard Business School Press, 2000).

Propst, Robert. *The Office: A Facility Based on Change* (Elmhurst: The Business Press, 1968).

# CASES IN DESIGN STRATEGY

The name of the game is: Show me! Theory and process are nice, but ultimately, it's the bottom-line issues that matter, even in the seemingly subjective, aesthetically charged arena of design. So this anthology concludes with "proof" that design does, indeed, deliver—in terms of competitiveness and market share as well as organizational coherence and effectiveness.

The case studies in this section cover a myriad of situations. In product design, John Barratt and Ken Dowd spell out the concepts driving the Boeing 787 Dreamliner project and their implications for the plane's interior architecture. On the other end of the scale, Dave Franchino describes his firm's redesign of the ubiquitous batting helmet used by school-aged kids. Addressing brand, Bonnie Briggs reveals the rationale and development effort behind Caterpillar's One Voice program. Moving on to facilities, Arnold Craig Levin explains how workplace design can be exploited to leverage business strategies. Rounding out the pragmatic focus of this section, two chapters emphasize the significance of context in design. Joe Duffy and Eric Block ponder the attributes of communications in a world where there is societal stratification, an erosion of trust, information overload, a desire to tune things out, and a democratization of design. And Lauralee Alben shares design tools an organization can use to both navigate and orchestrate major transformations in goals, strategies, and culture.

As in the previous sections, common threads can be found in this colorful tapestry of cases:

**Qualitative research is a must.** This effort looks in two directions. It starts with a thorough assessment of things as they currently stand. It must be richly textured and full of details. It should distill shortcomings and challenges. It should include a market analysis. And it has to clearly identify stakeholders and their attitudes and aspirations. It must also include a forward-looking component. What do stakeholders want? What are desirable outcomes? And what are constraints in fulfilling those desires? This is the targets-and-boundaries dimension of the research, and it is crucial to stimulating effective creativity and design.

**Build partnerships.** The best outcomes emerge when there is consensus among stakeholders with respect to both objectives and resources. Project criteria can be—and often are—modified. But an efficient process and successful responses to needed change are actually sustained by consistent relationships grounded in dialogue, trust, and commitment. Also, as an effort moves from conception through execution, the balance among partner contributions shifts, but the dependence on collaboration remains a constant.

**Have a step-by-step implementation plan.** It may be dry, but this is where the rubber meets the road. Of course, there has to be room for flexibility, and particulars and fine points can be added along the way. At the same time, it is essential to know what resources are available, and there must also be a path and a schedule, both of which must be updated regularly.

The cases in this section all have "happy endings." But that's not the point. These tales are really "wise beginnings," a foundation for your own initiatives. The lessons in this volume and in these case studies are of value to the degree that they inspire and guide your own success stories. Ultimately, this book is a "bon voyage" wish as you embark on your own design journeys.

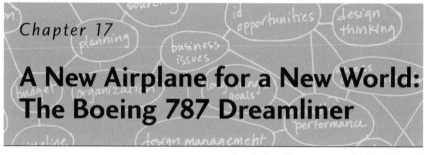

# Chapter 17

# A New Airplane for a New World: The Boeing 787 Dreamliner

## by John Barratt and Ken Dowd

*A multi-billion-dollar company wants to redefine the experience of commercial air travel. In partnership with a design firm known for its expertise in this special area, the two set forth on a collaborative venture to determine the needs and desires of travelers. John Barratt and Ken Dowd describe the strategies, processes, and circumstances involved in supporting the design of the Boeing 787 Dreamliner, the most successful commercial airplane launch in history.*

TODAY, THE CONCEPT of collaboration in design is considered somewhat conventional. Gone are the days when clients and designers met infrequently only to separate into self-contained production groups. With the advance of technology, collaborative design increasingly takes place across geographical and perceptual boundaries, creating teams that span the globe. Typically, however, these relationships, as liquid as their boundaries may be, develop with certain, and often anticipated, limitations.

Is it possible for designers to work seamlessly with clients? Can talent from both the client and design sides set aside personal, departmental, and company-driven egos for the greater good and create a single, exceptional team? The Boeing Company and Teague team—and their unique sixty-year working relationship—prove that exceptional talent can unite a team and lead the members to greatness.

This case study examines the distinctive collaborative design process and research strategy created and implemented by Teague and The Boeing Company to rejuvenate the spirit of flight through interior and architectural design channels. Due to the scope of the project, collaboration across varied disciplines was essential. The overarching design process for the purpose of a collaborative business paradigm, as well as the extraordinary design efforts produced by the collaboration between Teague and Boeing, will be discussed in this article.

## A DECADE OF DESIGN

Unlike the majority of product design efforts, the design of a commercial airplane requires an extended amount of time in terms of development and research. Based on the average replacement cycle of airplanes, as well as competitive market forces and available investment options, commercial airplanes—from inception to market—are introduced, on average, once a decade. Once every ten years. That is an almost inconceivable timeframe in this day and age of instant technology and shrinking shelf life. For the purpose of comparison, a single electronics company—such as Samsung or Nokia—can introduce in excess of three hundred mobile phones into the market in a single year. That's nearly one new mobile phone launch every day. At that rate, three thousand new mobile phones could be brought to market over a period of ten years.

That being said, the economic potential of an airplane is undeniably substantial. Once completed, an airplane's real estate is among the most valuable in the world. The revenue generated per square meter of an airplane is roughly six hundred times greater than that of the most expensive real estate in the United States. Therefore, the success or failure of one product within the aviation industry drastically affects not only the company that designs and manufactures it but also numerous other airline and flight-dependent companies worldwide.

## DREAM TEAM

Traditionally, a project of this scope is compartmentalized, undertaken in segments across teams that specialize in diverse disciplines. Boeing jetliners have been designed in the past in this way, and they have been successful; however, with the lofty goals of the 787 project came both the need and the desire to design a new process of collaboration and cross-team integration. The design team comprised designers, engineers, sales and marketing, differentiation, and manufacturing representatives, as well as partners and vendors. Representatives of these key areas would influence all areas of research, design, and development. For example, without precedence and with a seemingly counterintuitive logic, a designer would be responsible not only for design but also for providing solutions to marketing and sales obstacles, engineering issues, manufacturing challenges, and any other facet of the 787's development that might affect its final success. The same would apply to all other team members, regardless of their specialties or disciplines.

To ensure that all areas were represented in tandem, the team held meetings over a period of five years in addition to the daily collaborative process. These meetings were held every Thursday from 2001 to 2006, bringing the team together to forge new ideas, to perfect existing concepts, to discuss research findings, and to engage in philosophical discussions. In addition to weekly meetings, the co-location of the team afforded them daily interaction across disciplines as needed. The team also traveled together to aviation expositions across the globe to gain a group perspective of the industry's past, present, and future.

## INSPIRED DESIGN

The 787 Dreamliner was inspired by a preceding design: the Sonic Cruiser concept, unveiled by Boeing in 2001. This new transonic jetliner was designed to cruise at speeds 15 to 20 percent faster than any commercial aircraft currently on the market. However, the seismic economic global shifts after the terrorist attacks of September 11, 2001, halted the development of the Sonic Cruiser. The Boeing 7E7 (later christened the 787) represented a new concept based on fuel efficiency and low operating costs. In fact, the E in 7E7 stood for efficiency. It was clear from the outset that the commissioners of this airplane were expecting technological advancements that would make new efficiencies—from travel speed to interior travel comforts—possible.

Although it may seem like a very different starting point, the 7E7 benefited from the mental leap the industry had made in accepting the Sonic Cruiser. For one thing, it was clear that "just another airplane interior" would no longer be acceptable. An interior design as compelling, modern, and innovative as the exterior was required.

With this in mind, the creative forces at work began a new and inspired journey in the contrail of what was once the Sonic Cruiser.

## PRELIMINARY RESEARCH REVIEW

From the onset of the 787 Dreamliner project, team members were compelled to consider the passengers and their needs, and beyond them to address the needs and requirements of pilots, flight attendants, mechanics, modification engineers, leasing companies, and almost anyone who would come into regular contact with the new airplane. To ensure the 787 lived up to its moniker, A New Airplane for a New World, a new breed of research was required. What elements would passengers appreciate the most in a new airplane interior?

Prior to the debut of the Sonic Cruiser, a qualitative research method had been employed by Teague and Boeing across cultures to discover travelers' unexpressed desires around the flight experience. The researchers asked consumers to design their vision of an ideal travel experience and enumerate which elements of an aircraft interior would best allow for that experience. The findings from this research revealed, for instance, how the interior space should—and could—be modified to provide a welcoming point of entry for passengers boarding the airplane.

Gaining research momentum, Boeing launched the Passenger Experience Research Center (PERC) in 2002. Located adjacent to Boeing's Tour Center in Everett,

Washington, PERC was perfectly situated to receive a steady flow of the Tour Center's one hundred thousand annual visitors from around the globe. Empirical and qualitative research performed at PERC, which offered a scale model of the airplane's interior cabin, was designed by the Dreamliner team to test and rapidly iterate new ideas with the public in regard to passenger preference for cabin width, seat arrangement, adjacent empty seat alignment, stowage, and the like. This approach of testing full-scale designs generated rapid and invaluable insights and allowed, among other things, the team to validate reactions to various architectural features, such as larger windows.

Beyond the principal structural research, the Dreamliner team was compelled to further connect with passengers at a tactile level. That desire led to the initiation of a research program that looked at the ways in which passengers touched and interacted with an airplane. The team sought to make the operation of these interactive components, such as bin latches, more intuitive for a global, cross-cultural audience. The team focused on universal design as a theme in evaluating and developing design concepts[1] and ultimately proved that passengers prefer elegant, intuitive products that are as attractive as they are easy to use. In the past, details such as stow bin latches were typically designed or selected after the basic architecture was defined, leaving insufficient time for iteration and testing.

## RISING TO THE CHALLENGE

The Dreamliner team's goal was to produce a design that was excellent for the airlines and that would ultimately bring pleasure back into the flight experience for the passenger. With all 787 stakeholders, as well as the general consumer in mind, the design formula was expanded, cross-team integration was employed, seemingly unattainable goals were encouraged, and the design process began.

Using the passenger-focused research results as the backbone, in 2002 a three-month investigation began to search for ideas across three points of view: consumers, the airlines, and industrial/manufacturing concerns. Three teams managed by Teague representatives, each with five designers, were formed to represent each point of view. Each team was responsible for generating three individually distinct interior concepts. The consumer team, led by Rick Fraker, developed concepts around individual travelers, anticipating what their needs and wants would be. The airline team, guided by Ken Dowd, developed concepts centered on the requirements of airlines and their passengers. Finally, the industrial team, led by Craig Egenes, took on the manufacturing viewpoint, exploring technical solutions that offered manufacturing advantages.

Of the nine concepts presented, two were selected by the team as potential interior designs for the new 787. As these two were further developed, an additional subteam was commissioned to conceive a whole new design, again by focusing on the passenger experience. To gain a deeper understanding of the travel experience, this team logged many international travel miles. Eventually, the potential interiors were again narrowed down to two. At that point, Boeing narrowed its criteria for selection down to two premises: the extent to which the interior fulfilled the requirements from the qualitative research and whether or not the concept could realistically be turned into a constructible interior.

The Dreamliner team also sponsored multiple lean-design workshops to focus on the elimination of non-value-added details in both the process of development and in the design of the 787 itself. These workshops, often involving suppliers, were intended to radically change partner and manufacturing relationships and to develop efficient designs.

### THE 787 INTERIOR EXPERIENCE

As the Dreamliner team intended, the 787 interior is unlike any other. Combining research discoveries with an innovative design process, the team successfully achieved its initial goal to rejuvenate the spirit of travel. The outcome was both the interior "product" and a larger, reinvigorated flight experience in and of itself.

For the first time ever, the unarticulated needs of the flying public were embodied in the interior design. The unique research techniques employed in this effort formed a conscious differentiation strategy based on connecting the flying public to the emotional thrill of flying, recalling the magic we all experience during our first flight.

The all-composite aircraft features expansive inner architectures designed to elicit a "Wow" upon entry. By taking advantage of the large fuselage of the Dreamliner, Teague and Boeing were able to create a ceiling that sweeps dramatically upward (Figure 1);

in addition, the perceived height of this entryway was increased through the intelligent use of material layering and lighting (Figure 2). The entryway provides a contrast to the compressing feeling experienced in windowless jetways and connotes a welcoming sense to passengers.

As the passenger ventures further into the cabin, the open, welcoming theme is continued. Spaciousness is created in the Dreamliner in ways never before explored on an airplane. The patented LED lighting will allow the passenger to experience new levels of useable light, and the sky-colored ceiling continues to feel very light overhead, not heavy or compressing (Figure 3). This interplay between light and sculpted architec-

Figure 1. The Dreamliner's expansive inner architecture establishes the overall feel of spaciousness.

Figure 2. With the ability to replicate naturally occurring light patterns, the revolutionary LED lighting system eases passengers through their journey.

Figure 3. The interplay between lighting and sculpted architectural lines creates a feeling of spaciousness through the use of curves and light.

Figure 4. One of the most drastic design modifications, the 787 windows are 50 percent larger than those in other commercial airplanes. The shadeless electro-chromic windows can be darkened and lightened at the touch of a button.

tural lines began with the 777 design (which won an IDSA award) but was taken to new levels on the Dreamliner. The revolutionary LED light display also has the capacity to replicate day-to-night light patterns to ease passengers through their journeys.

The Dreamliner windows are another notable element of the Dreamliner design (Figure 4). The larger windows help connect people to the flying experience. In traditional airplanes, only the window-seated passenger is afforded a view. In the Dreamliner, which sports larger windows than any other current commercial airplane, all the passengers can see the sky. Moreover, the windows are electrochromic, dimming and brightening with a touch pad to control the amount of light entering the cabin. Because of this, they don't require shades. They are the only windows of their kind currently designed for commercial air travel.

The 787 is as desirable to potential buyers as it is to would-be travelers, with adjustable track seating, as well as modular color schemes that allow airlines to customize and brand the interiors. To bring the Dreamliner's innovative interior to life, Boeing opened a Customer Experience Center in late 2005. Built by and managed by Teague, the center was designed to facilitate an open dialogue between Boeing and potential airline customers, as well as to further establish the overall business case for a Boeing aircraft purchase. Providing compelling display mockups of the 787, 777, 737, and 747-8 as well as a customer-solutions studio that offers business solutions throughout the business cycle, from acquisition to operations and maintenance, the center is Boeing's ultimate business tool.[2]

Even better, the fuel-efficient 787 expends 20 percent less petroleum than similarly sized airplanes, while maintaining a speed comparable to that of today's fastest wide bodies.

## ALL THINGS CONSIDERED

While the team focused primarily on the inner architecture of the 787, they left no rock unturned in their mission to improve the flying experience. For the first time in history, the designers of the airplane interior had the opportunity to influence the design of the flight deck (Figure 5). The Dreamliner team worked closely with a group of pilots to determine the flight deck's design language. A series of focus groups were designed to better understand a pilot's emotional and psychological connection to the flight deck. In addition to sponsoring co-creation groups and benchmark studies, the team conducted research based on function and ergonomic flight requirements, as well as branding and identity. Finally, a design language based on research was built—dynamic, speaking of authority and control, and complete with iconic elements to match the overall form. For example, upon entry to the flight deck, the pilot experienced an arch suggestive of the door to the passenger cabin. The team also designed modern, ergonomically sound seats and adopted a color scheme that reflected the Dreamliner's new composite and titanium technology.

Figure 5. A new design language for the 787 flight deck improves the overall flying experience for the flight crew by exuding a sense of authority and control.

## A FUTURE PERFECT

To date, the launch of the 787 Dreamliner (Figure 6) is the most successful commercial airplane launch the world has ever witnessed. Since the launch of the 787 Dreamliner program, orders and commitments have been placed for more than four hundred airplanes from five continents. Firm orders for the 787 are valued at $59 billion at current list prices. The 787 is now in major assembly—slated to make its first flight in 2007, with certification, delivery, and entry into commercial service expected in 2008.[3]

Figure 6. Distinct exterior markings were developed exclusively for the Boeing 787 Dreamliner.

The creative alliance formed by Teague and Boeing effectively demonstrates the benefits of fully collaborative, open-source design processes. As they collaborated, Teague and Boeing reached out to experts from all areas of the globe. The goal was simple—to assemble a group of like-minded colleagues that through a collaborative process could create an enriched flying experience that honors the passenger and positions the 787 as the preferred cabin experience.

The design and successful launch of the 787 Dreamliner proves that a team of impassioned people united toward a common goal can achieve greatness.

### Endnotes

1. P. Guard, "Touchy Subject," *Aircraft Interiors International*, November 2005.

2. K. Spicer, "Customer Experience Center Helps Explain Why Boeing Is Best," *Boeing Frontiers*, March 2006.

3. The Boeing Company, 787 Dreamliner. August 20, 2006 (*http://boeing.com/commercial/ 787family/index.html*).

*Chapter 18*

# Designing for the Times

## by Joe Duffy and Eric Block

*The context for design is changing. Joe Duffy and Eric Block discuss how the erosion of trust, societal stratification, the age of information overload, "tuning out," and the democratization of design have shifted the ways in which people view brands, communications, and status. More significantly, they identify how businesses and design professionals can productively work together to respond to these new conditions.*

DESIGN FIRMS THAT assist clients in the context of branding and marketing are finding this a time of sea change. Recognizing and responding to the new lay of the land—in people's attitudes and behavior, in technology, and in broader trends in business and society—is critical if our discipline is to remain relevant, valuable, and sustainable. New thinking, new approaches, and greater collaboration with clients will make it possible for those clients to better understand and embrace the value of strategic design thinking.

In this chapter, we'll point out five significant trends shaping the lives of the audiences for the brands we are designing. We will also identify the implications of those trends for designers, and we'll discuss how we're addressing them every day in our own studio.

## TREND 1: THE EROSION OF TRUST

> "Consumers are making much more deliberate choices and being much
> more tough-minded about what they want. The investment question has to
> be: Are you generating heat? The companies that aren't . . . are in trouble."
> —**MICHAEL SILVERSTEIN**
> **BOSTON CONSULTING GROUP**

For the past several years, the World Economic Forum has been monitoring the level of public trust worldwide in various institutions—governmental, religious, and corporate. Public trust in national governments and the United Nations has declined significantly, and scandals at Enron and WorldCom, as well as a seemingly endless stream of head-lines about other corporate improprieties, have resulted in a level of trust in global com-panies that is at its lowest since the survey began. Unwelcome messages and broken promises add to the erosion of trust. As a result, a recent report by GFK/Roper[1] indicates that 81 percent of American consumers cite positive word of mouth as the most trusted source of information about what products to buy, far surpassing traditional communi-cation tools, such as media editorial coverage, advertising, or information on the Inter-net. (However, personalized electronic expressions, such as blogs and Web sites, might be considered another form of word of mouth.)

Brands are also vulnerable to the erosion of trust—which is ironic, because brands are meant to promote constancy and consistency and to evoke familial feelings. A great brand is a platform for innovation and forward thinking, but it also represents certain values and is meant to encourage a human connection. A strong brand looks, feels, acts, and is special. Human relationships rarely survive when one's counterpart can't be trusted; why would consumers' relationships with brands be any different?

Brands that no longer keep their promises can witness years of brand loyalty evapo-rating overnight. As designers, we must recognize the equities of the brands we work on

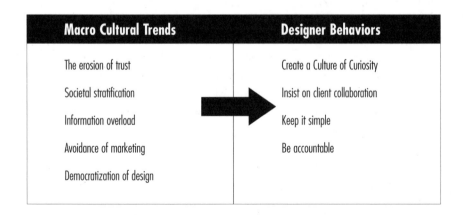

| Macro Cultural Trends | Designer Behaviors |
| --- | --- |
| The erosion of trust | Create a Culture of Curiosity |
| Societal stratification | Insist on client collaboration |
| Information overload | Keep it simple |
| Avoidance of marketing | Be accountable |
| Democratization of design | |

by thoughtfully considering which brand elements are critical to retain and which to eliminate as baggage. It's all designed to achieve the delicate balance of remaining fresh and relevant without losing the elements that have established a trusting relationship in the past.

## TREND 2: SOCIETAL STRATIFICATION

> "We are proud of those facts of American life that fit the pattern we thought, but somehow we are often ashamed of those equally important social facts which demonstrate the presence of social class. Consequently, we tend to deny them, or worse, denounce them and by doing so we tend to deny their existence and magically make them disappear from consciousness."
> —LLOYD W. WARNER, What Social Class Is In America

Marketers use the term mass brands to describe products that are designed to appeal to broad audiences. One could argue that in the future, there will be no such thing as a mass brand. This is an age of intense stratification in society: Baby Boomers, Gen Xers, and Millennials are described as separate age groups, each with vastly differing interests, tastes, and lifestyle needs reflected in their product purchases.

The growing population of audiences with varying ethnic backgrounds and the new wave of immigrants are also shifting the composition of society. Today, in America, 20 percent of the population possesses 84 percent of the wealth in our economy. Research has proven that social cohesion in our society is on the decline. One can only wonder how the fragmentation of media, as well as product choices, contributes to a dynamic in which people identify with close-knit communities of special interests rather than with broader concepts that might unite the nation. Once known as a melting pot, this country is demonstrating a resistance toward melting.

For designers, all this complexity makes the job of gaining insights into the appropriate brand audience more challenging. We can't be the students of just one culture; we need to research many sub-cultures and micro-cultures so that what we design is seen as relevant and accessible for whichever audience is intended.

## TREND 3: THE AGE OF INFORMATION OVERLOAD

As first chronicled in his landmark 1989 book, *Information Anxiety*, Richard Saul Wurman outlined the debilitating effects of too much data on modern lifestyles. Information overload and the stress it creates continue to grow with the proliferation of new media and the Internet. In a 2005 study by Hamermesh and Lee, "Stressed Out on Four Continents: Time Crunch or Yuppie Kvetch?,"[2] two professors of economics studied the causes of stress in four developed nations, Australia, Germany, Korea, and the United States. They learned that a greater demand on personal time comes with a greater abundance of goods that may be purchased; moreover, that stress is strongly correlated to a rise in personal income. So not only are people around the world overloaded with information, but the proliferation of product choices is itself a source of stress. The result is an increasingly intense desire for personal control and time management. The bestseller lists are crowded with self-help books, and there are dozens of periodicals meant to help people cope with too much choice and an overscheduled lifestyle.

For designers, this means the era of simplification is upon us. We must constantly balance the desire to introduce something new and different with the audience's ability to absorb it amid the cacophony of other things vying for their attention.

## TREND 4: TUNING OUT

Nowhere is the desire to avoid clutter more profound than in people's evolving relationship with advertising, marketing, and the media. As a result, all the traditional marketing communication tools are under siege. In its 2005 Marketing Receptivity Study, Yankel-

A Port for Creativity. The Sony Gallery in Shanghai, China, was designed to meet the high level of curiosity among Chinese consumers about all things new and Western. After ten months, the gallery welcomed its millionth visitor. Research indicated that more than 90 percent of visitors intended to visit again and would purchase Sony products in the future.

ovich Partners found that 54 percent of respondents agree they "resist being exposed to marketing and advertising," and 69 percent are interested in "products that help them block, skip, or opt out of being exposed to marketing." Indeed, 56 percent say they "avoid products that overwhelm them with marketing and advertising."[3]

Not coincidentally, the desire to avoid marketing is swiftly taking its toll on traditional media and the marketers that depend on it to spread their messages. McKinsey & Co. predicts that by the year 2010, television will experience a 23 percent decline in ads viewed due to switching off, a 9 percent loss of attention due to consumer multitasking, and a 37 percent decrease in message impact due to saturation.[4] Behaviors of next-generation consumers suggest even more radical shifts in media consumption thanks to TiVo and other digital video recorders, digital music and video players, satellite radio, DVDs, CDs, and other forms of information and entertainment not supported by advertising. The implications have left marketers scratching their heads. The national trade association of advertising agencies has gone so far as to hire a public relations firm to address their "image problem." How do you grow your brand when there is a shrinking audience for your message and many others have tuned it out completely?

## TREND 5: THE DEMOCRATIZATION OF DESIGN

> "How can you not see the power of design? Look around you: The evidence of design's power is everywhere. It's apparent in the mere fact that the bar has been raised. Customers expect, even demand, more from the design of everything they buy."
>
> —"MASTERS OF DESIGN," in Fast Company, June 2005

While each of the four trends have significant implications for designers, this fifth trend is the most profound. Simply stated, design matters to more people than ever before. As a result of pioneering brands like Apple, Nike, and Oxo, more people appreciate design's ability to enhance everyday life. Target's Design for All mantra has introduced designers and design sensibilities to the discount retail channel. Dozens of consumer magazines and hours of cable TV programming are devoted to design. People are increasingly able to choose the design that fits their own personal interests, passions, and lifestyles.

Many designers see the rise in the popularity of design as endangering the exclusivity of the craft. We believe this is akin to putting our collective heads in the sand; it's the exact opposite of the attitude that needs to be displayed by design leadership at this critical moment. At Duffy & Partners, we look at the rise in design's popularity as a good thing. Any trend that enhances the appreciation and interest in design needs to be embraced. As thought leaders at the center of a craft that is increasingly valued and substantive, our role must shift from practitioner only to practitioner, advocate, educator, and mentor. It is our responsibility to help people understand what design means and how to best use it for their own personal benefit. Design needs to hold a more important place in our culture.

Design that Sells Itself. Kimono Rose—a new fragrance collection from bath and beauty maker Thymes—quickly became the best-selling collection in the company's twenty-five-year history. Never supported with paid media advertising, Thymes uses the design itself as the major feature to attract attention to the product. Kimono Rose has been featured in People and other popular magazines, and the products were distributed to celebrities at last year's Academy Awards.

## FOUR SKILLS THAT ADDRESS THIS CHANGED WORLD

The trends just described are shaking the bedrock of convention about how modern commerce works. They buck more than one hundred years of attitudes toward branding and marketing. They also represent an incredible opportunity and responsibility for design firms and designers.

At Duffy & Partners, we are putting practices into place that address the trends. These practices—skills, really—are a key part of the process we embark on for every project. They are curiosity, collaboration, simplicity, and accountability.

### Skill #1: Create a Culture of Curiosity

> "Curiosity is the key to creativity."
> —AKIO MORITA, FOUNDER, SONY

Fostering a culture of curiosity is essential if a design firm wishes to remain relevant in the coming years. At Duffy & Partners, no design project is begun without a rigorous review of its context. Of course, this starts with a thorough understanding of the product category, the competition, the brand and its equities and iconography, any existing consumer research, and a synthesis of the business issues facing the client organization.

But it also includes healthy intellectual curiosity regarding what is most relevant to the audience for the project—curiosity about what is going on in their minds and lives that our design can help simplify, improve, or enrich.

The requirement for all our designers, young or old, is that they must be on the lookout for interesting developments taking place worldwide and across cultures—developments that can inform and inspire our thinking and our work.

### Skill #2: Insist on Client Collaboration

We find client collaboration to be crucial in both the strategic and the creative part of the design process. Design can be terribly subjective. Client collaboration, especially very early in the design process, is key to taking some of the subjectivity out of the equation.

Collaboration is also more critical than ever as marketers turn to design as a brand-building solution. Most traditionally schooled brand managers have little experience in evaluating, providing direction, or even in understanding design and the process behind it.

So how do you work with your clients to determine the most appropriate design solution for the brand? How do you collaborate to determine which design approach is right for the brand and its equities, its customers, and the client organization's core competency? Our response is to link strategy and design on a daily basis. Business and marketing strategy are just as critical to marketplace success as design creativity. Our strategists are experienced across all marketing disciplines. They collaborate with our clients to clearly understand what we need to accomplish for their business success, articulating "pictures of success" for the outcome of the design engagement. With this information, our designers explore different conceptual territories by designing visual collage boards—with color, typography, materials, icons, illustration, or photography—to evaluate a range of ways the brand's uniqueness can be communicated visually through design. At this stage, we insist the client be involved and contribute to the process in collaborative work sessions. We also get consumer input to determine what is being communicated, what expectations formed, what mood evoked, what works, and what doesn't. This consumer insight leads to refinement and a well-designed visualization of the strategic brief.

Then and only then do we start designing a product, package, identity, environment, or whatever the client needs to have created for the marketplace. And we use the original design collage board with our clients as a visual reference guide to evaluate the final design solution as it is being developed.

### Skill #3: Keep It Simple

We've already pointed to the epidemic of information overload and the desire to tune out unwelcome messages. As everything in the world seemingly gets more complex, we believe it is the responsibility of design to make things simpler. Simple in both the design solution and the process to get there. Simple in final expression. And, ideally, simple to execute, which increases the probability that the design will be successfully implemented in the marketplace.

Branding a Country. The brand identity for the Islands of the Bahamas needed to communicate its key point of difference from other Caribbean destinations—the understanding that the Bahamas are not one island but many, not one vacation experience but a myriad of choices. The identity and its brand language have driven an increase in visitors and in repeat visitors, as well as higher spending per visit.

Many client organizations are paralyzed with too much information. In this context, we must act as "reductionists" to distill the business problem and the subsequent design opportunity to its simplest articulation so that everyone key to the brand's success can understand and embrace what needs to be accomplished.

We also believe the audience for our design will continue to appreciate simplicity—expressed in respect for their intelligence, respect for their time, and respect for the role our designs will play in their lives.

Finally, we hold ourselves to a standard of keeping it simple within our studio. To trust our instincts and intuition. To use simplicity as a driver to achieve efficiency, so our time is utilized appropriately and focused on the work that matters. At the end of the day, we believe a culture that embraces simplicity is one that gets the freshest—and least adulterated—thinking and creativity, which in turn benefits our clients and their customers. We believe true creativity and innovation need not be at odds with simplicity.

## Skill #4: Be Accountable

In many ways, because of forces beyond our control, we are challenged to be more accountable for our creativity, our craft, and our decisions than ever before.

It is a natural outcome of the trends mentioned earlier. Corporate malfeasance has led to legislation dictating that corporate executives and their boards are accountable to their shareholders. Consumers are voting with their pocketbooks by avoiding marketers who add clutter to their lives. Marketers are turning away from traditional tactics and resources because they cannot directly link expenditures to proven returns on the investment. Once again, the design industry has the opportunity to behave differently. In this situation, "trust me, I'm the designer" will not cut it.

Our answer is to work closely with our clients to establish parameters of success and the methodology to measure it. Although each situation is unique and the process differs from project to project, we want to ensure that our clients understand that business results are what matter most and our desire is always to design for success in the marketplace, as well as for beauty.

With many clients, we've been able to develop contractual agreements that reward us for success in the marketplace—most often in the form of compensation based on sales performance; sometimes we are even offered an ownership position in the client company. While these arrangements are not always feasible, the idea behind them needs to find its way into any compensation approach involving our creativity. We like to be held accountable—to directly link our contributions to the business outcome. And true accountability transcends client work; it also means that we evaluate our work on its ability to hold up over time and on its impact on society, as well as the environment.

We think accountability is a strategy the industry should continue to elevate, because over time it will increase trust in our discipline and enhance the integrity of our client relationships.

## NEW IDEAS FOR A NEW AGE

Design is a wonderful thing. It can cut through the chaos and clutter of everyday life. It can communicate an impression about a brand in a fraction of a second—on the shelf, on the Web, on the showroom floor. It can be happily welcomed into the audience's home even if it's not blasted onto their TV or computer screens. It quite literally enhances people's everyday lives.

The key in this changing world is to never stop learning and to continually take stock of the importance of our work for our clients, their customers, the cultural stage, and society. Let's raise the intensity of the dialogue about how our industry can continue to evolve. Let's ensure that design remains part of the fabric of a vital society—something that unites us, not just the next new thing.

It is our collective responsibility to treat the importance of design with professionalism, enthusiasm, and confidence. We must always challenge ourselves to find new ways of thinking and working so that the craft is always rewarded for its contributions.

## Endnotes

1. Global Word of Mouth study, GFK Roper Consulting, June 20, 2006 (*www.gfkamaerica.com/ news/ WOMSpreadsAcrosstheGlobe.htm*).

2. D. Hamermesh and J. Lee, "Stressed Out on Four Continents: Time Crunch or Yuppie Kvetch?," discussion paper no. 1815, October 2005, The Institute for the Study of Labor (IZA), Bonn, Germany (*http://ssm.com/abstract=840748*).

3. 2005 Marketing Receptivity Study, Yankelovich Partners Inc., Topline Report, April 18, 2005 (*www.yankelovich.com*).

4. "McKinsey Study Predicts Continuing Decline in TV Selling Power," *Advertising Age*, August 6, 2006.

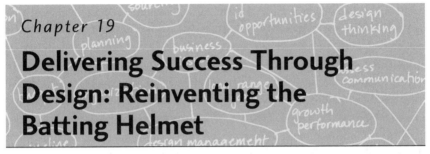

## Chapter 19
# Delivering Success Through Design: Reinventing the Batting Helmet

by Dave Franchino

*Sometimes collaboration is the key to a fresh and compelling approach to an old challenge. Dave Franchino narrates how Design Concepts helped develop an innovative youth batting helmet that has a distinctive profile, is easily adjustable, provides the best possible protection, and looks cool. Re-entering the market in 2002, Wilson Sporting Goods sold 200,000 helmets the first year and, in three years, saw its category share grow from zero to an impressive 30 percent.*

IF YOU'VE PLAYED or watched Little League baseball over the past couple of decades, you're all too familiar with the bucket helmet. It was the oversized, generic plastic helmet that every batter was required to wear—the helmet that didn't seem to fit anyone quite right. Too big, too clumsy, it blocked kids' vision and slipped off their heads. And safety? Safety was a myth. It was obvious that the helmet offered little or no protection. Where style was concerned, the word bucket said it all. We've all worn it or watched someone else wear it. At Design Concepts, Inc., our challenge was to redesign it.

Our client, Wilson Sporting Goods, approached our design firm to bring new creativity and insights to the youth batting helmet. The Wilson team came armed with a tremendous passion for their products and a keen ability to forecast trends.

## THE TIMES THEY ARE A-CHANGING

Today, there's a helmet for almost everything. Hugo Martin of the *Los Angeles Times* calls our enthusiastic acceptance of protective headgear "the helmetization of America."[1] Now more than ever, consumers are willing to buy equipment to protect themselves and their children against injuries. With baseball and softball near the top of the injury list, that seems wise. According to the U.S. Consumer Product Safety Commission, baseball is one of the five sports categories with the highest number of head injuries. And, as Martin points out, experts are stressing the need for good design in creating helmets that offer effective protection.

The days of kids grabbing a generic team helmet out of the ubiquitous equipment bag are coming to an end. Wilson Sporting Goods saw the movement in the marketplace toward families outfitting their own kids with safe, reliable products for both team and individual sports. From bike helmets to baseball bats, from soccer balls to hockey sticks, families were buying more and more of their kids' sports equipment. With this trend in mind, Wilson Sporting Goods executives saw the opportunity to design a new youth batting helmet.

The Wilson team defined style as the single most important element for entrance into the market. They theorized that design would be the most compelling factor for helmet sales. If it didn't look cool, kids wouldn't want it. It was time for the humble helmet to get a dramatic facelift.

Wilson's intuition proved to be spot on. More and more products and product categories that previously competed only on the basis of price, specifications, brand name, or distribution are finding themselves competing in completely new areas. Today, these products have to try to win at every stage of the user experience, which comprises the full range of customer emotions through the cycle of evaluation, acquisition, actual use, reflection, and eventual disposal.

Even manufacturers of such highly specialized products as medical devices find that their end users have grown accustomed to an array of choices and now demand exact attention to the customer experience. And a generation raised in the context of iPods, hip-hop, and MySpace can have excruciatingly sophisticated expectations for its safety products.

The desire to make a product look cool is, of course, nothing new. What is new, however, is applying cool to a dazzlingly broad range of products previously considered too mundane or pedestrian to warrant this effort. And increasingly, companies that shepherd these "mundane" and "pedestrian" products are recognizing that attention to the user experience can be a powerful strategic weapon against their competition.

In the absence of other, more-quantifiable data, consumers—parents and children alike—will infer a host of other attributes based on the visual appearance of a product. Does it look modern and therefore state-of-the art? Does it look safe? Does it look cool? Indeed, cool becomes the price of entry into many previously staid product lines.

While some companies find the increasingly relentless churn of style-sensitive products frustrating and long for the days of product-line stability, Wilson chose to embrace cool as an opportunity to create a meaningful strategic difference.

## GREAT EXPECTATIONS

With this as the backdrop, Wilson Sporting Goods outlined three mandates for the new helmet: great look, great fit, and great performance.

In order to infuse new perspectives into their products—to see things from a different creative vantage point—Wilson Sporting Goods hired Design Concepts' industrial design team to raise the bar and develop concepts for an exceptional product.

The decision for a well-known brand to partner with consultants in the process of design innovation can be an emotional step for many companies, but in many aspects it represents a logical continuation of the trend toward multi-organizational, multi-country collaboration. Indeed, while not to downplay the upheaval outsourced, offshore manufacturing has created, most firms now realize that actively embracing strategic partnerships and specialized collaboration actually creates more opportunity, better execution, and consequently more corporate security. Extending this philosophy to partnerships with firms that can help with innovation may seem like ceding control of your core business, but Wilson, like many other progressive firms, sees it differently. An outside innovation firm can bring a fresh perspective to solving problems, combining internal experience and market savvy with an external focus on trends, styles, manufacturing techniques, material advances, and so on. With this in mind, it becomes less a question of, "Should we partner with someone?" than of, "How can we leverage key partnerships more effectively than our competition does?"

Consequently, the firms that are the most successful are those best able to manage their strategic design partnerships—efficiently managing roles and responsibilities and combining the best capabilities of both organizations.

### Understanding The Playing Field

The Design Concepts team began by doing contextual research on the product. A clear understanding of the basics of the youth baseball industry laid the foundation for creative work. Learning more about the current state of youth baseball also raised questions and challenges that the new design needed to address.

### Great Look

Baseball, of course, is America's national pastime. It's a sport steeped in tradition. Understanding this, our industrial designers wondered how far from tradition consumers were willing to stray. Would parents embrace a new look if it were radically different from the design they grew up wearing? Would kids respond to a helmet unlike those they see worn by professional players?

The challenges were many. The new product would need to meet a lengthy list of requirements—the first of which was that the helmet needed to be something kids would actually wear, something they would want to own. Design Concepts and Wilson Sporting Goods agreed: Design was essential in connecting with both kids and parents.

Donald Norman, author of *Emotional Design: Why We Love (Or Hate) Everyday Things*, speaks to the idea of compelling design—design that strikes an emotional chord, design that motivates, connects, and generates product loyalty and success. In his book, Norman asks, "Can beauty and brains, pleasure and usability, go hand in hand?" That was the challenge for our designers.

And how do kids define cool?

Wilson and the Design Concepts team of researchers and designers watched and interviewed kids playing baseball and softball to find out how they wore the helmets and what they wanted in a better design. After creating nearly one hundred initial concept ideas, the team went back to the players armed with sketches and ready to learn more about what kids and parents needed in a new helmet. In fact, Wilson and Design Concepts went back to youth baseball games throughout the process to watch, listen, and gain valuable feedback clarifying everyone's comfort level with a break from tradition.

To add one more challenge to the design picture, the opinions and ideas of both boys and girls needed to be equally understood and represented. With boys and girls playing team sports, the styling needed to be compelling to baseball-loving kids regardless of gender.

In the end, our research confirmed what we knew. Kids want to wear what's in, what's cool. And change? Kids were more than ready for a change in style. They wanted something different, something exciting. Kids get it: Change is good.

### Great Fit

Wilson's expectation of a great fit was based on the idea that the helmet should fit every child well. In the past, helmet designs relied on compressed foam, which gave a loose fit or one that was much too tight. The new helmet needed to be truly adjustable to accommodate a good fit for every child—the elusive dream of one-size-fits-most.

In addition to tremendous conceptual challenges, the idea posed ergonomic issues. The helmet needed to be one general size and shape but fit children of every shape and size. The element used to adjust the size needed to be easy to use and easy to reach from the perspective of a child wearing and adjusting the helmet. It also needed to be adjustable by a parent or coach who might adjust the helmet while standing behind the child.

The helmet also needed to provide a comfortable fit that would get the child through this season and beyond. It needed to grow with the quickly changing sizes of young kids. The possibility that it could be worn for several seasons, possibly even worn by another child in the family, was even more attractive. Adjustability was a key factor for teams, as well, offering the opportunity for the helmet to be shared among players as needed. One-size adjustability was, however important, a lofty goal.

To solve several of these challenges, the helmet was designed with a simple adjustment feature—a velcro strap. Located on the back of the helmet, the strap was connected by cords to dual density foam padding inside the helmet. The strap was located at the back of the helmet to ensure that it would be worn securely and comfortably for the optimum fit and would be accessible for either an adult helping a child or a child putting on his/her own helmet. In addition, the location of the velcro strap made certain that the adjustment feature would not interfere with the way in which the ball might deflect off the helmet.

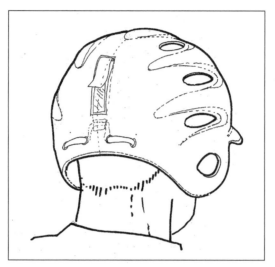

Concept sketches of the back of the Wilson helmet.

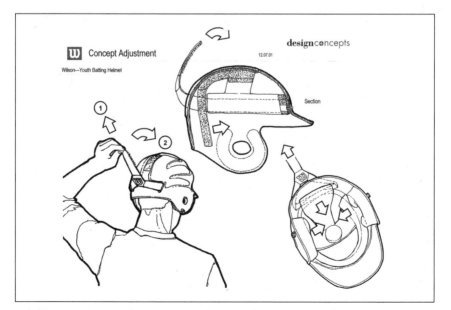

Refined concept sketches of the adjustability feature of the youth batting helmet.
Photo: Wilson Sporting Goods

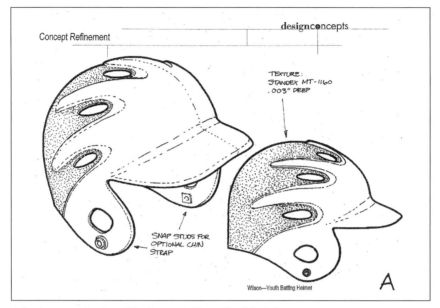

Refined concept sketches of the front and side profile of the helmet.

## Great Performance

While kids choose helmets based on design and style, parents use other criteria. Parents, who make the final purchasing decision, buy sporting goods products for their children based on safety and reliability, not to mention price. These factors were essential considerations when designing for the performance of the helmet.

To meet the need for a great fit, and thereby superior performance, the padding in the helmet was made of thick, comfortable foam. The lightweight foam absorbs energy and impact better than previous helmet designs and allows for a comfortable fit.

In the past, poorly fitting helmets could not provide maximum protection because they weren't used effectively and weren't fitting properly. The new helmet's easy-to-use adjustability feature made for a better fit that could provide greater protection. A more comfortable and effective fit combined with a greater sense of style improved the likelihood that the helmet would be worn correctly—the most important safety consideration.

Wilson Sporting Goods and its manufacturer ensured that the new helmet met the rigorous National Operating Committee on Standards for Athletic Equipment (NOC-SAE) standards for safety.

## GUERRILLA MARKETING

The final design submitted to Wilson Sporting Goods brought it all together, giving texture, color, and a modern, clean style to the helmet. The novel design was granted five patents. The product launched in 2002 with ten rich and saturated color choices.

Geometrically shaped perforations and vents, smooth and rough textured surfaces, and sturdy visors added to the helmet's sleek and attractive appearance.

Wilson went for dramatically high exposure, using marketing strategies designed for tremendous visibility to a national and international audience. To aggressively re-enter the market (from which they had been absent for roughly six years), they positioned themselves to make a huge splash in a huge pond.

The company offered to outfit each of the twenty kids on any of the sixteen teams participating in the 2003 Little League World Series. Fifteen of the teams—meaning three hundred players—wore the helmet during the Series. Broadcast on ESPN, with the finals televised nationally on the ABC network, the helmet caught the attention of kids and parents across the country. Monday morning after the first broadcast featuring kids wearing the helmet, Wilson's corporate headquarters received nearly 250 phone calls asking where the helmet could be purchased. As forecasted, the strong sense of design and the dramatic departure from the traditional bucket helmet appealed to kids' sense of style. The informal verdict was in: It was cool.

## IF YOU BUILD IT, THEY WILL COME

With product placement encouraging interest, and strong distribution channels at retailers, from big box to mom and pop, securely in place, Wilson was effectively poised to re-enter the marketplace. The company conservatively projected sales of the new helmet to reach a respectable 10,000 units within the first year. Remarkably, actual sales reached a staggering 200,000 units in the helmet's first year on the shelf. Within three years of re-entering the youth batting helmet market, the company's market share rose from 0 to 30 percent, selling approximately 750,000 helmets.

Young baseball player wearing the Wilson youth batting helmet designed by Design Concepts, Inc. Photo: Wilson Sporting Goods

The Wilson youth batting helmet in action. Photo: Wilson Sporting Goods

Today, youth batting helmets have grown to be the third-largest selling category in the baseball division of Wilson Sporting Goods. More than one hundred color combinations have been added to the line, continuing to make the helmet exciting to kids. Indeed, many new helmet products have been introduced, including a college helmet, a women's fast-pitch helmet, a catcher's helmet, and even a next-generation youth batting helmet. As of 2006, the entire batting helmet segment—80 percent of which is designed for kids—has grown to a $30 to $40 million market.

The success of the helmet sparked interest from retailers and consumers in other Wilson products and brought increased attention to the company's entire line of sporting goods. The company can now boast of its ability to outfit a player from head to toe. Most important, the reputation of the company for producing cutting-edge products with a contemporary, trend-setting style has been etched in the minds of consumers.

## CONCLUSION

By identifying design as a key differentiating business strategy, Wilson Sporting Goods committed itself and Design Concepts to infuse innovative thinking into every aspect of the helmet. With several design challenges, but few corporate constraints, Wilson utilized the full power of design. As Roger Martin, dean of the Rotman School of Management, asserts in *BusinessWeek Online*, "To get the full benefit of design, companies have to embed design into—not append it onto—their business."[2] Wilson fully committed to embedding creativity into this product.

The success of the youth batting helmet underscores the importance of design as a critical, differentiating business strategy. Wilson Sporting Goods' ability to embrace this important factor and combine it with consumer trend forecasting led to true market leadership. Wilson has retooled its philosophy toward innovation, and design is now a key factor in the development of new products. In the words of a company executive, design is the "driving force" behind new product development and in the invigoration of the existing product lines. In light of the youth batting helmet's success, design now influences strategic decisions from the outset of the process rather than serving as icing on the cake in the final stages of development.

### Suggested Reading

Martin, Roger L. "Designing Decisions," an interview with Doug Look for *Perspectives*, Illinois Institute of Technology's Institute of Design, May 17, 2006.

Norman, Donald A. *Emotional Design: Why We Love (or Hate) Everyday Things* (New York: Basic Books, 2004).

U.S. Consumer Product Safety Commission, "Gear Up, Strap It On—Helmets Can Save Lives and Reduce Injuries." March 29, 2006.

### *Endnotes*

1. Hugo Martin, "Today, Helmets for All," *Los Angeles Times*, July 24, 2005, p. 38.

2. Roger L. Martin, "Creativity That Goes Deep," *BusinessWeek Online*, August 3, 2005.

# Chapter 20

# How We Developed "Communicating Caterpillar: One Voice"

By Bonnie Briggs

*For Caterpillar, corporate voice requires wisdom, not rules. Recently the global company decentralized, and each unit, in the face of growing competition, has tried very carefully to define its mission and its products. As Bonnie Briggs explains, this complex situation has led to a strategy where, while there are certain uniform, corporate-wide identity standards, many critical communications elements are developed by individuals trained in understanding Caterpillar's voice generally rather than knowing how to look specifics up in a catalogue of design guidelines.*

THE DILEMMA FOR Caterpillar—the nearly seventy-five-year-old manufacturer of earth-moving equipment and diesel engines—wasn't that it was the first multinational challenged to reinvent itself in the face of intensifying global competition. Nor was it the first to decentralize, modernize, and grant individual business units unprecedented autonomy and responsibility. But Caterpillar does appear to be one of the few multinational enterprises to use corporate communications strategically to help accomplish the change.

On the face of it, Caterpillar would seem to be impervious to the kinds of competitive challenges that came its way starting in the 1980s. The Peoria, Illinois-based giant is a global competitor, after all. It has manufacturing facilities in twelve countries, marketing headquarters in seven, distribution facilities in thirteen, and independently owned dealerships in 128. The company employs more than 52,000 people worldwide, with

1994 sales of over $14.3 billion—and is the third largest exporter of industrial goods, as a percentage of sales, in the United States.

The global economic slump and events of the eighties shook the foundation of the organization and left a rapidly changing business environment in which the only certainty was change itself. Customers, fighting to survive, focused more and more on the equipment purchase price and examined every purchase with excruciating detail. Many felt they could no longer purchase Caterpillar® products on name alone. Struggling traditional competitors went out of business and emerging foreign competitors fought to expand their markets to remain in business, closing the gap which previously existed in product differentiation. This made the messages that Caterpillar and our competitors were communicating about the viability of our business, future plans, and the features and benefits of our products increasingly important.

Caterpillar also faced a host of other challenges that existing structures could not help it meet: we needed a way to compete in industries with well-established leaders and to take advantage of emerging opportunities; we needed focused resources for increasingly important businesses; and we needed a way to become more responsive and faster to market, which the marketplace was demanding. After seven decades of dominance in the construction industry, Caterpillar was challenged to operate successfully in expanding, fast-changing markets and to communicate coherently as it decentralized and diversified.

Beginning in 1987 Caterpillar embarked on a top-level strategic planning process and a six-year, $1.8 billion factory modernization designed to enhance production flexibility—enabling higher quality/lower cost manufacturing—and to shorten production time. In 1990 the company decentralized into profit centers and service centers—a move designed to shorten time to market, improve product quality and customer responsiveness, and bolster bottom-line accountability.

The "status quo" thought process became unacceptable. As Caterpillar repositioned itself for the future, employees saw the nature of their jobs change dramatically. The reorganization of 1990 had stripped away a familiar but outdated hierarchy of accountability, decision-making, product development, and communication.

While a leaner, more focused Caterpillar was delivering more and better products in less time, its business units were producing millions of dollars worth of videos, manuals, and brochures. Many were quite good individually. But since they were being done individually, duplication of effort was inevitable. Sometimes these messages competed with each other, and—hardly surprising—lacked coordination.

In 1990, the company installed a new corporate identity program, but that program did not deal with our most pressing communications issues.

Logo placement recommendations and color guidelines were not enough to coordinate communicators' efforts—nor were they intended to provide the core content and messages needed to clarify the company's central promise to its various audiences.

In the fall of 1992, working with an international communications consulting firm, we looked at everything that we were currently producing, along with much of what we had produced in the past. The consultants asked to be put on a dealer mailing list and learned firsthand the direction in which our marketing communications were going.

It became clear that the long-term consequences of failing to coordinate communications could be serious.

Business units had begun to create their own identities. At a time when dealers demanded more timely and effective sales materials, we were inadvertently making it more difficult for dealers to find the information they needed to sell product. And we were concerned that the Caterpillar and Cat identities were becoming fragmented and diluted.

Finding a solution called for a back-to-basics examination of the fundamentals. We needed to reconcile what Caterpillar was becoming with what we had been and to better understand how our corporate personality had evolved. We needed to define what set Caterpillar apart from the competition—as well as to agree on and validate the core ideas that link all parts of the company. And we needed to position ourselves to communicate who we are now to all audiences while looking confidently toward the future. We needed to capture and define that sense of oneness, culture, valuable history, and "voice,"[1] . . . before it was lost.

## DEFINITION OF THE NEW CORPORATE VOICE

The process began by defining the principal elements of Caterpillar's voice. First, the team considered the company's personality—a composite of qualities, some evolving, some unchanged since the beginning, which are the company's foundation. Discussing, refining, and agreeing on Caterpillar's evolving personality helped to eliminate confusion about the company's character. It also helped us understand and honor the qualities that are Caterpillar's heritage . . . which are important to retain.

The next task was to develop a communications positioning statement. It had to express the company's distinctive character and personality, and communicate our promise to our various audiences. Before doing anything else, the team gathered the views of key managers, dealers, and staff. Then a statement was hammered out which clearly expresses what Caterpillar is and does:

> Caterpillar enables the world's planners and builders to turn their ideas into realities. We are proud of our ability to create and support the best equipment and engines on earth. It's not only what we make that makes us proud—it's what we make possible.

This statement was not designed to hang on awall, but to reflect the way Caterpillar people work and the way we act toward customers and each other. And, last but not least, to influence what we say and how we say it.

If the voice concept was to become more than shelfware, there had to be general agreement on its core ideas. We thought that the best way to secure that agreement would be to make the concept real. We chose to prototype or "model" the voice concept using a representative cross-section of employee and dealer/customer materials. This exercise provided a tangible, powerful glimpse into what our voice could be.

Even after we secured executive management approval, however, the communications team recognized that the concept of a unified communications strategy might be misinterpreted as a return to centralized control. And we didn't want a top-down imposed solution, since that would clearly counter the ideas that drove decentralization. The new spirit required that each of the company's business units be persuaded to embrace a single, unified strategy.

Over the next six months, we set about presenting our case, building consensus among managers, employees, and dealers throughout the organization. Groups began to embrace the findings and recommendations to "own" them, and as owners, were committed enough to help strengthen them.

| Category: | Includes: | Examples: | Customer Benefits: | Process Defined as: |
|---|---|---|---|---|
| **Uniform** | Voice<br>Structure<br>Content | Product markings, signs, packaging, vehicles, P.R., stationery, institutional advertising, etc. | Stockholders are assured that the value of both the Cat and Caterpillar names are maintained. | "Uniform" follows corporate guidelines and procedures for form and content. |
| **Shared/Related** | Voice<br>Structure | Training materials, recruiting materials, product information, Specalogs, etc. | Audience understands type and purpose of communications because of consistent look/format. | "Consistent" format or "library" of materials. Ideal applications for electronic publishing and regional production. |
| **Singular** | Voice | Advertisements and promotion materials that are market-specific, facility communications, local promo materials, etc. | Caterpillar image and promise consistent with audience expectation: Positioning, values and competencies reinforced. | "Interpretative"…dependent upon professional guidance of agency or professional internal skills to understand and apply voice. |

Figure 1. Continuity categories for Caterpillar communications efforts.

## FIELD TEST FOR USABILITY

A series of field-test projects were chosen based on their applicability for other units. One example is the Aggregates Pilot Project, which focused on an industry that mines and crushes rock for paving and roofing materials.

It was an ideal opportunity to document the process of developing market-focused communications for a global industry while demonstrating the voice concepts. The project produced a market-focused communications strategy and materials but, more importantly, created a methodology for subsequent communications efforts in other markets.

There were a number of significant findings. An analysis of the life-cycle of communications needs, from an audience point of view, determined the minimum level of communications required to maintain a basic presence in a chosen market. Another study tracked how documents are used. We discovered that many documents are shared across many markets and could benefit from some level of continuity. Some communication materials are entirely unique to a particular market or audience and don't require coordination with other materials. That led to the identification of three distinct categories of communication: uniform, shared, and singular. Each category carries a different level of responsibility, on the communicator's part, to build in continuity—or said another way, to reflect Caterpillar's voice.

▲ The Uniform category is the easiest to recognize, since all creative and production decisions have already been made. It covers stationery, business cards, forms, packaging, product marking, signs, etc. Comprehensive identity guidelines exist to make design and production of these items simple, efficient, and uniform.

▲ The Shared materials category uses market research and audience testing to promote voluntary standardization of shared communications in our decentralized organization. We structure and design documents that are used across all markets in a consistent way, making it possible to use them in combination.

▲ The Singular category offers the greatest amount of leeway and challenge for communicators. Voice provides the only continuity tool for guidance on content and creative decisions for ads, trade shows, facility or market brochures, and other individual efforts for these pieces. However, voice offers no rules and again, participation is voluntary. The concept of voice relies heavily on good analysis and the ability to make the right choices.

## COMPANY-WIDE IMPLEMENTATION

By the end of 1993, there were strong pockets of support for the Corporate Voice program, mostly by the people who were involved in pilot studies or interviews. But many other employees had no idea that any of this was happening. The next step—perhaps the most difficult—was to help people understand how to use it. Drawing on pilot project experience that had been codified for information purposes, we began to document all that we had learned—with an eye toward implementation.

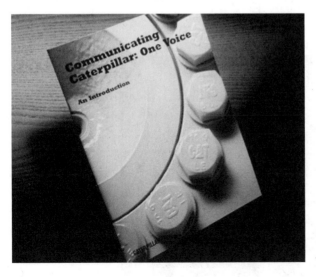

Figure 2. The brochure "Communicating Caterpillar: One Voice."

Our communications team developed a brochure entitled "Communicating Caterpillar: One Voice," to introduce employees to Caterpillar's values, competencies, attributes, and positioning. But we were afraid that by itself the brochure might be too easily dismissed.

When we polled employees, they strongly advised that the brochure should be distributed only after attending an orientation program or training session. After eighteen months of development work, there was still a risk that the entire effort could be dismissed as just another program—with a beginning and an end. We had nagging concerns that the term "voice" could be viewed negatively if perceived as controlling rather than enabling. And we had continuing concerns that the momentum could fade if interest and participation faded. Developing Caterpillar's voice was only the beginning— the concepts had to work. Again, going back to the original challenge, each step in the implementation process required acceptance by the people who had to use it. A voice training program seemed pivotal in the success or failure of the strategy.

Given the importance of training, the team was very sensitive to anything "off-the-shelf." The course had to be developed from a blank sheet of paper and specifically for Caterpillar. The course developers were inspired by training approaches that concentrated on "hands on" rather than lecture or "show and tell." While we knew the limitations on peoples' time, we also knew we couldn't deliver an effective training message in anything less than twelve hours. What evolved was a building-block approach to establishing the elements of Caterpillar's voice. People learned how to recognize it and analyze it through a series of demonstrations and exercises. We focused on teaching voice concepts, not communications skills—and we opened up the course to all those who plan, direct, or influence Caterpillar communications.

We learned from each session and improved the next one based on attendees' suggestions. Early in the program we were asked what other companies were doing to address communication and identity issues. We responded by inviting guest speakers from other companies to discuss the evolution of their companies' personalities.

Figure 3. Caterpillar's recruiting brochure illustrates design flexibility within "voice."

Figure 4. One business unit's holiday greeting to employees exemplifies flexibility in content and subject matter (Wheel Loader and Excavator Division).

Figure 5. Caterpillar employee benefits material offers well-written, well-organized, "accessible" information.

Figure 6. Gregory Poole Co.'s capabilities brochure builds on competencies and attributes similar to Caterpillar's.

Figure 7. The concepts of voice challenge a footwear licensee to tie into the "iron" in their communications and packaging.

Figures 8, 9. "Shared" communications use master formats and guidelines. Electronic templates facilitate worldwide production, language modifications, and consistency.

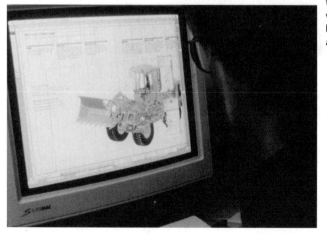

A segment of the workshop was devoted to corporate identity. It was important to distinguish between corporate identity—which was still based on a set of guidelines and standards with mandatory compliance—and voice, which gives people a set of tools or criteria through which they can make their own decisions. Both programs contribute to building the brand.

We're learning that real understanding occurs once people have a chance to work with the concepts. The workshop makes the concepts relevant and gives everyone a chance to problem-solve with a new set of "tools." The teamwork, and interdisciplinary participation, provides a perspective that is an important part of the training process. And because the course deals with fundamental corporate values and competencies, most attendees leave the workshop with an enlightened view of the company—and with a clearer understanding of how their communications can play a role in helping Caterpillar be successful.

During 1994 we saw the influence of Caterpillar's voice through many communications decisions and plans. Examples ranged from completely revised benefits and recruiting materials to a "workwear" clothing line that is packaged and displayed to reflect our in-the-iron prime products. Annual reports, brochures, and newsletters have changed tone, content, and style. Our Wheel Loader/Excavator Division applied the communication concepts to a range of media, from videotapes to coffee cups to holiday greeting cards. They even considered their lobby as a way to communicate Caterpillar's voice and accomplished it through giant machine photo murals and furniture with an industrial look. The transformation influenced other facilities to also look at their environment as a communications opportunity. Shared formats are improving the quality and timeliness of our product specification brochures and dealer sales support/training materials—and production efficiencies are delivering annual cost savings. Changes are taking place in Aurora, Geneva, Minneapolis, Peoria, San Diego, Sao Paulo, and Singapore.

A corporate advertising campaign is also playing a significant role in expressing Caterpillar's personality. Voice concepts guide how ads are developed and help determine message content. Our agencies are working with clearly defined strategies, enabling them to more accurately tell the Caterpillar story, consistent with the kind of company we are—truly reflecting the character of this company rather than "creating" an image.

Reflecting on the Caterpillar communications strategy, it is only fair to conclude that it's been an interactive learning process, taking a long-term view on all levels. The methods used to implement voice are working in conjunction with other communications initiatives and a strong overall corporate commitment to improve communications worldwide. Understanding that we're really just beginning our journey, we accept our communications challenges and continue to strive for incremental improvements. And even though we haven't "arrived" at our destination yet, we are confident that the path we're on is right for Caterpillar.

## SUMMARY

When Caterpillar reorganized several years ago, employees were empowered to solidify the company's leading position as a global competitor. They used that power to help the company respond quickly and effectively to a changing world economy and marketplace. But decentralization also changed the way the company communicated. Communications sometimes didn't reflect Caterpillar's personality or positioning in a clear and consistent way. That is why Caterpillar pursued the Corporate Voice Process—to educate employees so they would be able to express the company's personality and positioning in words and images that create a distinctive "voice" of Caterpillar.

> "Now, whenever this company expresses itself, it's in a single powerful voice—a voice that tells our employees, customers, dealers and shareholders what to expect, a voice that is unmistakably Caterpillar."
> —DON V. FITES, CEO, CATERPILLAR INC.

## *Endnote*

1. "Voice" is a term coined by Siegel and Gale to represent a corporation's unique personality.

*Chapter 21*

# Navigating a Sea Change

by Lauralee Alben

*Using the profound movements of ocean waters as an analogy, Laura-
lee Alben has devised a comprehensive analysis that helps organizations navigate major transformations—sometimes through uncharted
territory. The many elements of her methodology probe the context,
as well as the nature and breadth, of change and exploit design as an
essential vehicle for conveying new ideas and perceptions.*

WHAT DOES THE design discipline have to do with human rights in Uzbekistan, anthrax, or September 11th? Or tax-law reform in Australia? Or culture change in Procter
& Gamble? A few years ago, I would have said, "Not much." But by thinking deeply about
my professional experience and working hard on creating a new consulting model,
called Sea Change, I've had a chance to apply myself to these issues, and I've begun to
say out loud what I've always felt: Design sensibility and techniques are uniquely suited
to help us grapple with the diverse challenges of our modern condition—alienation
combined, paradoxically, with increasing interdependence; economic and political uncertainty; the development of new technologies at a blistering pace; and environmental
degradation. Complementing the traditional approaches employed in strategic thinking—numbers and words—design can bring new perspectives and ideas. No interpretation is necessary, no statistical analysis or complex reports required to experience the
insights that design can provide.

It's easy to think of design as creating a Web site for the Monterey Bay Aquarium, or architecting customizable appearances that give people computing freedom, or providing a new brand for the Mac OS—all projects I've been involved with. But working on Sea Change has taken me (and my colleagues in the Sea Change Consortium) into uncharted waters, where we find our skills tested and expanded and where we have had the stimulating opportunity to apply our expertise to critical issues usually seen as well outside the purview of traditional design. And if someone asks, "Hey, what's a nice discipline like you doing in a place like this?" we can now confidently answer, "A whole lot."

## DESIGNING FOR SEA CHANGE

Through magnificent ocean swells, forces are constantly at work shaping and changing the planet. Just as the ocean creates profound effects upon the land, so too, does design affect our lives. The real opportunity is to design for sea change—marked transformation both rich and surprising. This is the intent of the Sea Change Design Process,[1] a contextual, relationship-based approach to solving challenges in an integrated fashion.

Using proprietary techniques, Sea Change provides insightful ways to help organizations meet today's challenges by creating profound and sustainable change, congruent with their deepest values. It can be applied to a wide range of activities, from envisioning culture change and strategizing new business initiatives to the creation of products, services, codes of ethics, and law. At its core is a model, based on the natural system of the ocean, which creates a fluid framework connecting design, humanity, and our world into one interrelated whole. The ocean is an ancient and timeless archetype expressed in all art forms, legends, and myths. In this model, it serves as a metaphor, illuminating the design of our human experience.

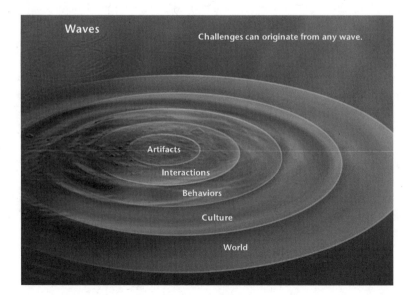

Waves

Challenges can originate from any wave.

Artifacts

Interactions

Behaviors

Culture

World

## BECOMING AWARE OF THE RIPPLE EFFECT

At every moment, we are all rocked by the ripple effects of a myriad designs launched into the world, sometimes purposefully, sometimes on a bet or a prayer. These ripples, originating from tangible and intangible artifacts, extend outward in ever-widening, concentric circles. They influence our feelings, thinking, ethics, and worldviews, which in turn affect our shared beliefs and practices. Expressed in culture, the ways in which we come together in communities, organizations, social systems, and countries affect our planet. Global events, both societal and environmental, send repercussions back around again, forming circular patterns of cause and effect that influence what and how we design. The "ripple effect" is a basic tenet of the Sea Change Design Model. We give considerable time to identifying and analyzing the implications and consequences of actions and artifacts on individuals, cultures, and the natural world over time. Before we do anything else.

Drop a pebble into water; skip a flat, smooth stone across a stream; watch rain pellet the surface of the ocean. The ripples that form from these actions produce a familiar effect. It is common wisdom that every action causes another, which causes another, and another. Every single action each of us takes affects untold others. We all know this principle. Whether we are conscious of it, and whether we choose to act on it at any given moment, is another matter.

Creation occurs when we choose to become aware of the ripple effect before acting, to think hard first, to design before we act. It is in the planning of meaningful actions that design, in its "meta" sense, can create purpose and potential, far beyond what would have transpired in the normal course of events. In an all-too-familiar scenario, which I have witnessed over and over, design is still often thought of and included near the end of the product-development cycle, to give something form and a face. Using design strategically, from the very beginning, is an altogether different way of thinking—one worth embracing.

What happens when you design the intentions and relationships you desire first? And then create the actions and artifacts to support those intentions? It becomes very clear that surprising, felicitous, and profound results are possible. Often, the appropriate actions required to accomplish a desired impact are quite different from the obvious, reactive ones that first came to mind, many of which can turn out to be irrelevant, redundant, or misconceived. The risks are high; the costs, both to the bottom line and to goodwill, higher still. Conversely, using design to create well-planned, transformative solutions can result in positive ripples economically, socially, and environmentally.

## SEEING THE FOREST AND THE TREES (OR RATHER, THE OCEAN AND THE WAVES)

A client once said to me, after seeing the Sea Change model for the first time, "Your model forces unity, partnership, and creativity. You want me to buck the entire culture of my organization, where specialization is prized, territories are to be defended, and the easy way out is considered pragmatic?" Delighted that he had grasped the potential of a successful culture change, I grinned and replied simply, "Yes!" There was a very long pause as he considered this, and finally he said, "Does your ocean metaphor include tsunamis?"

The ocean is constantly in motion, from the smallest capillary waves to the tides (longest of all waves, spanning half the earth's circumference). What is moving, however, is mostly energy—not water, except in the case of breaking waves and tsunami. Waves are generated from many sources, from very small disturbances: wind, gravity and, in the case of tsunamis, landslides, icebergs falling from glaciers, and underwater seismic and volcanic activity. These cause a major redistribution of water, setting up a huge rolling wave that travels incredibly fast. Depending on the shape of the shore, the power of the wave can be relatively benign or it can be magnified, causing enormous damage: In 1946, a tsunami thirty feet (nine meters) high traveled from Alaska to Hawaii in five hours, at roughly 470 miles per hour.[2]

Organizational tsunami can be equally devastating. They are caused by all sorts of events, originating either as a direct result of actions taking place upon the surface waters, or from the hidden depths below. It's important to understand the legacy of past waves, as well as to be alert to forces currently in motion that could cause future ones. These include changes in management from restructuring, mergers, transfers, and deaths; difficult product launches; unanticipated product releases by competitors; ground-swell consumer reactions (both negative and positive); and global events of an entirely different order of magnitude. Often, the impact is experienced in shock. Reactions can be very emotional, and are often unconscious and unexpressed. The ramifications are severe and lasting.

To even remotely predict or respond to these staggeringly powerful waves, you have to be aware of the circumstances that created them in the first place. However, it is not enough simply to be aware and to plan effective actions. Being in business means strategically managing systems in a relatively controlled environment on an ongoing, sustainable basis, not just solving one-off problems. To create sustainable solutions, it becomes critical to understand the complexities of the context, the relationships, and the flow of results that, taken together, form an integrated view of the business. This, of course, means taking the time to understand these interconnections, discouraging fragmented efforts, and forgoing the temptation to let speed to market drive everything at the expense of quality products and quality of life. Sometimes, a culture change is required.

When we use the Sea Change Process to design a thoughtful and implementable culture change, we look at everything in order to bring all the parts into an integral, meaningful whole. Often, an organization has never been viewed as such (that forest-for-the-trees problem, or its reverse). We often hear words similar to those of Pat Tinsley, former vice president of education and outreach for the Monterey Bay Aquarium: "The Sea Change Process has shifted not only how I approach my work, but also how I approach my life. It forces participants to challenge underlying assumptions, and to consider outcomes from a world view rather than from a corporate or personal view."

Using the model metaphor, we take into consideration the surface of the ocean, which represents all the identifiable components within the direct sphere of influence

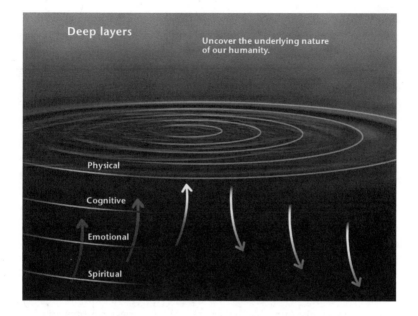

of the organization—products, people, the organization itself, resources, events, issues, world society, and the earth. We study other ripples on the surface—the competition, alliances, adversaries, and industry trends that can either support or hinder desired intentions.

## FATHOMING THE DEEP

To truly understand a problem or aspiration, we dive into the moving waters below the surface—the deeper levels of our humanity. Most ocean water stabilizes into three layers: the surface, the intermediate, and the deep or bottom layers. Stratification occurs mainly as a result of density, with the colder, saltier (denser) waters sinking to the bottom. However, these waters are constantly circulating, moving vertically through upwelling and downwelling from the warm surface, where the wind, waves, and currents combine, to depths of more than 14,000 feet. Huge, silent, slow-moving waves move the waters horizontally around the globe. It can take a particle of water thousands of years to travel from the sea ice at the polar ocean surface to the solar-heated tropics; from the submarine canyons of Monterey Bay to the coral cathedrals of the Great Barrier Reef; it makes its journey through this one magnificent ocean, connecting all of us.

The deep symbolizes our physical, cognitive, emotional, and spiritual layers, which eventually influence or are influenced by events or currents on the surface. These include the behaviors, motivations, thinking, and values of customers, clients, and employees. We have found that respectfully and sensitively exploring these depths helps to build trust and partnership within an organization. Surprising and influential things are revealed, bringing awareness to those participating in the process and a better understanding of the once hidden factors that have caused significant repercussions. Giving people the opportunity to express their feelings of excitement, frustration, and even pain, helps free up blockages and create new energy. It is always most moving to me when we tap into the spiritual layer, where wisdom, creativity, and a profound sense of belonging reside. When there is a lack of these things, when a sense of "family" or "home" is not present within an organization, employees withhold themselves, their talents, and their knowledge. There is less possibility for innovation and informed initiatives.

In a culture change, a high priority is given to uniting the people within an organization, inclusive of their areas of expertise, experience, and humanness. This requires asking lots of penetrating questions in order to understand how the culture is currently functioning and needs to change. What is the existing paradigm—the history, mission, principles, values, products, and practices? Who are the people employed by the organization (at all levels), and what are their deepest passions, concerns, emotions, and beliefs? Looking below the surface provides a wealth of information and insights, not readily recognizable on the surface, yet having a profound effect.

## READING THE WATERS

The most dynamic force in mixing the ocean's waters—surface currents driven by the force of the winds and the warmth of the sun—has a significant impact on circulation around the globe. From the tropics to the poles, currents redistribute the ocean's energy, affecting climates everywhere. They also redistribute water rich in nutrients and marine life, along with anything else that might happen along, from oil spills and sewage to tennis shoes. Currents are rivers of water, powerful catalysts that direct flow and have far-reaching influences upon the surface, the deep, and the atmosphere. Gyres (of which there are six on our planet) are massive, elliptical currents that continuously circulate water around the periphery of ocean basins.

We track the flow of design currents—actions and artifacts that connect the organization to its customers, consumers, or clients, and to the world. These dynamic relationships are interdependent, interrelated, and critical to success. Among other things, they provide a fundamental and vital purpose, one that results in brand equity, credibility, and customer loyalty. How cognizant is everyone in the organization of this fact? In what ways do consumers provide the basis for all product design and delivery efforts? How clear are the communications among functional groups and departments? Most important, is there a common view of what a product, service, or system is? Then there are the interconnections among the organization and its competition, partners, and outside suppliers, and the impact of its efforts on the world. A focus of our process is to identify, strengthen, or build gyres. These self-sustaining currents of influence are circular feedback loops that bring to the surface innovative solutions and new possibilities. We ask how all these relationships contribute to a cohesive, well-functioning, interdependent whole. Is there flow—results that reflect design integrity, economic prosperity, social responsibility, and environmental stewardship?

Finding new ways to approach the protection of human rights in Uzbekistan has been one of the most sobering uses of the Sea Change Model. Culture change on the level of a country is an extraordinary thing to envision. Advising on ombudsman law in a country renowned for human rights abuse requires temerity, wisdom, humility, and global street smarts, all of which Dean Gottehrer, an international ombudsman consultant for the United Nations, possesses in quantity. Uzbekistan, once infamous for its cities on the Silk Road, is now, as everybody knows, pivotal in the Afghanistan war. Uzbekistan's human rights issues now ripple out to America's military, the Green Berets, the State Department, and beyond.

Uzbekistan has been an unstable, volatile state for some time. Before designing ways to generate gyres that could encourage respect for human rights and court system reform, we needed to understand the country's global context and the critical relationships among many conflicting parts. Uzbekistan desperately needs geopolitical security, as well as international credibility and investment. It has a history of Soviet repression, conflicts among conservative Islamic, ethnic groups, and secularism; and an economy based on cotton, oil, and tourism. Add to this the environmental disaster of the dying Aral Sea, whose receding waters are used to irrigate the cotton fields and isolate the island where the results of Russian research into germ warfare are buried.

Dean Gottehrer remarked after our second day of working together, "It's often way too easy to focus on bits and pieces of problems or issues on which we are working. Sea Change encourages a more global view, which is useful in any situation where it may be difficult to see or consider the interrelationships, to develop resolutions, or to innovate alternative ways of working. By using this approach to look at human rights negotia-

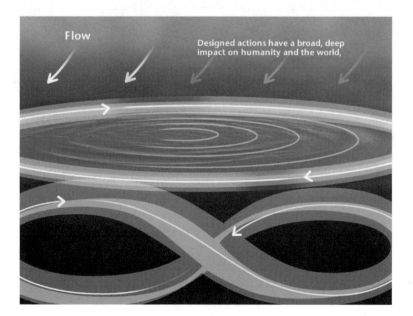

The **ripple** represents all the identifiable components within the direct sphere of influence—products, people, the organization, resources, events, and issues—viewed as an integral system.

**The ripple effect** is the implications or consequences of actions and artifacts on individuals, cultures, and the natural world, over time.

The **atmosphere** represents the universal influences that shape your challenge—global forces such as rapid change, increasing alienation, or economic uncertainty.

**Other ripples**—competition, alliances, adversaries, and industry trends—can either support or hinder desired intentions.

**Currents** are the actions and artifacts that connect the organization to its customers and the world. These dynamic relationships are interdependent, interconnected, and critical to success.

**Gyres** are self-sustaining currents of influence, circular feedback loops that surface innovative solutions and new possibilities.

The **deep waters** represent the deeper layers—physical, cognitive, emotional, and spiritual—of our common humanity. These include the behaviors, motivations, thinking, and values of customers, clients and employees that influence or are influenced by events and currents at the surface through **upwelling** and **downwelling**.

**The Sea Change Design Model™ uses a visual metaphor based on an integrated natural system—the winds of the atmosphere, the surface of the ocean and its flowing currents, and the circulating deep water below the surface.**

**The entire model consists of three cycles. It is used in each phase of Sea Change Design Process.™**

Context                Relationship                Flow

tions, I see a world rich in interconnections and consequences that we tended to overlook." Recently Dean wrote to me, "Who knew, those many months ago when we talked about Uzbekistan and the anthrax buried on an island in the Aral Sea, that anthrax would be a threat to our country and the impetus to help clean up the Aral Sea mess? But apparently that is what has happened."[3]

## FINDING OUR BEARINGS

In the Sea Change Process, we also monitor the winds of the atmosphere—the universal influences that shape all of us. These are not hard to miss, given how constantly we struggle with them—rapid change, increasing alienation, economic uncertainty, global wars. When events like the terrorist acts of September 11, 2001, happen, the true impact on economics, politics, society, and the environment are not readily apparent at first. These events take on universal implications affecting the entire world in one way or another, over time. Lately, in our Sea Change workshops, September 11th has been coming up a lot. Attendees are feeling its economic impact on productivity and profitability, as well as, of course, the emotional toll it has taken.

These events sprang from deep, complex causes, and will have lasting effects on America's national security, the legal system, industry (especially the airlines, to state an obvious one), purchasing and investing habits, technology, culture, national psyche, and on and on. And then there are the continuous waves of global impact. In order to manage responses tempered with foresight and wisdom, we must become aware of the world context—understanding the disjunctions in the relationships among people, systems, and countries; and then negotiating the breaks in terrain in order to design sustainable solutions.

Thomas Friedman has a kindred perspective. In *The Lexus and the Olive Tree: Understanding Globalization*, he writes, "I believe that this new system of globalization—in which walls between countries, markets, and disciplines are increasingly being blown away—constitutes a new state of affairs. And the only way to see it, understand it, and explain it is by arbitraging all six dimensions . . ."[4] He refers to the dimensions of technology, finance, culture, politics, ecology, and national security.

The Sea Change Design Process, and design in general, can be especially useful in finding your bearings in this uncertain world. As an antidote to growing alienation, design is human-centric, requiring partnership and multidisciplinary collaboration. In response to frenetic change, the design process is iterative, producing adaptability, responsiveness, and resilience. Ill-defined, seemingly intractable problems of ever-growing complexity can be approached with design's intentionality, meant to manifest things. Using systemic thinking to simply see and to synthesize challenges is the very nature of design. If we can visualize our problems, at least we have a better chance of getting our hands around them. And finally, as a counterbalance to the chaos that seems so pervasive in our lives today, design, done with imagination and integrity, makes our relationships clear, uniting us in our efforts to temper, and even embrace, the uncertainty. This is the essence of Sea Change. Our definition of design is the conscious planning of meaningful acts that influence our relationships to one another, those yet unborn, and the web of life, of which we are a part.

Dr. Lewis Mehl-Madrona writes in his book, *Coyote Medicine*: "Finding direction means recognizing that life actually has a purpose. Once we believe it does, then we have it in our power to heal ourselves. To me that is proof enough that our lives are meaningful."[5] The traditions, tools, and techniques of design can help orient us as we venture outside current boundaries and borders into the unknown world of possibility. And there, in that world of sea changes, lies hope and healing.

## ACKNOWLEDGMENT

My thanks to Michael Rigsby, Jon Butah, Sydney Hudspith, and Terry Swack for their inspiring conversations, careful wordsmithing, and unwavering partnership and belief in Sea Change.

### Suggested Reading

Burke, James, and Ornstein, Robert. *The Axemaker's Gift* (New York: G. P. Putnam's Sons, 1995).

Capra, Fritjof. *The Web of Life* (New York: Doubleday, 1996).

NOAA & Monterey Bay Aquarium. *A Natural History of the Monterey Bay, National Marine Sanctuary* (Monterey: Monterey Bay Aquarium Foundation, 1997).

Remen, M.D., and Rachel Naomi. *My Grandfather's Blessings: Stories of Strength, Refuge and Belonging* (New York: Riverhead Books, 2000).

Whyte, David. *The Heart Aroused: Poetry and Preservation of the Soul in Corporate America* (New York: Doubleday, 1994).

Wilbur, Ken. *The Theory of Everything: An Integral Vision for Business, Politics, Science, and Spirituality* (Boston: Shambala, 2000).

Find related articles on *www.dmi.org* with these keywords: case study, corporate culture, cultural change, interactivity, partnership.

## SEA CHANGE FOR THE MONTEREY BAY AQUARIUM'S WEB SITE

The three phases of the Sea Change Process bring a design-centered orientation to solving complex, ill-defined problems and aspirations. What is exciting is the diverse range of challenges that benefit from the application of the Sea Change Model consistently over time, from strategic planning, new business initiatives, and culture change to research and development efforts, new products, services and systems, and global and environmental initiatives. What is unique is the focus, emphasis, and techniques used in each phase. The consulting process is flexible, scalable, and customized to fit the specific challenge.

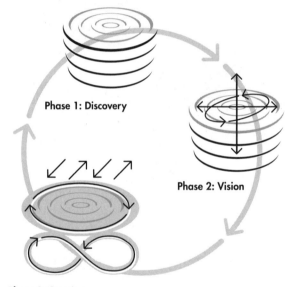

## PHASING IN THE E-QUARIUM

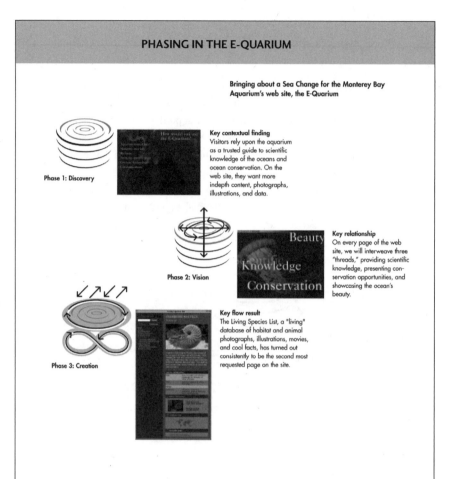

Bringing about a Sea Change for the Monterey Bay Aquarium's web site, the E-Quarium

**Phase 1: Discovery**

**Key contextual finding**
Visitors rely upon the aquarium as a trusted guide to scientific knowledge of the oceans and ocean conservation. On the web site, they want more indepth content, photographs, illustrations, and data.

**Phase 2: Vision**

**Key relationship**
On every page of the web site, we will interweave three "threads," providing scientific knowledge, presenting conservation opportunities, and showcasing the ocean's beauty.

**Phase 3: Creation**

**Key flow result**
The Living Species List, a "living" database of habitat and animal photographs, illustrations, movies, and cool facts, has turned out consistently to be the second most requested page on the site.

### Phase 1: Discovery

In the Discovery Phase, we use the Sea Change Model to create the broadest possible awareness of the general conditions, influences, and deep human values that form the context of the challenge. The outcome of this phase is a consensus definition of the deep challenge. For the Monterey Bay Aquarium, we helped examine the organization in relationship to the E-Quarium; its services, exhibits and practices, traditions and innovations, and competition, as well as its visitors' values and desires. One of the key contextual findings was that there was very little connection between the physical aquarium and the existing Web site. In fact, the original Web site was one of the best-kept secrets around, and yet, it was heavily used by teenagers (29 percent of the site's visitors)—kids who typically don't visit the aquarium (hey, it's not a mall!). What an opportunity to achieve the mission in ways new to the aquarium's culture.

## PHASING IN THE E-QUARIUM

### Phase 2: Vision

In the Vision Phase, we identify the key relationships that can create "self-sustaining currents of influence." We envision multiple courses of action that can create these key influences. The outcome of this phase is a detailed picture of the desired future state and a plan of action. The aquarium needed to build and strengthen many relationships. Among them was providing compelling content that answered a wide range of visitors' needs. This included making interconnections among many types of media and content across the site in ways that helped achieve the aquarium's conservation mission, preserve its reputation for scientific accuracy, and inspire awe within the hearts of visitors.

### Phase 3: Creation

In the Creation Phase, we design and implement the plan of action in a fashion that is iterative, feedback-sensitive, timely, and cost-effective. The outcome of this phase is "flow"—new energy that creates sustainable, felicitous results, new ideas for future actions, and broad and deep impact in the world. The E-Quarium continues to evolve in response to visitor needs and the aquarium's goals. Eight months after launch, revenues from the online ticketing far exceeded projections, the number of unique visitors tripled, and just as important, the E-Quarium received the Webby's People's Voice Award for science, high praise from the people for whom we originally designed it.

**THE MONTEREY BAY AQUARIUM RIPPLE EFFECT**

Sea changes are legend, as are their designs, as varied and profound as the challenges they spring from. One of them took place in 1978, with the founding of the Monterey Bay Aquarium. Launched by four marine biologists and Hewlett-Packard cofounder David Packard, it began a ripple effect that continues today. Their vision to share the ocean's wonder, and their concern for its survival, brought forth an aquarium that is world renowned for the design of its pioneering and popular exhibits on jellyfish and deep-sea creatures; cutting-edge conservation and research programs for sea otters, bluefin tuna, and other open-ocean fishes; and landmark education and outreach programs. Since 1984, more than 30 million visitors have joined the aquarium in creating a sea change of its own—conservation of the world's oceans.

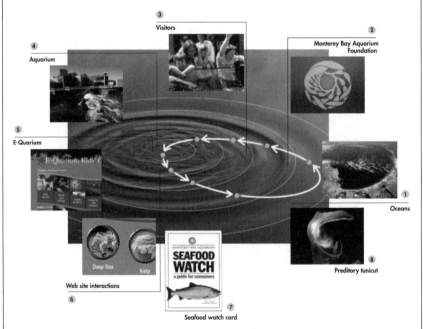

1. The oceans of our planet cover more than 70 percent of its surface and make up 99 percent of its living space. Yet in many respects, we know more about outer space than we do about inner space—life in the oceans here, where we live. The aquarium founders understood that this needed to change and that designing an aquarium would provide very effective ways to increase people's awareness and en-

## THE MONTEREY BAY AQUARIUM RIPPLE EFFECT

courage their feelings of stewardship toward the oceans. America's largest national marine sanctuary provided the perfect location; the relatively pristine waters of the Monterey Bay are exceptionally rich in marine life and diversity of habitats, from kelp forests to the deep sea. Seawater is piped directly into the aquarium at a rate of two thousand gallons per minute, filtered during the day to enhance viewing of the breathtaking exhibits and the 300,000 plants and animals living within their habitats.

2. As part of their initiative, the founders created The Monterey Bay Aquarium Foundation, whose global mission is to inspire conservation of the oceans. Today, more than four hundred staff and nine hundred volunteers contribute to the nonprofit aquarium work of the scientific-based institution, which emphasizes innovation and quality. (There are no performing porpoises here.) It has a $35 million annual budget, supported by revenues generated from admissions, events, gift and bookstore sales, and grants.

3. Taking its role seriously as a trusted guide, the aquarium provides visitors with moving experiences designed to reach their hearts and minds, encouraging them to become more connected with the oceans. The aquarium inspires, informs, and helps them to invest in and get involved with conservation issues.

4. The aquarium is built on the footprint of the Hovden Cannery, one of the first on Monterey's Cannery Row and the last to close when the sardine fishery collapsed due to intense overfishing, which came at a time of natural fluctuation in sardine populations. The site serves as a fitting reminder of the ecological change and upheaval that we humans can cause.

5. In 1998, the aquarium launched a new Web site (*www.montereybayaquarium.org*) to serve as its virtual home. This E-Quarium connects visitors and the oceans, visitors and the aquarium, and visitors with each other. AlbenFaris provided strategic planning, branding, design, and content development, working with a large team of aquarium staff and outside consultants. Our intent was to augment the ripple effect already in motion—to leverage the momentum, reputation, and equity of the physical aquarium.

6. Along with e-commerce, the Web site includes the E-Quarium Kids' Habitat Guide; an interactive kelp forest tour; ocean conservation content, and games like "The Deep Sea Memory Game."

### THE MONTEREY BAY AQUARIUM RIPPLE EFFECT

Working closely with the aquarium staff, we generated many "currents of influence." As with all circular currents or gyres, what goes around comes around. As the E-Quarium reached more and more people, the aquarium responded to feedback, data, and an avalanche of mail, like this letter from Lenor Friedman, of San Francisco—which, in turn, influenced business in many ways, from online ticketing to conservation content.

Lenor wrote, "I am eleven years old. I have already written to the President about protecting dolphins because they are my favorite animal. He wrote me back saying that he would do something to help them. I love your aquarium so much that I went there to celebrate my birthday. I think you could make it even better though if you put a section where people could complain about any marine mammals that they think are being treated unfairly."

7. As often happens with gyres, many surprising and felicitous results occur. Witness what happened in 1999, when the aquarium designed and placed a small icon for its "Seafood Watch" wallet card on the E-Quarium's home page. Another gyre, with momentum of its own, quickly formed. Part of a campaign to increase public awareness of ocean wildlife conservation practices, including seafood buying and the status of fisheries, the card provides seafood recommendations rated Best Choices, Proceed with Caution, and Avoid. Tens of thousands of printable cards have been downloaded from the site. The Ocean Conservancy and the White House Council on Environmental Quality have requested cards. The Yosemite Concession Services Corporation no longer serves Chilean sea bass at its properties in Yosemite National Park. Bon Appetit Management Company adopted the Seafood Watch guidelines, distributing the cards to its 150 clients around the world, which include The Getty Center, corporate headquarters for ExxonMobil and Oracle, and the food services at Stanford University. And on and on it flows.

8. True to the intentions of the founders, both the aquarium and the E-Quarium have spurred concerned individuals and organizations into taking actions that ripple back to the ocean habitats and the wondrous life within them. Understanding the consequences of our actions as we explore, harvest, and mine the deep sea, will have a significant impact on our chances for survival. From what the aquarium marine biologists tell us, we won't get another chance to get it right unless we inhabit another planet.

## *Endnotes*

1. The Sea Change Design Process and the Sea Change Design Model are both trademarks of Alben Design.

2. Tom Garrison, *Essentials of Oceanography* (Belmont, CA: Wadsworth Publishing Co., 1995).

3. Judith Miller, "U.S. Agrees to Clean Up Anthrax Site in Uzbekistan," *New York Times*, October 23, 2001.

4. Thomas Friedman, *The Lexus and the Olive Tree: Understanding Globalization* (New York: Anchor Books, 2000), p. 23.

5. Lewis Mehl-Madrona, *Coyote Medicine* (New York: Scribner, 1997), p. 125.

## Chapter 22
# Solving the Right Problem: A Strategic Approach to Designing Today's Workplace

by Arnold Craig Levin

*Work environments need to be aligned with the core dimensions of an organization's business. As Arnold Levin highlights, aesthetic options are not the issue. What matters are workplaces that support a company's processes, structure, strategies, people, and reward system. To stress their value-added contribution, designers, he argues, should anchor their proposals to these management-related concerns.*

WITHIN THE DESIGN profession, there has been much talk of design strategies, workplace strategies, and strategic design. To a large extent, such talk has been in response to an increasingly competitive design market, but it is even more urgently aimed at clients who have become ever more sophisticated, as well as somewhat skeptical, about the value of "design for design's sake." These clients want to see a measurable return on investment in the design of today's workplace. For decades, workplace design has been sold on the merits of good design, effective branding, and attractiveness to clients. However, today's businesses are far more sophisticated when purchasing design services, and they are also reacting to senior management's demands that they provide the same value proposition they would when developing an IT or HR strategy.

All of this has left the profession struggling to demonstrate value. Most firms have given up on the Holy Grail of showing how effectively designed workplaces will make their clients' organizations more productive. It is virtually impossible to demonstrate productivity with a mostly knowledge-based workforce that is not producing tangible products.

As a result, the concept of workplace design strategies has been incorporated into the lexicon of most firms engaged in workplace design. This is a response to the vacuum left by years of neglect on the part of the design profession—a vacuum that has resulted in a situation in which form has come before substance and in which the importance of form has failed to be substantiated beyond the ego gratification of the designer or the image-consciousness of the client.

Approaching the problem through workplace design strategies has become a way of framing design in such a way as to show the client its value is more than a functional and aesthetic endeavor. The term "workplace design strategy," or workplace strategy, is fairly widely used, though a review of the literature shows that it has not been concisely defined. In a Google search, workplace design strategy comes up with no responses, while workplace strategy comes up with resources relating to everything from IT strategy to HR strategy to violence in the workplace—but not to any resource related to the design of the workplace. As I discuss in this chapter, when I interviewed eighteen persons involved in developing and carrying out workplace design strategies within their organizations, I got a fairly broad range of definitions (which is an important factor alone in understanding the designer-client relationship and the use of language in describing the approach to take on a given workplace design project).

For the purposes of this chapter, it is important therefore to define workplace design strategy to better understand the context in which I discuss these issues and to understand the differences between this term and workplace design. A simple definition of workplace design comes from Horgen, Joreff, Porter, and Schon in *Excellence by Design*. They refer to workplace design as the process of creating and or modifying the workplace. It involves a design process that includes: ". . . the activities of programming, design, building, maintenance, management, and renovation. The term workplace-making connotes the idea of unfolding in time, with a beginning (the design problem) and an end (the new workplace in use)."[1]

With workplace design strategy, the emphasis is on strategy as a differentiator to workplace design. The phrase takes a long-term view of design solutions that affect the workplace through a deep understanding of the organization's long-term, as well as immediate goals, and as such takes into consideration the underlying organizational resources of the business. Using Mintzberg and Quinn's definition of strategy helps define this way of utilizing workplace design: "A strategy is the pattern or plan that integrates an organization's major goals, policies, and action sequences into a cohesive whole. A well-formulated strategy helps to marshal and allocate an organization's resources."[2]

Along the same lines, there are many different terminologies given to the practice of workplace design, as well as to those who are practitioners. Practitioners can include designers (those with an interior design or environmental design degree) and architects, along with design firms (firms not practicing as licensed architects, although they may be licensed interior designers), and architectural firms. For the purpose of this chapter, I use the terms "designer" and "design firm" to include all professionals practicing workplace design, as well as their organizations.

The problem facing designers is manifest in a number of ways. First, this lack of demonstratable value has put the design consultant in the position of competing for design commissions, often on the basis of fee. Without proven or at least perceived value, the services offered by these consultancies have been commodified to the point of either giving design services away or not providing services adequate to do justice to the client's project.

Secondly, and this has potentially far greater implications for the effectiveness of the completed design, the position of the design consultant within the supply chain has been marginalized to a point where access to the visionaries within the client organization has been extremely limited and in many instances, nonexistent. The role of facilities manager as the point person for the project on the client side has severely hampered the relationship between consultant and client visionary and therefore has hampered the potential impact of the design and problem-solving capabilities of the designer.

This has not always been the case, and looking at the problem from a historical viewpoint, one can see just how this change in dynamics has adversely affected the results of workplace design and subsequently its perceived value. In her PhD dissertation, "Tower, Typewriter, and Trademark" (2005), Alexandra Lange explores the roles of corporate leaders in the design process of the multitude of new corporate headquarters designed after the Second World War, and most significantly in the 1950s and 1960s. These corporate presidents were intimately involved in the selection of the architect and were the primary interface with that architect when it came to defining culture and design image. While one can point to the negative aspects of the hierarchical nature of this approach, as well as to the problems caused by lack of stakeholder involvement, this relationship served to establish a strong design direction and, in many cases, avoided the safe way out in favor of more-innovative methods (at least for those times) of design strategy. It was not until the design of IBM's New York headquarters that the president was eased aside for political purposes and a facilities management role was created to carry out the project. Lange credits this event as signaling the rise of the FM profession, as well as the cause of subsequent compromised design solutions. The importance of this dynamic as part of the workplace design strategy process was echoed in my own research, where within those organizations that cited a perceived value in creating a workplace design strategy as an integral component of their organization's real estate strategy, involvement at the highest senior management level, along with a champion within these ranks, was deemed critical.

I believe the design of the workplace is a business problem first and foremost and that design is the methodology by which that business problem can be solved.[3] This chapter attempts to show that a vacuum has been created as the result of several factors the design profession must address. This vacuum has marginalized the perceived value that design consultancies provide, and to address the problem, we must view the role of design as it relates to work environment at a different level (strategic), use different tools to develop these strategies, and frame the design problem as a business problem, eventually presenting solutions to this problem, at least partially in the context of business.

## A LITTLE HISTORY

Workplace design as we know it is a relatively new field, one that evolved only after the end of the Second World War. Although Frederick Taylor's writings on scientific management in 1911 dealt with the workplace and had lasting effects on both the planning of the workplace and on perceptions of the value of its design, the workplaces that resulted were, with few exceptions (such as Frank Lloyd Wright's design of the Johnson Wax building in Racine, Wisconsin—which fully embodied the factory-like approach outlined by Taylor), not designed by design professionals. It was not until the years after World War II, which saw major changes in American business, that design began to take a greater role. The emergence of the modern architectural movement had profound effects on the role of architects and designers as facilitators of change. High-rise office buildings, meant to symbolize the importance of the organizations within, required considerable planning if they were to contain the many workers employed in those postwar years.

This was also a time in which European modernism reigned. The role of modernism and all that it embodied inspired designers to approach office design as a problem to be solved. It took the role of design beyond the functional and aesthetic realms that were design's previous focus and shaped an entirely new framework from which the designer and architect could create. Peter Blake in his *No Place Like Utopia* focuses on this paradigm shift: ". . . most of the modern architects between the two world wars seemed concerned with the creation of a democratic, egalitarian social order; they were concerned with problems of housing for everyone, with problems of planning humane and healthy communities for all, with sheltering a human family that was about to burst at its seams."[4]

While this implies strong political and social consciousness, it represents the underlying belief within the modern movement that problem-solving went beyond the aesthetic and form-giving roles with which designers were preoccupied. Making the transition from this hypothesis, the designers originally engaged in the creation of corporate workplaces at the end of World War II used design to define a corporate vision or ethic and as such became facilitators of change, as well as a resource for the organization. The natural progression of this would have been for designers to increase their knowledge of and involvement in organizational design and to learn to utilize workplace design as a facilitator of organizational change. However, as I discuss below, and with exceptions such as the pioneering work of Frank Duffy, the profession lost its way.

The approach lost ground with the rise of Post-Modernism. Form began to take precedence over function, and the so-called star syndrome began to emerge within the design profession. The emphasis on form as a driver of design strategies contributed to alienating the designer from the client and further created a disconnect between designer and client in an area of business that had the potential to be a significant enabler of business strategy. As British architect and educator Neal Leach opined: "Architects have become increasingly obsessed with images and image-making to the detriment of their discipline. The sensory stimulation induced by these images may have a narcotic effect that diminishes social and political awareness, leaving architects cosseted within their aesthetic cocoons, remote from the actual concerns of everyday life."[5]

Although Leach was writing about the field of architecture, this mindset has carried over into the profession of workplace design and contributes to client conceptions (or misconceptions) about the value, or lack thereof, in workplace design strategies. The effect on the design profession has been to demonstrate client value through the venue of workplace strategy. In a survey of the leading design firms engaged in designing workplaces, most had a group dedicated to workplace strategies. This issue is seen as so crucial to the implementation of value-centered services within an area in which the perceived value of design has been marginalized that most national and international real estate brokerage firms also have created workplace strategy groups. Clearly, a need to demonstrate tangible value through elevating the role of workplace design to a strategic plateau is perceived at both ends of the occupier service professions. (These include those professionals traditionally involved in the design of the workplace, such as architects and designers; real estate consultants involved in procuring space; and a new breed of consultants called project managers, involved in ensuring the seamless implementation of the project.).

The U.K.-based consultancy DEGW was one of the first design firms to incorporate strategic services as an integral component of its practice. The more conventional architectural practices, such as Gensler and HOK, have also integrated workplace strategy practices within their offerings. On the real estate service side, both Cushman and Wakefield and JLL (two global commercial real estate service firms) have incorporated workplace strategy components. This is indeed evidence that workplace strategy is now viewed as a critical asset.

The struggle to convince business organizations of design's value is probably the single most critical issue affecting the design profession, and the evolution of the client base has contributed to this difficulty. A preponderance of office workers is now engaged in what we call knowledge work, and the nature of that work affects the way in which it is carried out, the form the workplace needs to enable it, and the way in which the workplace is perceived.

The nature of knowledge work poses two challenges for the design consultant. The first: What is the best way to design work environments that enable the most vital work processes, knowing that different types of work environments are needed to enable the vast array of knowledge-work needs? While there are certainly commonalities among knowledge workers, each business organization has its own culture, business model, and business processes that requires unique applications to best support these workers. The one common denominator is that the work is, for the most part, intangible, but how that work is done—that is, the technology interfaces that are involved—varies among organizations.

Figure 1. A typical floor from Capital One's Future of Work design. Notice the open, collaborative desking typology, featuring short-stay rooms in the background.

Capital One, for instance (see Figure 1), has developed a workplace design strategy based on maximum worker flexibility that relies heavily on collaborative work processes (both face-to-face and long-distance). Branded The Future of Work, the strategy incorporates initiatives such as partitionless open-bench-type work environments to house workers. Some are designated for permanent on-site staff, while others are "touch-down spaces" for workers who are entirely mobile. A hierarchy of meeting spaces, from open collaborative areas to two-person short-stay rooms and project rooms allow for the various types of privacy needs required during the course of a day. Providing staff with a variety of wireless tools, and setting up their facilities to accommodate wireless technology, these workers are encouraged to work anywhere within or without a particular facility. The value within Capital One is for the workplace to fully support and enable the type of knowledge work required.

Figure 2. Time Warner headquarters in New York City features a typical office floor, with perimeter private offices and open administrative work areas.

Conversely, Time Warner (Figure 2) believes its knowledge workers require a more conventional and conservative setting. The new headquarters facility was designed using a private office strategy, but acknowledges the need to provide additional amenities, such as collaborative space and fitness facilities, to support the type of staff the company believes is integral to its business model.

Understanding this shift in focus for knowledge workers acknowledges that value for any workplace initiative is perceived through its enabling processes rather than its tangible assets. This is the second challenge for design consultants to embrace—understanding the need to focus on process as the central element that informs the design brief. This new reality was underscored by a report of the Brookings Institute on understanding the intangible sources of value within business organizations.[6] This report completely negates the value of physical assets for creating wealth within organizations, thereby further casting doubt on the value of the physical workplace. The underlying message is that it is intangible assets (work processes to support knowledge workers) that create value and in which value resides. Design consultants therefore need to focus on developing workplace design strategies that enable work processes as the basis of any strategy.

## RESEARCH FINDINGS

During the course of conducting research for my PhD on the factors that inform perceptions of the value of workplace strategies within organizations, I interviewed eleven firms. Six were American-based, and five were based in the U.K. Within the five American organizations, I extended the interviews to the U.K. subsidiaries of three. Eight of the firms were private-sector companies representing finance, manufacturing, communications, media, consulting, and energy. Two of them were from the public sector and represented national governments.

My intent was to examine management's perceptions of the value of workplace strategies. The importance of studying perceptions is that perceptions shape action. Whether one can quantifiably demonstrate value is of little merit, if perceptions already militate against it.

My findings highlighted a gap in perception between the design community and the very organizations they are attempting to influence. My results point to a design profession that has become so caught up in its own language surrounding the value and benefits of design that to a certain degree it has become, as Neal Leach pointed out, numb to design's true potential.

From the eleven companies, only two interviewees expressed the belief that their firms did not value the role of workplace strategies within their organizations. Of the remaining nine who individually perceived value and who believed their respective organizations perceived value in adopting workplace strategies, all were in agreement with the following:

▲ Without a relocation, move, or change in real estate holdings, the value of workplace strategies would decrease or potentially not have come about. The primary driver for all workplace strategies undertaken was a reduction of real estate costs.

▲ The reduction of real estate costs drove many of the respondent firms to develop workplace transformation as a strategy. However, it is clear that such transformation was not the initial motivator.

▲ Having to develop a business case that outlined costs and benefits affected the perceptions of senior management.

▲ There were differing definitions for the phrase workplace strategy.

▲ Only one interviewee mentioned the word design in the context of workplace strategies and as a component of that strategy. The absence of that term was stunning.

▲ There was no one approach represented by these strategies. They varied from the conventional (private offices predominate) to more open work settings to transformation, where an entirely new way of working was introduced. Those who perceived value did so not on the basis of a particular strategy but on the business case that strategy made to the organization.

Although there were many other findings, these represent the issues most affecting the role of design firms in developing a strategic approach to workplace design. With few exceptions, ultimate value is perceived as stemming from cost reduction, even in instances of organizations adopting more-progressive forms of workplace strategies. These strategies would not have come about were it not for the need to address real estate cost issues. This is a mindset that design consultants need to adopt in approaching the design of the workplace and in developing appropriate workplace design strategies.

As I explained earlier, a variety of definitions were given for workplace strategy by those interviewed. Below are some of the major components and definitions provided.

▲ Intangible drivers of workplace design strategies, such as maximizing flexibility, minimizing costs, and maximizing the use of space

▲ The ability to provide accommodations to effectively support the business (accommodations, meaning workspace, technology, HR policies, and other influences)

▲ How we configure and deploy workspace and technology to facilitate and integrate work processes to enhance productivity. Real estate savings must also be considered: Invest in amenities whose effect on productivity can be measured.

▲ Workspace strategy, meaning finding the most functional, efficient, and cost-effective design for an office environment—using the available space and the furniture in it to help optimize employee performance

▲ Workplace strategy, implying a recognition that the workplace can be a positive factor in supporting the delivery of an organization's business objectives, that it affects the way people work and their productivity at work, and can be an enabler of cultural change; it exploits that understanding in order to procure and make best use of an appropriate range of workplaces, whether they are office-based, home-based, or mobile

▲  Identifying and accessing a broad array of drivers for each organization, including business metrics, branding, market realities, culture, work processes, organizational structure, and work-style characteristics, and the strategies of HR, IT, operations, and support services

The responses to the question of defining workplace strategies demonstrate a somewhat limited, micro, and cost-focused perspective. In addition, in some instances, the definitions take the form of what could be described as parts of a strategy, but not necessarily a definition of a strategy. This is important in understanding the difficulty some respondents had in defining an area they were actively engaged in developing. It goes toward giving some insight into recognizing why some do not perceive value in workplace strategies and the task that is before design consultants in shifting language and paradigms. From these interviews and preliminary analysis, we can make the assumption that workplace strategies need to take on a different dimension; they need to frame the problem as a business, as well as a design, problem. Therefore, analysis methodologies and deliverables also need to be expanded. I discuss these analysis methodologies in the next section.

Design firms trying to make use of and define workplace strategy have tended to emphasize issues of collaboration and innovation. Although these are all critical components, they are themselves not a workplace strategy. A workplace strategy, as the research indicates, should be a business response to the client's problem. Design is merely the vehicle through which this response is delivered.

What then should the design consultant use as the basis of analysis to begin this shift? Organizational design has much to offer toward understanding workplace strategy issues from a business perspective. The research for my MBA dissertation on the relationships between organizational design and workplace design uncovered many similarities in the approaches of the two methodologies. However, although the literature in the field of organizational design uses terminology such as architecture and design, there is an incredible absence of any reference to their physical aspects as they relate to the places in which organizations reside.

I propose that design consultants engaged in developing workplace design strategies begin to explore and make use of the assessment tools and methodologies employed in the business consulting arena, particularly those that are part of the organizational design field. As my MBA research indicated, the striking similarities of problem definition and needs create the ability to incorporate these processes into the lexicon of the design consultants processes. Incorporating methodologies and tools that have been used by organizational designers offers an extremely robust way of assessing business needs to develop a workplace design strategy that addresses the needs discussed in this chapter. It offers a level of analysis that provides the design consultant with the information needed to utilize the business model as the basis of strategy development and to frame the strategy brief as a business case.

## HOW DOES IT DIFFER FROM CONVENTIONAL METHODOLOGIES?

If we take the view that workplace strategies need to address issues of a broader nature and structure their design recommendations to include a business case, the methodologies one uses need to include those of organizational strategy. For this, the concept of organizational congruence holds the most resonance. As Jay Galbraith explains in *Designing Organizations*, for an organization to be effective, all the categories in what he refers to as the STAR model need to be in alignment.[7] The components of the STAR (see Figures 3a and 3b) model are processes, structure, strategy, people, and rewards.

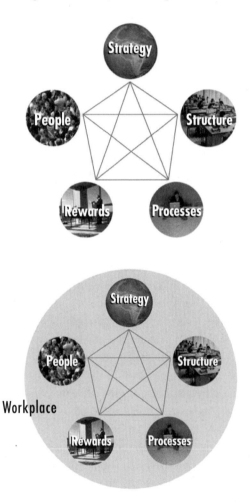

Figure 3a. Jay Galbraith's STAR model illustrates organizational congruence theory relating to key organizational resources: strategy (business, IT, HR, marketing, finance); structure (organizational); processes (work); rewards (perceptions of nonfinancial rewards by employees—i.e., entitlement of work space); and people (demographics, skills, cultural fit).

Figure 3b. The STAR model establishes a context and basis for workplace design strategies.

If the design profession were to adopt this model as the core of a workplace strategy analysis, it might include these five components:

▲ Process: Work process; technology interface; collaboration

▲ Structure: Management and organizational structure; business units; technology infrastructure; culture

▲ Strategy: Brand strategy; change management and workplace transformation; business strategy

▲ People: Demographics; motivation; retention and hiring; HR policies

▲ Rewards: Understanding how employees perceive the workplace in terms of undefined sources of compensation; entitlement (for example, "I deserve an office because of my title")

The STAR model works well as the basis for analysis, but it also works as a tool to define the performance metrics that the proposed workplace strategy needs to match— an essential component of the business case. Another feature of this form of analysis is that, for the most part, it relies on an analysis of intangible organizational assets. If we frame our workplace design strategies in this analytical context, we begin to reframe the value perception of the role of workplace strategies as an organizational asset. In order to change perceptions, the way we present, analyze, and engage the occupier needs to shift.

## WHY IT IS IMPORTANT AND WHAT IT MEANS FOR THE DESIGN PROFESSION

This new way of viewing the issues of workplace strategies is important because it raises the level of analysis to an organizational level, beyond the references of aesthetics and form. All this is not to suggest that we ignore the visual aspects of design. What differentiates a mediocre workspace from a great one is that very design element. In addition, design thinking—the way designers see a problem—is an added value that should be brought to bear on this form of organizational analysis.

Adopting this framework has serious implications and consequences for the design profession. To engage in this form of analysis in a meaningful and insightful way, the experience of the design professional needs to be widened to include business skills and potentially suggests the inclusion of a business degree as part of one's skill set.

Award-winning design solutions are no guarantee of workplace design excellence. Two of the organizations studied have won design awards for their completed workspace designs; however, neither mentioned design solutions as part of the value criteria for their workplace strategies. Their design strategies were successful because they were informed by a workplace strategy presented to senior management as a business case, not as a conventional design solution. Awards themselves do not testify to the success of a design solution. As Neal Leach suggests, architects have become anesthetized to the true benefits of design as a tool for change. It is as if we have been solving the wrong problem really well. With this new framework, designers can begin to solve the right problem really well.

### Suggested Reading

Albrecht, Donald, and Broikos, Chrysanthe (eds.). *On the Job: Design and the American Office* (Princeton, NJ: Princeton Architectural Press/National Building Museum, 2000).

Blair, Margaret, and Wallman, Seven (co-chairs). *Unseen Wealth: Report of the Brookings Task Force on Understanding Intangible Sources of Value* (Brookings Institute, 2000).

Lange, Alexandra. "Tower, Typewriter, and Trademark: Architects, Designers and the Corporate Utopia, 1956–1964". A dissertation submitted in partial fulfillment of the requirements for the degree of Doctor of Philosophy, Institute of Fine Arts, New York University, May 2005.

Levin, Arnold. "Workplace Design: A Component of Organizational Strategy." A dissertation undertaken as part of the award of Master of Business Administration, Design Management, Harrow Business School, University of Westminster, 2001.

## *Endnotes*

1. Torid Horgen, Michael Joroff, William Porter, and Donald Schon. *Excellence by Design: Transforming Workplace & Work Practice* (New York, John Wiley & Sons: 1999).

2. Henry Mintzberg, and James Quinn (eds.), *Readings in the Strategy Process, 3rd ed* (Upper Saddle River, NJ: Prentice Hall, 1996).

3. This hypothesis is supported by research conducted originally as part of the author's MBA dissertation on the connections among workplace design strategies and organizational design strategies, as well as by the author's current research toward the completion of his PhD on the perceptions of the value of workplace design strategies by those within business organizations who are responsible for managing them.

4. Peter Blake, *No Place Like Utopia: Modern Architecture and the Company We Kept* (New York: Knopf, 1993), p. 46.

5. Neal Leach, *The Anaesthetics of Architecture* (Cambridge: MIT Press, 1999).

6. Margaret Blair and Steven Wallman, *Unseen Wealth: Report of the Brookings Task Force on Understanding Intangible Sources of Value* (Brookings Institute, 2000).

7. Jay Galbraith, *Designing Organizations: An Executive Briefing on Strategy, Structure, and Process* (San Francisco: Jossey-Bass, 1995).

# About DMI

DMI connects design to business, to culture, to customers—to the changing world. We bring together business people, designers, educators, researchers, and leaders from every design discipline, every industry, and every corner of the planet. The results are transformational. Over the decades, DMI has been the place where the world's most experienced, creative, and ambitious design leaders gather to share, distill, and amplify their knowledge.

DMI is a non-profit (501c3) educational organization, with more than 1,500 members in 44 countries. The Institute was founded at the Massachusetts College of Art and Design in Boston in 1975, and although it spent several formative years in London it is presently based in downtown Boston. DMI has long-standing relationships with Mass Art, Harvard, London Business School, many of the world's leading design schools and most of the country design councils.

Our vision is to improve organizations worldwide through the effective integration and management of design and design principles for economic, social, and environmental benefit. Our mission is to be the international authority, resource, and advocate on design management, and our objectives are to:

▲ Assist design managers to become leaders in their profession

▲ Sponsor, conduct, and promote research

▲ Collect, organize, and make accessible a body of knowledge

▲ Educate and foster interaction among design managers, organizational managers, public policy makers, and academics

▲ Be a public advocate for the economic and cultural importance of design

The heart of DMI is to connect design leaders to the inspiration, knowledge, and community they need to achieve their goals. Over the years, DMI has created the largest body of knowledge about design management in the world. The Institute has produced 30 case studies with Harvard Business School, published 70 issues of the *Design Management Review*, adding up to over 800 articles, produced over one hundred conferences and two hundred workshops/seminars. This book is an anthology of some of our best articles about building design strategy and leadership.

Our Web site is: *www.dmi.org*

# Authors' Biographies

**Lauralee Alben**, president of Alben Design LLC, is a pioneer of the creative economy and consults with several of the world's most innovative organizations: Apple Computer, Procter & Gamble, and Intel. Alben conducts Sea Change Design Workshops and coaches executives to help bring about strategic solutions to challenges such as corporate innovation capability, sustainability, human rights, and women's leadership. Well respected as a thought leader, she is an internationally acclaimed speaker who gives keynote lectures to corporations, professional conferences, and academia, including the Women's Forum for the Economy and Society in France, TED, DMI, Intel, SUN, and Stanford University. Alben received the inaugural Muriel Cooper Prize from the Design Management Institute.

**Jeremy Alexis** is an assistant professor at the IIT Institute of Design. He holds both a Bachelor of Architecture and a Master of Design degree from the Illinois Institute of Technology. Alexis has spent the majority of his professional career leading interdisciplinary teams tasked with defining next-generation products, services, and business models. He has worked with clients such as Unilever, Motorola, Citibank, Pfizer, American Express, Target Corporation, and Zebra Technologies. He currently teaches the research and demonstration (year-long capstone) class, as well as classes on economics and design, concept evaluation, design decision-making, and problem framing.

**John Barratt,** president and CEO of Teague, is responsible for positioning the company for future success by building and strengthening partnerships with some of the world's leading brands. Barratt began his career in industrial design, gaining global experience in operational and strategic roles with Exatiss Concept Design and Philips Design. His industry experience established his true passion—building, leading, and inspiring great teams to achieve extraordinary results.

**Eric Block** has spent his career using a combination of business acumen and creativity to build effective ideas that inspire customers to action. He founded Duffy & Partners in 2004 with Joe Duffy after seventeen years with Fallon Worldwide, most recently as chief operating officer. Block has developed branding solutions for clients including United Airlines, Jim Beam, Federal Express, Coca-Cola, McDonald's, and Purina. He was also the VP of Creative Services for Fox Television in Los Angeles.

**Bonnie Briggs** is best known for her work with Caterpillar in creating a strategic role for design and brand management. There, she initiated an effective brand education program, establishing a single "voice" for the global brand and developing the tools for growing brand value. Bridging the understanding gap between identity, brand, marketing, and management have been the goal. Briggs has lectured and published extensively in North America, Europe, and Asia. Her approach to brand education has been a benchmark for other companies. Currently, she is principal of B.OnBrand, a corporate brand consulting firm in Lexington, Kentucky.

**Alonzo Canada** is a relationship lead for Jump Associates. He has particular expertise in integrating the directives of brand positioning, competitive strategy, and consumer insights to create compelling experiences for ordinary people. He holds two master's degrees, one in design from Stanford University and one in fine art from Mills College.

**Andy Cargile** is director of user experience for Microsoft Hardware. He and his team are responsible for creating exceptional user experiences with consumer products at the interface between people and computers. Over the last twenty-five years, he has worked in user research and interaction design in small startups, large corporations, and higher education. Cargile thrives on helping to create products that solve meaningful needs and make a difference to people. He holds a Master of Design from the Institute of Design and an MS and BS from Stanford University.

**Ravi Chhatpar** is the strategy director of Frog Design's Shanghai studio. His focus is in innovation and growth strategy. He helps clients find novel ways to be successful in new markets, whether in China, Asia, or globally. His client portfolio includes experience with leading Fortune 100s and global brands across industries, including consumer electronics, technology, mobile, healthcare, media, and financial services. Before Frog, Chhatpar spent several years in Tokyo, building an e-business strategy and delivery capability for NEC. He has an AB in biology and economics from Harvard University.

**Joshua L. Cohen** is a shareholder of RatnerPrestia, a firm specializing in intellectual property law. He holds engineering and law degrees and co-chairs RatnerPrestia's patent procurement group. Cohen has lectured about strategies for protecting design innovations to the Design Management Institute, the Industrial Designers Society of America, the Product Development and Management Association (PDMA), and the American Intellectual Property Law Association. He is currently president of PDMA's Philadelphia chapter and is the past president of The Benjamin Franklin American Inn of Court, an organization chartered to advance excellence, ethics, and professionalism in the field of intellectual property law.

**Michael Cooper** excels at bringing together diverse groups to solve complex issues and to create unique workplaces. His clients include Amerada HESS Corporation, Apache Corporation, McKinsey & Company, Torch Energy Advisors, Accenture, Tesoro Petroleum (the joint venture between Texaco and Shell), and Mission Resources. Cooper has a Master of Architecture degree from Rice University and a joint undergraduate degree from Pace University and the Pratt Institute, and he also studied at the Georgia Institute of Technology. He is one of the founding principals of Ziegler Cooper Architects.

**Kenneth Dowd** has spent the past forty years creating innovative and provocative designs for automotive and aerospace industries. Dowd began his design career working for Ford Motor Company and currently serves as the vice president of Teague's aviation studio. With an inventive imagination and a deep-rooted knowledge of design process and philosophy, Dowd has seamlessly fused industry and aesthetics to produce some of the most powerful and functional designs recognized within the realm of transportation.

**Joe Duffy,** principal and chairman of Duffy Design, has led the design studio since 1984 and is one of the most respected and sought-after creative directors and thought leaders on design in the world. Duffy's work includes brand and design solutions for leading global companies. His work is regularly featured in leading design publications and exhibited around the world. In 2004, he received the Legacy Medal from AIGA for a lifetime of achievement in the field of visual communications.

**Mark Dziersk** is the Vice President of Industrial Design of laga, a design and innovation partner to the world's leading companies. Dziersk is a fellow of the Industrial Designers Society of America. He is a twenty-year member of IDSA and has held several of its leadership positions, including that of president. Dziersk has earned more than a hundred U.S. product design and engineering patents and garnered numerous awards, among them the Industrial Design Excellence Award, *ID* magazine's Annual Design Review Design Distinction, and the Appliance Manufacturer's Excellence in Design. Currently, he is an adjunct professor for the Master of Product Development Program at Northwestern University in Evanston, Illinois.

**Dave Franchino** is president and principal of Design Concepts, Inc., a product development and design firm located in Madison, Wisconsin. Before joining Design Concepts, Franchino worked within the automotive industry as lead engineer and project manager on the team that designed and manufactured the first line of Saturn cars. He has taught courses in design at the University of Wisconsin-Madison. Franchino is a board member of the Association of Professional Design Firms. He holds a master's degree in mechanical engineering from Stanford University and a bachelor's degree in mechanical engineering from the University of Wisconsin-Madison.

**Ken Fry** is design director at Artefact, a Seattle-based design consultancy. He started his career with Microsoft as a user experience designer in 1994 and has spent his career leading design and research teams to launch dozens of hardware and software products. Fry has been recognized with several awards. In his time as design manager for Microsoft's hardware division, his group was among the five most recognized corporate design organizations. His experience led him to teach design courses at Seattle University and the University of Washington, where he received degrees in industrial design with a focus on interaction design.

**Ryan Jacoby**, an associate partner at IDEO, leads the organization's business factors discipline. He also leads the consumer experience design practice in IDEO's New York office. Jacoby is passionate about applying design thinking to business strategy, especially strategies for growth. While at IDEO he has focused on growth projects in industries such as retail, financial services, food and beverage, sporting goods, entertainment, and consumer products. He holds a BS in systems engineering from the University of Virginia and an MBA from Stanford University, where he focused on design, marketing, and strategy.

**Frans Joziasse** is one of the two founding partners of PARK, an international network of strategic design management consultancies that works with clients such as Audi, LEGO, Roca, Siemens, Johnson Controls, Hyundai & KIA Motors, and Reckitt Benckiser. He holds an MBA in design management from the University of Westminster (London) and lectures/teaches at several universities in Europe and the United States. In 2003, Joziasse developed the strategic design management module for the Master's in Design Management program at the INHOLLAND University, in Rotterdam, where he teaches.

**Gert L. Kootstra** is the managing consultant for Census Design Management BV. Kootstra studied publicity design at the Academy of Fine Arts and subsequently obtained a Master's degree in brand management from the Erasmus University. He is also the program director and core lecturer for the EURIB Master of Design Management course, and the author of a handbook for managers: *Design Management: Design effectief benutten om ondernemingssucces te creëren* (*Design Management: Efficient Use of Design for the Creation of Business Success*), which was published in Dutch by FT/Prentice Hall (Pearson Education) in 2006.

**Claudia Kotchka** is vice president for design innovation and strategy at Procter & Gamble. She joined P&G's marketing department after earning her CPA and spending five years at Arthur Andersen & Co. Kotchka led the marketing for such products as Crest, Pampers, Pantene, and Head & Shoulders, and she gained a reputation as an innovator and change agent. In 2001, P&G charged her with building design into the company's DNA. In 2005, she was named one of twenty Masters of Design by *Fast Company* magazine and one of the Best Leaders of 2005 by *BusinessWeek* magazine.

**EunSook Kwon** is an associate professor and the director of the industrial design program at the University of Houston's Gerald D. Hines College of Architecture. Kwon has published and lectured throughout the world about creative design thinking and design strategy development. She has consulted numerous corporations and has conducted private education programs for government agencies and corporations. Kwon holds a BFA in industrial design from Seoul National University, two master's degrees in industrial design from Seoul National University (MFA) and the Ohio State University (MA), and a PhD in arts education from Ohio State University.

**Arnold Craig Levin** is a director of Bennett Strategy, which specializes in developing workplace strategies for an international spectrum of clients. Levin has developed a unique facilitation process, along with a workplace design strategy process, that has been particularly successful in defining workplace goals, enabling design strategies to successfully connect to business strategies. Prior to Bennett Strategy, Levin was design principal in Mancini Duffy's Washington, D.C., office, where he also directed its Centre for Workplace Innovation. Levin received a design degree from Pratt Institute and a MBA from the Harrow Business School of the University of Westminster, London.

**Thomas Lockwood** is the president and a board member of DMI. He is responsible for all aspects of the Institute, including research, content, education, and editorial direction, as well as the production of DMI's events throughout the world. Prior to joining the public sector, he directed global brand and design strategy at Sun Microsystems and StorageTek, and ran his own design consultancy for many years. One of his most enjoyable projects was designing the racing skiwear worn by the U.S. Nordic Ski Team in the Olympics. He holds a PhD in design management from the University of Westminster in London as well as an MPhil, MBA, and BA in marketing and in visual design. He is considered an international expert in the areas of design and brand strategy, methods, operations, and management, is a design advisor to corporations and countries, and serves on numerous boards and advisory councils around the world.

**Kevin McCullagh** is the founder of Plan Strategic Ltd., a product strategy consultancy based in London, U.K. While at Plan and in his previous position as director of Seymour Powell Foresight, McCullagh has consulted to design, marketing, and corporate strategy departments of brands including Ford, HP, Mars, Nokia, Orange, Samsung, Shell, Strategos, Unilever, and Yamaha. His background spans design, marketing, engineering, and academia; and he regularly writes, speaks, broadcasts, and curates conferences on design, technology, and society.

**Pete Mortensen** is the communications lead of Jump Associates. He writes and speaks with a highly illuminating and lyrical style about questions of culture, design, and business. A journalist by training, he has written for *Spin Magazine* and *Wired News* and is the co-editor for *Wired*'s Cult of Mac blog. Mortensen holds a dual bachelor's degree in journalism and English literature from Northwestern University.

**Dev Patnaik** is the managing associate and a founder of Jump Associates. He draws upon a background in design, research, and strategy and has worked with firms in the United States, Asia, and Australia, to explore new opportunities for growth. Patnaik works with leaders of new business groups to increase the impact of their internal teams. He is also an adjunct professor at Stanford University, where he teaches design research methods to undergraduate and graduate students.

**Diego Rodriguez** is responsible for IDEO's global business consulting capability. In addition, he is an associate consulting professor at the Hasso Plattner Institute of Design at Stanford University, where he teaches design-thinking classes on marketing and venture strategy. Rodriguez has a BS in mechanical engineering; an AB in values, technology, science, and society, with honors, from Stanford University; and an MBA with distinction from Harvard Business School. Prior to IDEO he held a wide variety of operating roles at Nissan, Intuit, and HP.

**Joseph W. Synan** is a leadership and team effectiveness consultant. The focus of his work is helping leaders and teams by facilitating consensus-building and helping them to lead, envision, and plan better together. Synan is founder and president of Leadingwell Associates and the past president of the American Leadership Forum. He holds three degrees in nuclear engineering—two from MIT and one from Notre Dame. He completed the University of Virginia's executive business program in 1977 and obtained a master's in theology at the University of St. Thomas in 2001.

**Jos Vink** worked in advertising after he graduated in business administration from Erasmus University in Rotterdam. In 1999, he started at Blauw Research. Initially, he worked on multi-client image research projects. After heading marketing and communications at Blauw, Vink became responsible for the communication research unit. Since December 2004, he has been managing partner at Blauw Research.

**Sohrab Vossoughi** is founder and president of ZIBA Design, the company he started in 1984. The recipient of more than thirty patents and over two hundred design awards, Vossoughi was named one of the top five innovation gurus in the United States by *BusinessWeek* in 2005. He continues to direct projects for start-ups and Fortune 50 clients including Procter & Gamble, Nike, Microsoft, Xerox, and Hewlett-Packard. Born in Tehran, Iran, in 1956, Vossoughi moved to the United States in 1971. He is a graduate of San Jose State University's Department of Industrial Design.

**Robyn Waters**. Known as the "Trendmaster," Robyn Waters, president of RWTrend, is a keynote speaker, author, and hired-gun visionary for corporate America. She has more than thirty years of experience in tracking and translating trends into sales and profit. As Target's former vice president of trend, design, and product development, Waters helped a small regional discount chain become a national fashion destination. She is the author of *The Trendmaster's Guide* and *The Hummer and the Mini: Navigating the Contradictions of the New Trend Landscape*.

**Laura Weiss** is currently a director of IDEO's Software Experiences practice leadership team, where she oversees programs in service design. Prior to joining the firm, Weiss was a consultant with Integral, Inc., a Cambridge, MA.-based management consulting firm specializing in innovation management. At IDEO, she has contributed analytical business tools and methodologies to the development and management of a variety of strategic innovation programs for clients as varied as JP Morgan Invest, AT&T, Juniper Financial, Hewlett-Packard, and Steelcase. She holds an MBA from the MIT Sloan School of Management, a Master of Architecture from Yale University, and a Bachelor of Architecture with honors from Cornell University.

# Index

# Books from Allworth Press

Allworth Press is an imprint of Allworth Communications, Inc. Selected titles are listed below.

**AIGA Professional Practices in Graphic Design, Second Edition**
*edited by Tad Crawford* (6 × 9, 320 pages, paperback, $29.95)

**Green Graphic Design**
*by Brian Dougherty with Celery Design Collaborative* (6 × 9, 212 pages, paperback, 100 b&w illustrations, $19.95)

**How to Think Like a Great Graphic Designer**
*by Debbie Millman* (6 × 9, 256 pages, paperback, $24.95)

**Design Disasters: Great Designers, Fabulous Failures, and Lessons Learned**
*edited by Steven Heller* (6 × 9, 240 pages, paperback, $24.95)

**Creating the Perfect Design Brief: How to Manage Design for Strategic Advantage**
*by Peter L. Phillips* (6 × 9, 224 pages, paperback, $19.95)

**Designing Logos: The Process of Creating Logos That Endure**
*by Jack Gernsheimer* (8½ × 10, 208 pages, paperback, $35.00)

**The Graphic Designer's Guide to Better Business Writing**
*by Barbara Janoff and Ruth Cash-Smith* (6 × 9, 256 pages, paperback, $19.95)

**The Graphic Design Business Book**
*by Tad Crawford* (6 × 9, 256 pages, paperback, $24.95)

**Business and Legal Forms for Graphic Designers, Third Edition**
*by Tad Crawford and Eva Doman Bruck* (8½ × 11, 208 pages, paperback, includes CD-ROM, $29.95)

**The Graphic Designer's Guide to Pricing, Estimating, and Budgeting, Revised Edition**
*by Theo Stephan Williams* (6¾ × 9⅞, 208 pages, paperback, $19.95)

**The Graphic Designer's Guide to Clients: How to Make Clients Happy and Do Great Work**
*by Ellen Shapiro* (6 × 9, 256 pages, paperback, $19.95)

**Editing by Design: For Designers, Art Directors, and Editors**
*by Jan V. White* (8½ × 11, 256 pages, paperback, $29.95)

**How to Grow as a Graphic Designer**
*by Catharine Fishel* (6 × 9, 256 pages, paperback, $19.95)

**Design Management: Using Design to Build Brand Value and Corporate Innovation**
*by Brigitte Borja de Mozota* (6 × 9, 256 pages, paperback, $24.95)